MITIGATION AND AGGRAVATION AT SENTENCING

This innovative volume explores a fundamental issue in the field of sentencing: the factors which make a sentence more or less severe. All sentencing systems allow courts discretion to consider mitigating and aggravating factors, and many legislatures have placed a number of such factors on a statutory footing. Yet many questions remain regarding the theory and practice of mitigation and aggravation. Drawing on legal and sociological perspectives and examining mitigation and aggravation in various jurisdictions, the essays provide practical illustrations of specific factors as well as theoretical justifications. After the foreword by Andreas von Hirsch, a number of contributors address broad conceptual issues raised at sentencing. These contributions are followed by several empirical chapters, including an exploration of personal mitigation in English courts. The authors are leading scholars from a range of common law jurisdictions including England and Wales, the United States, Canada, Australia, New Zealand and South Africa.

JULIAN V. ROBERTS is a professor of criminology in the Faculty of Law, University of Oxford, and a member of the Sentencing Council of England and Wales. He is editor-in-chief of the *European Journal of Criminology* and associate editor of the *Canadian Journal of Criminology and Criminal Justice*.

CAMBRIDGE STUDIES IN LAW AND SOCIETY

Cambridge Studies in Law and Society aims to publish the best scholarly work on legal discourse and practice in its social and institutional contexts, combining theoretical insights and empirical research.

The fields that it covers are studies of law in action; the sociology of law; the anthropology of law; cultural studies of law, including the role of legal discourses in social formations; law and economics; law and politics; and studies of governance. The books consider all forms of legal discourse across societies, rather than being limited to lawyers' discourses alone.

The series editors come from a range of disciplines: academic law, socio-legal studies, sociology and anthropology. All have been actively involved in teaching and writing about law in context.

Books in the series

Diseases of the Will
Mariana Valverde

The Politics of Truth and Reconciliation in South Africa: Legitimizing the Post-Apartheid State
Richard A. Wilson

Modernism and the Grounds of Law
Peter Fitzpatrick

Unemployment and Government: Genealogies of the Social
William Walters

Autonomy and Ethnicity: Negotiating Competing Claims in Multi-Ethnic States
Yash Ghai

Constituting Democracy: Law, Globalism and South Africa's Political Reconstruction
Heinz Klug

The Ritual of Rights in Japan: Law, Society, and Health Policy
Eric A. Feldman

The Invention of the Passport: Surveillance, Citizenship and the State
John Torpey

Governing Morals: A Social History of Moral Regulation
Alan Hunt

The Colonies of Law: Colonialism, Zionism and Law in Early Mandate Palestine
Ronen Shamir

Law and Nature
David Delaney

Social Citizenship and Workfare in the United States and Western Europe: The Paradox of Inclusion
Joel F. Handler

Law, Anthropology and the Constitution of the Social: Making Persons and Things
Edited by Alain Pottage and Martha Mundy

Judicial Review and Bureaucratic Impact: International and Interdisciplinary Perspectives
Edited by Marc Hertogh and Simon Halliday

Immigrants at the Margins: Law, Race, and Exclusion in Southern Europe
Kitty Calavita

Lawyers and Regulation: The Politics of the Administrative Process
Patrick Schmidt

Law and Globalization from Below: Toward a Cosmopolitan Legality
Edited by Boaventura de Sousa Santos and Cesar A. Rodriguez-Garavito

Public Accountability: Designs, Dilemmas and Experiences
Edited by Michael W. Dowdle

Law, Violence and Sovereignty among West Bank Palestinians
Tobias Kelly

Legal Reform and Administrative Detention Powers in China
Sarah Biddulph

The Practice of Human Rights: Tracking Law between the Global and the Local
Edited by Mark Goodale and Sally Engle Merry

Judges beyond Politics in Democracy and Dictatorship: Lessons from Chile
Lisa Hilbink

Paths to International Justice: Social and Legal Perspectives
Edited by Marie-Bénédicte Dembour and Tobias Kelly

Law and Society in Vietnam: The Transition from Socialism in Comparative Perspective
Mark Sidel

Constitutionalizing Economic Globalization: Investment Rules and Democracy's Promise
David Schneiderman

The New World Trade Organization Knowledge Agreements: 2nd Edition
Christopher Arup

Justice and Reconciliation in Post-Apartheid South Africa
Edited by François du Bois, Antje du Bois-Pedain

Militarization and Violence against Women in Conflict Zones in the Middle East: A Palestinian Case-Study
Nadera Shalhoub-Kevorkian

Child Pornography and Sexual Grooming: Legal and Societal Responses
Suzanne Ost

Darfur and the Crime of Genocide
John Hagan and Wenona Rymond-Richmond

Planted Flags: Trees, Land, and Law in Israel/Palestine
Irus Braverman

Fictions of Justice: the International Criminal Court and the Challenge of Legal Pluralism in Sub-Saharan Africa
Kamari Maxine Clarke

Conducting Law and Society Research: Reflections on Methods and Practices
Simon Halliday and Patrick Schmidt

Culture under Cross-examination: International Justice and the Special Court for Sierra Leone
Tim Kelsall

The Gacaca Courts and Post-Genocide Justice and Reconciliation in Rwanda: Justice without Lawyers
Phil Clark

Water on Tap: Rights and Regulation in the Transnational Governance of Urban Water Services
Bronwen Morgan

A Sociology of Constitutions: Constitutions and State Legitimacy in Historical-Sociological Perspective
Chris Thornhill

Mitigation and Aggravation at Sentencing
Edited by Julian Roberts

MITIGATION AND AGGRAVATION AT SENTENCING

Edited by

Julian V. Roberts

CAMBRIDGE
UNIVERSITY PRESS

CAMBRIDGE UNIVERSITY PRESS
Cambridge, New York, Melbourne, Madrid, Cape Town,
Singapore, São Paulo, Delhi, Tokyo, Mexico City

Cambridge University Press
The Edinburgh Building, Cambridge CB2 8RU, UK

Published in the United States of America by Cambridge University Press, New York

www.cambridge.org
Information on this title: www.cambridge.org/9780521197809

First published 2011

Printed in the United Kingdom at the University Press, Cambridge

A catalogue record for this publication is available from the British Library

Library of Congress Cataloguing in Publication data
Mitigation and aggravation
at sentencing / edited by Julian V. Roberts.
p. cm. – (Cambridge studies in law and society)
ISBN 978-0-521-19780-9 (hardback)
1. Sentences (Criminal procedure) – England – Congresses. I. Roberts, Julian V.
KD8406.A75.M58 2011
345.42′0772–dc22

2011010610

ISBN 978-0-521-19780-9 Hardback

CONTENTS

TABLES

CONTRIBUTORS

EDITOR

Julian V. Roberts is Professor of Criminology, University of Oxford, and a member of the Sentencing Council of England and Wales. His books include *Punishing Persistent Offenders, The Role of Previous Convictions at Sentencing* (with A. von Hirsch), *Understanding Public Attitudes to Criminal Justice* (with M. Hough), *The Virtual Prison* (Cambridge University Press).

CONTRIBUTING AUTHORS

Andrew Ashworth is Vinerian Professor of English law at the University of Oxford. He is the author of *Sentencing and Criminal Justice* (5th edn, Cambridge University Press). Other recent volumes include *Principled Sentencing* (3rd edn, with A. von Hirsch and J. V. Roberts) and *Proportionate Sentencing* (Oxford University Press, with A. von Hirsch).

William W. Berry III is an Assistant Professor of Law in the School of Law at the University of Mississippi. He has published a number of articles on sentencing in the United States. His current sentencing scholarship focuses on the intersection between the philosophical justifications for punishment and the practical administration of penalties such as the death penalty.

Arie Freiberg is Professor and Dean of Law at Monash University and the author of *Sentencing in Victoria* and *Pathways to Justice*. He has published many articles and chapters in the area of sentencing and he is the chair of the Sentencing Advisory Council in Victoria. Recent publications include *Penal Populism, Sentencing Councils and Sentencing Policy* (with K. Gelb).

Mike Hough is Professor of Criminal Policy, Birkbeck, University of London, and Co-director of the Institute for Criminal Policy Research at Birkbeck, University of London. His current research interests include sentencing, youth justice and public trust in justice. Until 2011 he was president of the British Society of Criminology.

Jessica Jacobson is a Senior Research Fellow of the Institute for Criminal Policy Research at Birkbeck, University of London. She has been involved in a number of sentencing projects and her publications include *Mitigation: the Role of Personal Factors in Sentencing* (with M. Hough) and *Unjust Deserts: Imprisonment for Public Protection* (with Mike Hough).

Andrea King is a Senior Legal and Policy Adviser at the Law Commission in New Zealand. She managed the Sentencing Establishment Unit, based in the Law Commission, which developed New Zealand's draft sentencing guidelines.

Austin Lovegrove is an Honorary Fellow at the University of Melbourne. His research interests are in sentencing, and cover public opinion, judicial decision making and guidelines. He was a member of the Victorian Committee of Inquiry into Sentencing, which reported in 1988.

Allan Manson is Professor of Law at Queen's University in Canada and the author of *The Law of Sentencing*. He is also the principal editor of *Sentencing and Penal Policy in Canada* (2nd edn).

Nicola Padfield is a senior lecturer at the University of Cambridge. She is also a Crown Court Recorder and the editor of the practitioners' monthly, *Archbold Review*. She is the author of a number of books; her *Criminal Law* is in its seventh edition. Her current research focuses on parole and recall.

Kevin R. Reitz is the James Annenberg La Vea Professor at the University of Minnesota Law School. He is Reporter for the American Law Institute's project to revise the sentencing and corrections articles of the Model Penal Code. He is co-author, with Henry Ruth, of *The Challenge of Crime: Rethinking Our Response*.

Joanna Shapland is Professor of Criminal Justice in the School of Law at Sheffield. She has published very widely in the field of criminal justice. Publications include *Between Conviction and Sentence*. Her latest book is *Restorative Justice in Practice: Evaluating What Works for Victims and Offenders* (with G. Robinson and A. Sorsby).

Felicity Stewart is the Principal Legal Policy Officer at the Victorian Sentencing Advisory Council. Previously she worked as a criminal lawyer at Victoria Legal Aid, as a Judge's Associate in the Supreme Court of Victoria and as the Legal Assistant to the Lord President of the Court of Session and Lord Justice General of Scotland.

Stephan Terblanche is Professor in the Department of Criminal and Procedural Law at the University of South Africa. He is the author of *A Guide to Sentencing in South Africa* and *Report on the Sentencing Framework Bill*.

Andreas von Hirsch is Honorary Professor at the Law Faculty of the University of Frankfurt. He is Emeritus Honorary Professor of Penal Theory and Penal Law at the University of Cambridge, and Honorary Fellow at Wolfson College, Cambridge. Much of his earlier writing has appeared under his anglicized name of Andrew von Hirsch.

Kate Warner is a Professor of Law at the University of Tasmania, where she teaches criminal law, evidence and sentencing. She is the Director of the Tasmania Law Reform Institute and a member of the recently established Sentencing Advisory Council. She writes the annual Sentencing Review for the *Criminal Law Journal*.

Warren Young is Deputy President of the New Zealand Law Commission. He has previously held positions as Deputy Secretary for Justice and as Director of the Institute of Criminology, Professor of Law and Assistant Vice Chancellor (Research) at Victoria University of Wellington. He was the Law Commissioner responsible for the report *Sentencing Guidelines and Parole Reform* that led to the enactment of the Sentencing Council Act 2007 in New Zealand.

FOREWORD

Explicit guidance for sentencing decisions, and an explicit rationale to guide them, has been a notable feature of sentence-reform efforts over recent decades. In England and Wales a system of sentencing guidelines is in place, based on statutory standards and guidelines provided by the Sentencing Council. Meanwhile, an extensive literature on sentencing theory has developed – for example, that based on notions of desert and proportionate sanctions, or on notions of 'limiting retributivism' (von Hirsch and Ashworth 2005: ch. 9 and appendix 2).

Yet, curiously, little attention has been paid to aggravating and mitigating circumstances affecting the sentence. The first systematic effort at sentencing guidance in England and Wales, the Criminal Justice Act 1991, established a system of statutory guiding principles; these norms were aimed at helping to establish gradations of sentence for various crimes, based chiefly on offence-seriousness. However, the legislation omitted any guidance on aggravating or mitigating circumstances affecting sentence. It was only a decade and a half later, in 2004, that the Sentencing Guidelines Council (since replaced by the Sentencing Council of England and Wales) adopted a list of aggravating and mitigating factors. Sentencing theorists and scholars have, if anything, been still more neglectful of the subject; this is the first major book devoted to the topic.

Yet aggravation and mitigation are matters of great importance in the determination of sentence. Such factors may substantially affect the severity of the sentence and raise complex ethical and practical questions.

Consider the mitigating factor of provocation by the victim, and a simple case. A young woman lives with a partner who regularly abuses her. After numerous incidents of mistreatment, her partner returns from the pub one evening under the influence of alcohol, again beats her badly, and then falls into a drunken semi-stupor. While he is in that state, she goes into the kitchen, finds a heavy skillet, and smashes it into his face. He suffers a fractured nose, jaw and cheekbones, extensive lacerations and severe trauma, and must be hospitalized. She is charged with aggravated assault, is duly convicted and appears for sentencing. Should her sentence be mitigated, on grounds of severe provocation on his part?

It would seem that it should be. The seriousness of her offence depends on its harmfulness and culpability. The harm is unaffected by the victim's provoking conduct, but her culpability should be reduced in recognition of her victim's gross misconduct towards her, even as a matter of common-sense moral judgement. How, then, should this case be handled?

Sweden's statutory sentencing guidelines, in effect since 1989, address such questions.[1] That scheme provides guidance on the grading and severity of ordinarily applicable sentences. It also includes an explicit catalogue of circumstances of aggravation and of mitigation. One of the listed mitigating factors is provocation: that the crime was committed in virtue of the victim's 'obviously [injurious or] offensive' behaviour towards the defendant. Under that standard, the defendant in the hypothetical case would qualify as having been provoked by the victim's gross misconduct towards her, and the sentence would be reduced substantially.

Addressing mitigating and aggravating factors explicitly in this fashion will evoke a series of important further questions. One is that of the sentencing rationale. Consider, again, the mitigating factor of provocation. The traditional English common-law account of provocation (which concerns only homicide cases and their statutory classification) utilizes a theory of impaired volition: whether the defendant's capacity for self-control was affected by the victim's misconduct.[2] Several authors, including Arie Freiberg and Felicity Stewart in the present volume, point out that provocation does not necessarily involve diminished volition, and favour a culpability-based account instead.[3]

A second set of interesting questions relates to the criteria for applying the stated norms of aggravation or mitigation. If provocation as a mitigating factor is based on the victim's wrongful conduct towards the defendant, how heinous must the provoking conduct be? Must serious violence be involved (as in the just-cited hypothetical case)?

1 Swedish Criminal Code, ch. 29 §3(1).

2 See, e.g., Horder (1992). However, the common-law doctrine combines this subjective loss-of-self-control standard with a further (and very different) element of culpability: that the loss of self-control was 'reasonable' in the circumstances. For a critique of this approach, see Narayan and von Hirsch (1996).

3 For an account of why provocation is a matter of culpability, see Narayan and von Hirsch (1996).

Lesser forms of violence? Gravely insulting conduct? Infringement of domestic obligations (e.g. marital infidelity)? My inclination would be that only serious misconduct by the victim should count, but how serious this needs to be should be clarified.

Making aggravation/mitigation explicit and examining their rationale can have a third function: helping to decide whether a given factor is worth introducing or retaining at all. Consider the traditional 'equity factor' in English judicial practice of reducing sentence on account of a defendant's 'social contributions' – for example, his assistance to public charities, or his good military record. Such an approach presupposes a 'social accounting' conception that treats criminal punishment as concerned with the defendant's general worthiness or unworthiness. I am sceptical that the criminal sanction should have this function – and whether it would be consistent with notions of personal liberty and fair accountability for criminal conduct (see discussion in von Hirsch and Ashworth (2005), appendix 1). But this, again, is a matter that needs further debate.

It has been suggested, however, that aggravation and mitigation are subjects not well suited to being addressed through sentencing guidelines; and that these matters are best left to the discretion of individual judges. One argument is that aggravation/mitigation should take greater account of rehabilitative factors (or of 'personal mitigation') than desert-orientated guidelines permit – so that these subjects should be exempt from the guidelines. But if that assumption is correct – that aggravation/mitigation should focus on rehabilitation or personal mitigation more – then why cannot this concern be dealt with through explicit standards on the subject? Why not, in other words, have desert-orientated guidelines for the normally applicable sentence, and aggravation/mitigation standards with a somewhat differing emphasis? The rationale for this shift in emphasis would need to be explained. But taking this approach would at least help to ensure greater consistency among the sentencing decisions of judges than were matters of aggravation and mitigation simply left to individual decision-makers' discretion.

Another claim is that matters of aggravation and mitigation are too complex and elusive to be addressed in sentencing guidelines, and should be left to judges' discretion; that they are of 'infinite' variety. The argument puzzles me. Were it valid, then how could even individual judges deal with such matters? After all, none of us (whether judges or academic penologists) seem to possess the skills of mathematicians and cosmologists in dealing with trans-finite quanta.

An inquiry into aggravation and mitigation, their rationale, criteria and application, is long overdue. This important volume does great service in examining this area and opening it for discussion.

Andreas von Hirsch

REFERENCES

Horder, J. (1992). *Provocation and Responsibility*. Oxford University Press.

Narayan, U. and A. von Hirsch (1996). 'Three Conceptions of Provocation', *Criminal Justice Ethics*, winter/spring.

von Hirsch, A. and A. Ashworth (2005). *Proportionate Sentencing: Exploring the Principles*. Oxford University Press.

ACKNOWLEDGMENTS

This volume originated in a sentencing seminar held at Worcester College on 29 February 2008. A number of scholars made presentations, some of which ultimately gave rise to the chapters published here. Additional chapters were commissioned on topics of cross-jurisdictional importance.

I am very grateful to Worcester College, Oxford, and the Research Support Fund at the Faculty of Law, University of Oxford, for supporting the seminar and the subsequent volume.

I would also like to acknowledge the support of Finola O'Sullivan from Cambridge University Press.

Julian V. Roberts
Worcester College and Centre of
Criminology
University of Oxford

CHAPTER ONE

PUNISHING, MORE OR LESS: EXPLORING AGGRAVATION AND MITIGATION AT SENTENCING

Julian V. Roberts

This volume explores an under-researched yet fascinating domain in the field of criminal sentencing: the circumstances that may justify imposition of a harsher or more lenient sentence. At sentencing, courts must weigh a wide range of offence and offender-related factors in order to determine the severity of the sentence. Some factors influence the sentence by affecting the seriousness of the crime, others because they reflect a higher or lower level of culpability on the part of the offender. Mitigating and aggravating factors are often taken for granted by members of the public (and possibly some legal professionals) – we all have intuitions about whether factor X should result in a more lenient or a harsher sentence. Certainly, for many factors the relevance is obvious: committing an assault against someone while disparaging their ethnicity or religious beliefs obviously makes the assault more serious; there is an additional element of harm (contained in the affront to the victim's identity). Similarly, if, immediately after committing the crime the offender assists the victim, apologizes for his conduct and makes amends, this justifies a more lenient sentence. But many problematic circumstances exist.

Consider intoxication – a circumstance commonly associated with offending and which is explored by Nicola Padfield in her chapter in this volume. Should the fact that the offender was drunk at the time of the offence result in a more lenient sentence? One justification is that the offence was uncharacteristic of the offender. On this line of reasoning intoxication sustains a more general claim that the offence was 'out of character'. At the same time there is a strong counter-argument in cases in which the offender has a history of heavy drinking: he or she may be seen as being more culpable for failing to exercise some restraint regarding a known problem. According to this analysis intoxication should aggravate the sentence – as in the case of an offender who drinks heavily knowing that this often results in criminal assaults in pubs. Indeed, a number of guideline schemes identify intoxication as an aggravating factor.[1] Empirical research by Wilkins found that the fact that the offender was under the influence of alcohol emerged on lists of mitigating *and* aggravating factors (Wilkins 1983). As with a number of other factors, then, intoxication may aggravate or mitigate, depending upon the particular circumstances of the offence and the offender.

Intuition alone is often a poor guide to principled sentencing. Some guidance for sentencers with respect to the interpretation of this circumstance would be helpful. If the role of a particular circumstance is subject to variable interpretations, the case for guidance surely becomes unassailable. This does not mean that guidelines with respect to an ambiguous factor such as intoxication need to be heavy-handed and prescriptive – laying down that drunkenness should *never* mitigate or *always* aggravate – but it is surely possible to give some guidance as to its role at sentencing, with the intention of promoting a consistent approach.

CHAPTER OVERVIEW

I begin by noting some justifications for providing guidance for sentencers with respect to mitigation and aggravation. This is followed by a brief discussion of the guidance provided to courts in common law jurisdictions. Throughout, I illustrate the discussion with examples from various jurisdictions, although the primary focus is on the guidelines in England and Wales. After identifying some limitations on sentencing factor guidance, I offer suggestions for improving matters. The chapter concludes with a brief overview of the remainder of this volume.

JUSTIFICATIONS FOR GUIDANCE

The absence of comprehensive guidance regarding sentencing factors is regrettable, for several reasons.

[1] For example, the crime seriousness guideline issued by the Sentencing Guidelines Council (now the Sentencing Council of England and Wales) identifies 'commission of offence while under the influence of alcohol or drugs' as an aggravating factor indicating higher culpability. (All the English guidelines are now available at www.sentencingcouncil.org.uk.)

The power of sentencing factors to influence sentence severity

If mitigating and aggravating factors had only a minimal impact on sentencing, it might be reasonable to leave the matter to judicial discretion. However, these factors can exert a powerful influence over sentence outcomes; they may well determine whether custody is justified and necessary, or may mean a significant difference in the duration of any custodial term imposed. Research in England and Wales has demonstrated that personal mitigation still plays the largest role in tipping the balance away from the imposition of a term of custody (Hough et al. 2003: 37) while Jacobson and Hough (2007) found that in approximately one-third of the cases which they observed, judicial recognition of personal mitigation changed what would have been a custodial sentence to a community-based sanction. In the light of this it is vital that sentencers consider and apply factors in a uniform manner. The concepts of equality and fairness that underlie the criminal law require sentencers to apply mitigating and aggravating factors consistently.

The potential variability of application

A second justification for guidance concerns the absence of consensus; sentencers often disagree with respect to the weight and significance of various sentencing factors. Research has repeatedly demonstrated considerable variation in the judicial response to some sentencing factors. In an older Canadian study Hogarth found that 'there was little agreement among magistrates . . . each magistrate seemed to establish his own criteria for assessing the relevance of, and the weight to attach to, different types of information' (1971: 371). Shapland (1981) also found little consensus among barristers in England and Wales with respect to the factors deemed relevant to speeches of mitigation, while Corbett (1987) noted that 'aggravating and mitigating value judgments were made of the same fact' (p. 211). Most recently, Jacobson and Hough (2007: 17) report considerable variation in sentencers' reactions to mitigating factors. It seems clear that some factors are susceptible of different interpretations – hence the need for guidance.

Guiding the 'intuitive' sentencer

A third justification for providing structure and guidance concerns the phenomenology of sentencing. Determining which factors should mitigate or aggravate is the element of sentencing most likely to arouse intuitive reactions to punishment. There are several dangers here. First, as noted earlier, our intuitions are not always good guides to the determination of a principled sentence. Second, intuitions, by definition, vary widely; one person's view of personal mitigation may be very different from another's. Even if two sentencers agree on the relevance of a particular factor, they may diverge on its relative weight, one considering it to be important enough to make a difference between community and custody, the other as being insufficient to change the appropriate sanction to this extent. For this reason, sentencers should be provided with some guidance and encouraged not just to give free rein to their intuitive responses.[2] In addition, lay sentencers may be overly influenced by sympathy for a particular defendant, or swayed against some kinds of offenders. There is a natural human tendency to be more lenient towards people we like, or people whom we perceive to be similar to ourselves. Social distance is inversely related to the level of tolerance we have for wrongdoing.

Promoting public confidence in sentencing

A final justification for guidance concerns the relationship between sentencing and the community. If sentencing factors are not conceptually sound and systematically applied, the public image of sentencing will suffer. Poorly understood sentencing factors can be the source of much public and media criticism of sentencers;[3] when a defendant is spared custody through the application of an important mitigating factor it is important to ensure that the relevance of the factor is clear to the community – and guidelines represent a vehicle to communicate with the public. Otherwise, public misunderstanding of sentencing and criticism of sentencers will grow. Promoting public understanding of sentencing is a statutory function of many sentencing authorities. For example, the enabling legislation of the Sentencing Council of England and Wales states that the Council 'may promote awareness of matters relating to the sentencing of offenders' (s. 129(2)). Similarly, section

[2] It would be strange if no parallels existed between legal models of sentencing and intuitive reactions to claims for mitigation; however, there are important differences between the two spheres. State punishment invokes a separate set of considerations. For example, the purposes of sentencing identified in s. 142(1) of the Criminal Justice Act 2003 in England and Wales include deterrence and incapacitation; these objectives are not invoked in an everyday context.

[3] The author of the first English sentencing text (Cox 1877) observed that 'The province of the Judge and Magistrate is so little understood by the public that complaints are sometimes made of the severity of a Judge. The writers of sensational articles in the newspapers take especial pleasure in this work. It is at once so easy to write about and so pleasant to read . . . The degree of mitigation is a question that can only be determined by such knowledge of all the facts as the Judge alone can acquire . . . but which are quite unknown to the public, to the reporters and to the commentators' (p. 19).

100J(1)(e) of the Crimes (Sentencing Procedure) Act 1999 in New South Wales requires the Sentencing Council in that state to 'educate the public about sentencing matters'. Many sentencing factors may strike the public at first glance as being questionable. As Roberts and Hough note in their chapter here, mitigating sentence because the offender pleaded guilty or because it was his or her first conviction may generate public anger – at least until the principle underlying these common factors is adequately explained.

CONCEPTUAL FRAMEWORKS

Despite the importance of sentencing factors, as Ashworth notes, 'The concepts of aggravation and mitigation have tended to attract little close examination or theoretical discussion' (2010: 156; see also Walker, 1999). Classifications of sentencing factors have been proposed. For example, the Victorian Sentencing Committee identified five categories of mitigating factors (1988: 258). More recently, Jacobson and Hough have proposed a framework of categories for factors relating to personal mitigation (2007; see also their contribution to this volume). Guideline schemes do not always reflect a coherent conceptual foundation, and more structure for sentencers may be desirable.

STRUCTURING DISCRETION AT SENTENCING

Sentencers in England and Wales, the United States and a number of other jurisdictions receive guidance on a wide range of issues relating to the determination of sentence. However, even the most detailed and prescriptive guidelines will fail to ensure consistency of approach in sentencing unless adequate direction is also provided with respect to sentencing factors, both mitigating and aggravating. At present, guidance regarding sentencing factors tends to be modest. Guideline schemes around the world generally adopt a laissez-faire approach to the use of sentencing factors. Even in the relatively restrictive US-based systems which restrict judicial discretion, guidance regarding the application of other factors is quite limited. This state of affairs may reflect the view that consideration of mitigation and aggravation is more properly left to the exercise of judicial discretion, with only minimal direction from the legislature, the guidelines authority or the Court of Appeal. Consistent with this perspective a number of scholars – including some contributors to this volume – are of the view that additional guidance regarding mitigating or aggravating factors is unhelpful or unwise.

As will be seen, there is considerable variation across the common law world with respect to the degree and nature of guidance regarding sentencing factors.

SOURCES OF GUIDANCE

The legislature: statutory sentencing factors

Legislatures affect sentencing factors in the first instance by creating the judicial discretion to consider mitigation at sentencing. For example, section 166 of the Criminal Justice Act 2003 states that: 'Nothing in [provisions relating to the determination of sentence] . . . prevents a court from mitigating an offender's sentence by taking into account any such matters as, in the opinion of the court, are relevant in mitigation of sentence'. Section 718.2a of the Criminal Code of Canada is more affirmative, directing courts that 'A sentence should be increased or reduced to account for any *relevant* aggravating or mitigating circumstances relating to the offence or the offender' (emphasis added).

The second way in which legislatures affect the application of sentencing factors is through codification of specific factors. Almost all[4] common law jurisdictions have placed certain mitigating and aggravating factors on a statutory footing. According to some statutes, judges are directed to consider these factors when determining the seriousness of the offence. Thus, sections 2 and 3 of Chapter 29 of the Swedish Criminal Code 1988 specify a number of factors that enhance or diminish the penal value of the crime. In addition, section 5 of the chapter specifies eight additional mitigating circumstances that a court shall consider 'to a reasonable extent'. These include factors such as whether the punishment would have a disproportionate effect on the offender due to advanced age or ill health.

In most jurisdictions the number of codified factors is generally small: in Finland the principal sentencing statute specifies only five factors which increase the severity of the punishment, while the Canadian Criminal Code lists only a handful of aggravating factors and no mitigating factors. The absence of mitigating factors in the Canadian sentencing regime reflects a trend found elsewhere to provide more guidance

[4] Tasmania is an exception: its sentencing legislation does not identify any factors.

with respect to aggravation than mitigation.[5] In England and Wales, five sentencing factors have been placed on a statutory footing. The Criminal Justice Act 2003 provides no indication regarding the relative weight of the factors, their potential to move a case over the custody threshold, or whether they are more important than other sentencing factors emerging from the case law. The statute thus provides only limited guidance to sentencers regarding the sources of aggravation and mitigation. This reflects the existence of the sentencing guidelines issued by the Sentencing Council and which presumably are designed to supplement and interpret the statutory framework.[6]

The Court of Appeal

Until the advent of sentencing councils and commissions to disseminate guidelines, the appellate courts have been the traditional source of guidance at sentencing. Evaluating the adequacy of appellate guidance regarding mitigating and aggravating circumstances is beyond the scope of this chapter. However, numerous academic commentators and commissions have identified the limitations on appellate guidance in general and the area of mitigation and aggravation in particular. Most sentence appeals address a specific point of law or provide a test for whether the sentence imposed was 'manifestly unfit'. Guideline judgments in which the court sets out the mitigating and aggravating factors relevant to the offence are relatively rare. Walker, for example, described the degree of guidance from the English Court of Appeal in the following way: 'What emerges is the unsystematic approach of the Court of Appeal, resulting in contradictory decisions and special pleading.' (1985: 43). Elsewhere, the Canadian Sentencing Commission (1987) noted that 'Research undertaken by the Commission has shown that a significant number of judgments just enumerate factors without specifying whether they are considered to be aggravating or mitigating' (p. 321). More recently, however, the Court of Appeal in England and Wales has provided

[5] The explanation for this asymmetry is unclear; it may reflect greater consensus around aggravating factors. For example, if one agrees that hate motivation is an aggravator, it surely operates across all offences and offenders. There may be less agreement about the relevance and weight of different mitigators, in which case it is hard to be more prescriptive.

[6] Other jurisdictions provide more comprehensive lists of statutory factors. Thus the Crimes (Sentencing Procedure) Act 1999 in New South Wales identifies twenty-one aggravating and sixteen mitigating factors. S. 9 of the Sentencing Act 2002 in New Zealand notes ten aggravating, seven mitigating and one statutorily excluded sentencing factor (see the chapter by Young and King in this volume).

detailed guidance for sentencers.[7] The primary source of comprehensive guidance is the guidelines authority.

Sentencing guidelines

The first challenge for any guidelines authority is to resolve the question of justification or relevance: On what basis is factor X a legitimate consideration which may aggravate or mitigate sentence? One response is to define relevance in terms of the statutory purposes of sentencing or the principal components of a proportionate sentence, namely harm and culpability. If factor X enhances culpability or signifies greater harm, then it should be considered at sentencing. This approach may be too restrictive; it is easy to conceive of factors which are unrelated to harm or culpability.

Two examples are the discount offered to offenders who plead guilty and who assist the state in its prosecution of other offenders. The justification for reducing sentences on these grounds lies outside any sentencing rationale and is located in the wider objective of constraining the costs of justice, enhancing the crime control function of the criminal justice system and sparing victims and witnesses from having to testify. On occasion the principles of sentencing, then, give way to broader goals. In these examples the role of a guidelines authority is no less clear, however. Courts need guidance on the magnitude of the discount, its relevance to variables such as the timing of the plea, the complexity of the case and other variables. This guidance is provided in some jurisdictions (see, e.g., the guideline issued by the English Sentencing Council, discussed below). The picture becomes even more complicated when we enter the zone of personal mitigation. A myriad of factors is taken into account here, many of which are hard or impossible to justify on a sound retributive principle or utilitarian basis.

The United States

Under most US sentencing guideline schemes the role of mitigating and aggravating factors is generally to justify the imposition of a sentence that is outside the range prescribed by the guidelines, or to move the case from the normal range up to an aggravated or down to a mitigated range.[8] For example, the Utah guidelines manual notes that 'There are

[7] See, e.g., R *v*. Saw, which sets out factors for the offence of domestic burglary.

[8] In the landmark decision in *United States v. Booker*, the US Supreme Court held that the federal sentencing guidelines are merely advisory rather than bindingly presumptive in nature. Mitigating circumstances therefore may be reasonably described as mitigating factors rather than 'departures' in the stricter sense of the pre-*Booker* era (see also the discussion in the chapter by Will Berry in this volume).

occasionally circumstances that compel deviation from the guidelines' (Utah Sentencing Commission 2010: 12). Directions are provided to courts with respect to the consideration of the sources of mitigation and aggravation. A non-exhaustive list of factors is provided, and courts are directed that 'in considering all aggravating and mitigating factors in a particular case, the number of each should not merely be added up or otherwise mechanically applied in the balancing process. Rather, the totality of the mitigating factors should be compared against the totality of the aggravating factors' (p. 12). Elsewhere, aggravation and mitigation create separate guideline ranges. For example, the sentencing guidelines in North Carolina provide sentencers with three sentence ranges: presumptive, aggravated and mitigated (North Carolina Sentencing and Policy Advisory Commission 2007).

Sentencing Council of England and Wales

The first definitive English guideline was issued in 1999, and many offence-specific guidelines have since appeared (see Ashworth and Wasik 2010 for a review). The English guidelines provide sentence ranges for categories of seriousness – most offences are divided into three levels. Each guideline also contains a non-exhaustive list of relevant mitigating and aggravating factors. In addition, the previous Sentencing Council issued a guideline for the determination of offence seriousness which is applicable to all offences. In that guideline the Council provides two lists containing a total of thirty-one generic aggravating factors that arise from a higher level of culpability or a greater degree of harm (or sometimes both conditions). These are described as being the most important aggravating circumstances with application across many offence categories. The lists are non-exhaustive. They include both statutory and non-statutory factors but make no commentary on the relative importance of the two. They are then followed by four factors that indicate when an offender's culpability is unusually low or that the harm is less than usually serious.

There is an imbalance in the lists reflecting the asymmetry to which reference has already been made: thirty-one factors are identified that enhance sentence severity, while only four factors are noted which may reduce the level of culpability or harm. Similarly the domestic violence guideline identifies seven aggravating but only two mitigating factors. The sexual offences guideline is also asymmetrical; there are 189 citations to aggravating factors, yet only 45 in mitigation (the same factors are cited across offences). For sixteen common offences in the

Magistrates' Courts Sentencing Guidelines only a single mitigating factor or none are specified. One danger is that this asymmetry will concentrate sentencers' attention on aggravation rather than mitigation. The asymmetry is curious, since research suggests that the need for guidance is less pressing with respect to aggravating factors. For example, Wilkins (1983) found a high degree of consensus regarding aggravating factors but much less consensus with respect to mitigating factors.

Guilty plea discount

With respect to one important sentencing factor – the guilty plea – the Sentencing Guidelines Council (now the Sentencing Council) has provided clear and detailed advice.[9] The Council's definitive guideline makes it clear that the reduction for a guilty plea 'derives from the need for the effective administration of justice and not as an aspect of mitigation' (Sentencing Guidelines Council 2007: 4). The definitive guideline published in July 2007 specifies the range of the reduction in sentence as well as the circumstances that justify different levels of reduction. This level of guidance reflects the importance of this factor in terms of sentencing and the administration of justice. With respect to other aggravating and mitigating factors, however, guidance is less comprehensive or precise.

Providing enhanced guidance

In all the guideline schemes a number of elements are missing, or require greater elucidation. At this point, some sentencers (and sentencing scholars) may roll their eyes and think, 'Here comes another exercise in box ticking!' Yet it is surely possible to provide structure and guidance without unduly limiting a court's discretion to craft an appropriate disposition. What other elements might a guidelines authority reasonably provide to sentencers? In my view, a number of issues need to be addressed.

The rationale for mitigating or aggravating sentence

First, it would be useful for a guidelines authority to articulate the rationale for considering specific mitigating and aggravating factors. This is not simply an academic exercise; awareness of the justification

[9] Not once, but twice. A definitive guideline was issued by the former Council (the SGC) in 2004. After further study and consultation this was revisited by the SGC and a second definitive guideline issued in 2007. Curiously, less than two years later, in 2009, the Coroners and Justice Act created a statutory obligation on the new Sentencing Council to issue a guideline on the discount for a guilty plea. Were the legislative drafters unaware of the existence of the definitive guideline?

for mitigation will focus sentencers' attention on the question of relevance. The *Overarching Principles: Seriousness* guideline in England[10] provides only a limited rationale for the invocation of any specific factor. Sentencing factors are particularly relevant when they indicate a higher or lower level of culpability or harm. Some sentencing factors, however, are unrelated to these concepts, and are applied because they are relevant to the statutory objectives of sentencing identified in section 142 of the Criminal Justice Act 2003. Still other factors are taken into account for more practical reasons, relating, for example, to the administration of justice. Sentencers should be encouraged to use this section to guide their application of the factors.

It is important to consider whether a factor is relevant to one of the sentencing objectives or principles. Some factors may be relevant independent of any link to the statutory objectives, but in general the coherence of the sentencing process is impaired if many factors unrelated to the sentencing purposes or principles are taken into account. A clear statement of the rationale for any specific factor would also help members of the community and crime victims to understand why the factor was taken into account at sentencing. As Ashworth notes, 'a key requirement is that the justifications [for factors] be strong and specific' (2010: 157). A good example of an ambiguous or controversial factor is positive actions by the offender which speak to his or her good character but which are unrelated to the offence.

Worthy conduct unrelated to the offence

Consider an offender who has performed some commendable action for the community – a mitigating circumstance in many jurisdictions. This contribution to the community is sometimes recognized in guideline schemes[11] and sentencing statutes. For example, section 6 of the Sentencing Act 1991 in the state of Victoria states that 'any significant contributions made to the community by the offender' is a relevant factor to be considered at sentencing. The classic case is the offender who performs an act of exceptional bravery shortly before or after conviction. The theory justifying this kind of leniency is unclear,[12] yet sentencers sometimes mitigate sentence on this basis. There is a strong

[10] Available at www.sentencingcouncil.org.uk.

[11] The definitive assault guideline issued by the Sentencing Council in England and Wales cites 'exemplary conduct' as a relevant factor – see www.sentencingcouncil.org.uk.

[12] There may be an argument that in considering punishment for transgressions against the state, it is legitimate to take into account conduct of the defendant which has contributed to the

intuitive appeal to a policy of mitigating sentences for offenders who have a history of very creditable social behaviour.

An important guide for probation officers and social workers preparing pre-sentence reports (PSRs) takes an expansive view of the issue, noting that '*Any* situation where an offender has helped or is helping an individual or the community to improve or enhance their life could be considered. Examples could be – driving the local community bus; shopping for an elderly person; housework or caring for grandparents; any charity that helps others' (Gilyeat 1993: iv). This approach seems unprincipled. These are all worthy activities, but can they reasonably be used to mitigate punishment for unrelated criminal conduct? As Gross noted, 'not every kind of creditable activity is properly taken into consideration and we find it difficult to decide where to draw the line' (1979: 451) – hence the need for some guidance for courts.

Most jurisdictions permit courts to recognize a mitigating factor that is unrelated to the principal theoretical orientation of sentencing. For example, the Wisconsin Sentencing Commission provides a list of 'additional factors' that do not relate to the primary sentencing rationale. The list includes items as diverse as the contents of the victim impact statement and whether the offender suffered public humiliation or loss of employment as a result of having been convicted (Wisconsin Sentencing Commission 2010: 8). However, these factors should not carry the same weight as more fundamental sentencing factors – those relating to crime seriousness or culpability. Moreover, if a factor is unrelated to culpability or harm, there is a greater need for guidelines to provide a justification.

The standard of proof for contested facts

Although the rules of evidence are relaxed at sentencing, courts must nevertheless ensure some evidentiary foundation for the invocation of specific sentencing factors. In most common law jurisdictions a clear asymmetry has emerged with respect to the standard of proof. If contested by counsel for the defendant, aggravating factors must be proven to the criminal standard of proof beyond a reasonable doubt. The burden of proof on the offender, however, is simply to establish mitigating factors on a balance of probabilities.[13] Judicial education initiatives

community. However, this view is still subject to the criticism that that positive acts have an adventitious element – opportunities to contribute to the community may arise by chance – and nor are these opportunities equal across social strata.

[13] In Canada, the different standards of proof were codified in 1996; see s. 724(4)(3) of the Criminal Code. The Law Commission of New Zealand proposed a similar codification in its report on the subject (Law Commission of New Zealand 2001).

can address this issue, but there may also be a role for sentencing guidelines which could make these standards clear to sentencers and counsel. If counsel have the standard of proof clearly in mind, they are more likely to pay attention to the factors that they put before the court in their submissions.

The interests of fairness require that when entertaining submissions on sentence, or considering specific mitigating or aggravating factors, sentencers should keep the standard of proof in mind. For the least serious offences, disputes over claims for mitigation are unlikely to arise. However, for serious crimes, sentencers should consider the question whether the claim for mitigation has some foundation or is simply speculative. Counsel should be prepared to lead some evidence; the claim for mitigation must have an 'air of reality' before it is accepted by the court to a civil standard. In the event that the claim is disputed by the crown, the latter should be required to disprove the factor beyond a reasonable doubt. Guidelines typically make no reference to this issue.

Weighting sentencing factors

Some guidance may be useful regarding the relative weight to be accorded different aggravating and mitigating factors – they are clearly not all equally important. The circumstances identified by the English Sentencing Council in its *Overarching Principles: Seriousness* guideline represent a wide range, some important, others less so. For example, by virtue of their statutory nature as well as their relevance across all cases, prior convictions should carry more weight than factors such as 'causing gratuitous damage to property over and above what is needed to carry out the offence'. Courts should be provided with some sense of the relative power of these factors to influence the quantum of punishment. This is not to say that precise weights could or should be assigned to factors, rather that if a factor is particularly important, sentencers should be aware of this fact – otherwise they are free to develop their own hierarchies of impact. Courts could benefit from knowing how much impact mitigating or aggravating factors may have – raising, lowering or otherwise changing recommended dispositions.

This suggestion may seem overly prescriptive, but it is worth noting that this degree of guidance is provided in some guideline schemes.[14] For

[14] The guidelines devised by the Law Commission of New Zealand offer possibly the most comprehensive and thoughtful model for the use of mitigating and aggravating factors. Regrettably, they have yet to be implemented (see the chapter by Young and King in this volume).

example, in Sweden the existence of statutory mitigating factors permits the court to impose a sentence below the statutory minimum. Allowing a factor this much influence is controversial, but at least sentencers have an indication of the extent to which a mitigating factor may reduce the custodial term. In a similar fashion the sentencing statute in Alaska identifies two gradations of mitigation. If the presumptive sentence is four years or less, mitigating factors may reduce the sentence by up to this amount. If the presumptive term is longer than four years, mitigating factors may reduce the sentence by up to 50 per cent. Regardless of the sentence length, aggravating factors may increase the presumptive sentence up to the statutory maximum.[15]

Placing limits on the impact of sentencing factors provides sentencers (and other parties) with an idea of the extent to which these factors can affect the sentence. Moreover, it would surely be useful to indicate to courts whether sentencing factors taken together or on an individual basis can make the difference between custody and a community sentence. Some guidance should be provided with regard to the factors which have the potential to move the offender above or below the custodial threshold. Several jurisdictions create two tiers of factors. For example, in Missouri the system of advisory sentencing guidelines incorporates two levels of aggravating factors: 'serious' and 'other'. If a serious aggravating factor is present, its impact on sentence severity cannot be offset by mitigating factors, although this is not true for the 'other aggravating factors' (Missouri Sentencing Advisory Commission 2007: 15).

In England and Wales, the Council's *Overarching Principles: Seriousness* guideline makes no distinctions among the thirty-one aggravating circumstances related to harm or culpability. Similarly, the *Overarching Principles: Domestic Violence* definitive guideline offers no guidance as to which among the aggravating factors should carry more weight. Different guidelines sporadically distinguish between factors that '*could* be taken to indicate a higher level of aggravation' (the offender's intention and the impact on the victim in cases of hate-motivated crime) and others such as the fact that the offender has ejaculated or has caused the victim to ejaculate which will increase the seriousness of the of the offence 'in *all* cases'.[16] These issues could and should be treated more systematically.

[15] Alaska Statutes: AS 12.55.155(a)(1) and AS 12.55.155(a)(2).
[16] p. 31 (emphasis added), available at www.sentencingcouncil.org.uk.

Excluded factors and controversial factors

The English guidelines do not specify factors that should *not* be considered in mitigation or aggravation. It would be both unrealistic and undesirable to construct a sentencing guideline which would specify all relevant mitigating and aggravating circumstances. However, greater consistency of application would be promoted by identifying problematic factors that should not mitigate or aggravate, or by specifying the way in which factors should be considered. Most sentencing guideline systems identify a number of factors that should be excluded from consideration. For example, the proposals made by the Australian Law Reform Commission identify circumstances which should not aggravate sentence.[17] Similarly, many US guidelines identify specific grounds which should not be considered by a sentencing court. For example, in Minnesota, the guidelines exclude the race, gender and social or economic status of the offender (Minnesota Sentencing Guidelines Commission 2010).

Establishing a list of proscribed as well as permitted factors also compels the guidelines authority to confront the underlying principles, and consequences of, various mitigating factors. The offender's employment status is often cited by sentencers as justifying the imposition of a mitigated sentence, in order to preserve the offender's source of income, or possibly to prevent the infliction of collateral harm on his or her dependants. Research has repeatedly demonstrated that employment status is a significant predictor of whether a custodial sentence is imposed (see, e.g., Moxon 1988). However, the application of this factor obviously disadvantages the unemployed or offenders with poor employment histories. Visible or immigrant minority offenders may be particularly affected, which is why a number of commentators have advocated the prohibition of this factor and why some sentencing guidelines (such as those in Minnesota) explicitly exclude it.

Ambiguous factors: remorse and the offender with 'attitude'

Other factors are particularly likely to generate conflicting opinions among sentencers, and hence require clarification regarding their application. Consider the expression of remorse, a mitigating circumstance

[17] These are a not guilty plea, prior convictions, declining to participate in a restorative justice program, and declining to co-operate with the authorities (Australian Law Reform Commission, 2006).

recognized by the Council's guideline regarding seriousness. Despite the reservations of some retributive theorists (e.g., Bagaric and Amarsekara 2001), courts that perceive the offender to be genuinely remorseful often mitigate sentence. But what of the offender who not only lacks remorse but demonstrates a contumelious attitude to the court and the crime victim? Should offenders who adopt such an attitude be punished more harshly? Is there a continuum with remorsefulness on one (mitigating) pole and defiance on another (aggravating) pole? A number of jurisdictions such as Delaware consider the *absence* of remorse to constitute an aggravating factor at sentencing (Delaware Sentencing Accountability Commission 2010), and some sentencers in other jurisdictions may sympathize with this position. For controversial factors of this nature it would be useful to clarify the asymmetry of effect whereby remorse mitigates but its absence may not aggravate.

Personal mitigation

Finally, guidelines around the world tend to be laconic with respect to personal mitigation. In his sentencing text Thomas argued that allowance for mitigation should not be considered to be an entitlement of the offender (1979: 174). Times may have changed since he expressed this opinion. Today, personal mitigation is generally accepted as a fundamental element of the sentencing process. The English Council's *Overarching Principles: Seriousness* guideline notes only the statutory provision in the Criminal Justice Act 2003 which authorizes courts to take account of any matters that are relevant in mitigation of sentence (see above) and then states that courts should 'consider any offender mitigation. The issue of remorse should be taken into account at this point along with other mitigating features such as admissions to the police in interview'. The *Magistrates' Court Sentencing Guidelines* simply direct magistrates to consider 'offender mitigation' and offer three or four examples. Research by Jacobson and Hough (2007) also revealed that many different personal mitigating factors were taken into account by sentencers, and that while agreement was expressed with respect to some factors, participants disagreed on many others. The authors suggest that the Council needs to provide better guidance in this area, beginning with the principles on which personal mitigation is based (see discussion in Shapland, this volume; Jacobson and Hough 2007).

To conclude, a comprehensive sentencing guidance system for the exercise of discretion with respect to sentencing factors would:

- articulate a rationale for mitigating and aggravating factors;
- provide a list of the principal mitigating and aggravating factors of potential application to all offenders as well as specific lists for different offence categories;
- encourage sentencers to consider the justification for invoking specific factors;
- clarify the different standard of proof for contested claims for mitigation and aggravation;
- distinguish between factors of low and high importance;
- identify specific factors that should *not* be considered in mitigation or aggravation; and
- encourage sentencers to identify in their reasons the most important sentencing factors taken into account.

CONCLUSION

Over a generation ago, scholars called for more judicial guidance regarding the criteria for mitigation and aggravation. Thus Ashworth lamented the absence of 'any thorough consideration of the claims of the various personal factors' and argued that 'this is a sphere in which discretion has led largely to anarchy' (1987: 30–1; see also Corbett 1987). The search for relevant sentencing factors should involve a systematic inquiry into principled adjustments to the quantum of punishment. My contention here is that courts would benefit from more detailed and structured guidance regarding the use of mitigating and aggravating factors at sentencing. This guidance need not be restrictive or impede a court's ability to impose a just sentence; it would result in more consistency in the use of these factors and, ultimately, more equitable and proportionate sentencing outcomes.

OUTLINE OF THIS VOLUME

Our volume is divided into four parts. Part one contains a number of contributions which deal with conceptual issues, beginning with Andrew Ashworth, who explores the justifications for aggravation and mitigation at sentencing, and the difficulties of finding principles on which to base many common mitigating factors. Allan Manson addresses the links between mitigation and the culture in which sentencing takes place. He argues that once we move beyond the basic concepts of gravity and culpability, there are cases where only a cultural inquiry will properly account for the fine-tuning that determines when a factor leads legitimately to mitigation. Joanna Shapland then raises a number of questions about the relationship between personal mitigation and desistance.

Part two explores specific issues which have cross-jurisdictional relevance, beginning with Nicola Padfield, who, as noted, discusses the controversial factor of intoxication at sentencing. Arie Freiberg and Felicity Stewart then address the relationship between provocation as a partial defence and the sentencing process. Is provocation best conceptualized as a partial defence or as a mitigating factor post-conviction? Kate Warner addresses the relevance of social background factors at sentencing, including ethnicity and race.

Part three contains empirical findings relating to mitigation and aggravation, beginning with Jessica Jacobson and Mike Hough, who report findings from a study of mitigation in England. The volume then turns to explore the views of the public with respect to sentencing factors. As with other issues, contributors take divergent perspectives. Julian Roberts and Mike Hough discuss quantitative and qualitative research in England, and argue that argue that there is considerable correspondence between community opinion and the guidelines in England and Wales. Austin Lovegrove draws on Australian research to argue that the community is strongly supportive of personal mitigation and that the English guidelines discourage sentencers from giving personal mitigation its appropriate weight. Both chapters agree that the view of the public as punitive sentencers uninterested in mitigation and focused exclusively on the seriousness of the crime is unfounded.

The final part of the volume explores a number of practical issues. Warren Young and Andrea King discuss the development of guidance for problematic factors at sentencing, drawing on the guidelines currently being developed in New Zealand. Kevin Reitz discusses a very important issue that receives very little attention in the literature: proof of aggravating and mitigating factors at sentencing. Will Berry explores the implications of the landmark ruling from the US Supreme Court in *Booker*.

Our volume concludes with a chapter by Stephan Terblanche, who discusses sentencing factors in the South African context and notes the difficulty of determining whether specific factors influenced the sentencing outcome.

REFERENCES

Ashworth, A. (1987). 'Criminal Justice, Rights and Sentencing: A Review of Sentencing Policy and Problems', unpublished ms. at Worcester College, Oxford.

(2010). *Sentencing and Criminal Justice*, 5th edn. Cambridge University Press.

Ashworth, A. and Wasik, M. (2010). 'The Story of the Panel and Council', in Sentencing Guidelines Council, *Annual Report, 2009–2010*, available at www.sentencingcouncil.org.uk.

Australian Law Reform Commission (2006). *Same Crime, Same Time: Sentencing of Federal Offenders*. Sydney: Australian Law Reform Commission.

Bagaric, M. and Amarsekara, K. (2001). 'Feeling Sorry – Tell Someone who Cares: The Irrelevance of Remorse in Sentencing', *Howard Journal of Criminal Justice*, 40: 364–76.

Canadian Sentencing Commission. (1987). *Sentencing Reform: A Canadian Approach*. Ottawa: Supply and Services Canada.

Corbett, C. (1987). 'Magistrates' and Court Clerks' Sentencing Behaviour: An Experimental Study', in S. Lloyd-Bostock (ed.), *The Psychology of Sentencing*. Oxford: Centre for Socio-Legal Studies.

Cox, E. (1877). *The Principles of Punishment as Applied in the Administration of Criminal Law, by Judges and Magistrates*. London: Garland Publishing.

Delaware Sentencing Accountability Commission (2010). *Benchbook of the Delaware Sentencing Accountability Commission*, available at http://cjc.delaware.gov/SENTAC/Benchbook/2010%20SENTAC%20%20Benchbook.pdf.

Ford, P. (1972). *Advising Sentencers*. Oxford: Basil Blackwell.

Gilyeat, D. (1993). *A Companion Guide to Offence Seriousness*. Ilkley: Owen Wells.

Gross, H. (1979). *A Theory of Criminal Justice*. New York: Oxford University Press.

Hogarth, J. (1971). *Sentencing as a Human Process*. Toronto: University of Toronto Press.

Hough, M., Jacobson, J. and Millie, A. (2003). *The Decision to Imprison: Sentencing and the Prison Population*. London: Prison Reform Trust.

Jacobson, J. and Hough, M. (2007). *Mitigation: The Role of Personal Factors in Sentencing*. London: Prison Reform Trust.

Law Commission of New Zealand (2001). *Proof of Disputed Facts on Sentence*, Report 76. Wellington: Law Commission of New Zealand.

Minnesota Sentencing Guidelines Commission (2010). *Minnesota Guidelines and Commentary*, available at www.msgc.state.mn.us/guidelines/guide10.pdf.

Missouri Sentencing Advisory Commission (2007). *Recommended Sentencing User Guide. 2006*. St. Louis: Missouri Sentencing Advisory Commission.

Moxon, D. (1988). *Sentencing Practice in the Crown Court*. London: Home Office.
North Carolina Sentencing and Policy Advisory Commission (2007). *Structured Sentencing. Training and Reference Manual*. Raleigh: NCSPAC, available at www.nccourts.org/Courts/CRS/Councils/spac/Documents/yo_finalreporttolegislature.pdf.
Sentencing Guidelines Council (2007). *Reduction in Sentence for a Guilty Plea*, available at www.sentencingcouncil.org.uk/guidelines/guidelines-to-download.htm.
Shapland, J. (1981). *Between Conviction and Sentence*. London: Routledge & Kegan Paul.
Thomas, D. (1979). *Principles of Sentencing*, 2nd edn. London: Heinemann.
Utah Sentencing Commission (2010). *2010 Adult Sentencing and Release Guidelines*. Salt Lake City: Utah Sentencing Commission.
Victorian Sentencing Committee (1988). *Report of the Victorian Sentencing Committee*. Melbourne: Victorian Sentencing Committee.
Walker, N. (1985). *Sentencing: Theory, Law and Practice*. London: Butterworths.
(1999). *Aggravation, Mitigation and Mercy in English Criminal Justice*. London: Blackstone Press.
Wilkins, L. (1983).*Consumerist Criminology*. London: Heinemann.
Wisconsin Sentencing Commission (2010). *Sentencing Guidelines*, available at http://wsc.wi.gov.

TABLE OF CASES

R *v*. Saw and others [2009] EWCA Crim 1.
United States *v*. Booker (2005) 543 US 220.

CHAPTER TWO

RE-EVALUATING THE JUSTIFICATIONS FOR AGGRAVATION AND MITIGATION AT SENTENCING

Andrew Ashworth

In an important essay Julian Roberts has drawn attention to the paradox that aggravating and mitigating factors play a crucial role in sentencing, particularly in terms of quantum and around the custody threshold, and yet 'most guideline systems around the world adopt a laissez-faire approach' to these factors (Roberts 2008a: 274). Sentencing statutes or guidelines may list the relevant factors, and may even group them, but only rarely do they provide any guidance as to the relative weight of those factors or as to the impact they should have on sentence. The role of aggravating and mitigating factors is therefore left largely without structure, unbridled and untamed, a tendency that undermines the rationale of sentencing guidelines in providing common starting points and shared standards. It may also impair public understanding of sentences handed down by the courts.

In order to achieve their objectives, therefore, sentencing systems should deal with aggravating and mitigating factors in a more structured way. The most suitable form of those structures, and particularly the respective roles of principle and of quantification, is a pressing subject. However, this chapter is concerned with a logically prior task – that of scrutinizing the justifications for factors commonly accepted as aggravating and mitigating. It is therefore a prelude to those important architectural decisions, which will in any event depend on the nature and style of the particular sentencing system. Although this enquiry will examine the extent to which aggravating and mitigating factors are related to one or more of the purposes of sentencing, it is not assumed that such a link is necessary if the particular factor is to be accepted. It is quite possible that some factors will be supported by other social justifications that are valued sufficiently highly to override the relevant purpose of sentencing; it should not be assumed that the traditional 'purposes of sentencing' constitute a comprehensive set of goals worthy of pursuit in a sentencing system. It is also possible that insufficient justifications for a particular factor will be found at the level of principle. But consideration will also be given to the reasoning which provides the 'best fit' for existing practices, so that the arguments are not conducted entirely at a theoretical level but are brought closer to prevailing practice (where that is different).

CHAPTER OVERVIEW

The chapter begins by describing briefly the approach taken by the sentencing guidelines in England and Wales. It then sets out to assess the links between the purposes of sentencing and various aggravating and mitigating factors; to examine the justifications for the various extraneous mitigating factors, both in principle and for the 'best fit'; and to consider the proper role of mercy in sentencing. In conclusion, it returns to consider the implications of the analysis for sentencing guidelines.

THE GUIDELINES IN ENGLAND AND WALES

General structure

The definitive sentencing guidelines for England and Wales differ from those employed across the United States. The usual structure is for each offence to be divided into three or four categories or levels of seriousness. Each level of seriousness is assigned a range of sentences, with a starting point usually in the middle of the range. The English guidelines deal with aggravating and mitigating factors in a number of ways. The principal source is the guideline *Overarching Principles: Seriousness* (Sentencing Guidelines Council 2004), which contains a list of aggravating and mitigating factors, including the few that have statutory authority. The list is not intended to be exhaustive, and in respect of personal mitigation it is open-ended. In addition to referring to this general list, most of the offence guidelines go on to identify particular factors as aggravating or mitigating in two contexts.

First, some offence guidelines use factors (particularly aggravating factors) as determinants of offence-seriousness for the purpose of distinguishing between categories or levels of the offence. An example is the guideline on *Causing Death by Driving* (Sentencing Guidelines Council 2008a: 10–11), which ranks the relevant aggravating factors by directing that certain factors, such as the consumption of large amounts of drugs or alcohol or a prolonged and deliberate course of very bad driving, place an offence of causing death by dangerous driving in the highest of the three levels or categories.

Second, whether or not aggravating or mitigating factors are used to determine the level or category applicable to the particular case, a guideline will usually list a number of aggravating and mitigating factors which may or may not be found on the general list but which are likely to be particularly relevant to the offence in the guideline. Thus the guideline for the offence of causing death by dangerous driving lists seven 'additional aggravating factors' and six 'additional mitigating factors' (Sentencing Guidelines Council 2008a: 11).

The methodology of English guidelines

Once a sentencer has identified the relevant seriousness-based category of the offence, the next step is to place the offence at the appropriate point within the indicated range by reference to the relevant aggravating and mitigating factors. This is a matter of judgement, since the guidelines provide no general rankings or weightings. Account must be taken of previous convictions,[1] and for offenders with many previous convictions the criminal record may sometimes have the effect of moving the case from one offence category up to the next-higher category (see, e.g., the guideline *Theft and Burglary in a Building other than a Dwelling* (Sentencing Guidelines Council 2008b: 8)). Offender mitigation should then be assessed. However, once all these aggravating and mitigating factors have been taken into account, the English guidelines do provide for a quantified reduction in the case of an offender who pleaded guilty. The revised guideline *Reduction in Sentence for a Guilty Plea* (Sentencing Guidelines Council 2007) provides for a sliding scale of reductions, from one-third, for a guilty plea entered at the earliest opportunity, to one-tenth, for a guilty plea at the door of the court.

The English system of sentencing guidelines has been changed by the Coroners and Justice Act 2009 (Ashworth 2010b). The Act created a

[1] S. 143(2) of the UK Criminal Justice Act 2003 provides that each previous conviction renders the current offence more serious, taking account of how relevant and how recent that previous conviction is. For discussion of this complicated provision, see Roberts (2008b) and Ashworth (2010a: 206–18).

single Sentencing Council, and courts 'must follow' guidelines (whether created by the new Council or by the previous Sentencing Guidelines Council) unless it would be contrary to the interests of justice to do so. The Council's first guideline, on assaults, introduces several changes of format (Sentencing Council 2011), but the former guidelines remain in force until replaced. The Council is required (among other things) to prepare a guideline on the totality principle in relation to sentencing for multiple offences, and to consider providing guidance for 'determining the weight to be given to previous convictions of the offender' and to any other aggravating and mitigating factors that it considers to be of particular significance. How might the Council carry out this last obligation?

CONNECTING THE FACTORS WITH THE PURPOSES OF SENTENCING

English law, like that of many other jurisdictions, has a statutory list of sentencing purposes. According to section 142 of the Criminal Justice Act 2003, a court must have regard to the following five purposes when sentencing an adult:

(a) the punishment of offenders;
(b) the reduction of crime (including its reduction by deterrence);
(c) the reform and rehabilitation of offenders;
(d) the protection of the public; and
(e) the making of reparation by offenders to persons affected by their offences.

The relevant guideline, taking its cue from the following section of the Act, section 143, states that courts must 'pass a sentence that is commensurate with the seriousness of the offence' (Sentencing Guidelines Council 2004: 1), seriousness being determined by culpability and harm. All offence guidelines are drafted in terms of culpability and harm, and it is doubtful whether section 142 would be interpreted as allowing a judge to depart from a guideline if he or she takes the view that a different purpose of sentencing should be pursued in a particular case. Thus both the guideline on causing death by dangerous driving (Sentencing Guidelines Council 2008a: 10) and the guideline on theft in breach of trust (Sentencing Guidelines Council 2008b: 10) make it clear that the court's primary task is to assess the seriousness of the offence and to identify the sentencing range or category that most closely reflects it.

This emphasis on assessing harm and culpability indicates the centrality of proportionality judgments in English sentencing, and consequentially draws in many of the aggravating and mitigating factors. Indeed, in the lists of factors in the definitive guideline (Sentencing Guidelines Council 2004: 4–5), the aggravating factors are divided into 'factors indicating higher culpability' (including previous convictions, planning, use of weapon, abuse of trust, and operating in a gang or group) and 'factors indicating a more than usually serious degree of harm' (including multiple victims, vulnerability of victim, and additional degradation of victim). The list of mitigating factors is short, and refers only to factors indicating a lower level of culpability. All these factors therefore relate to proportionality. That is a central element in desert theory, and perhaps in what the Act refers to as 'the punishment of offenders'. It is also relevant to theories of deterrence such as that of Bentham, who devoted a whole chapter to 'the proportion between punishments and offences' and set out various principles such as 'venture more against a great offence than a small one' and 'induce a man to choose always the least mischievous of two offences' (Bentham 1948 [1789]: ch. XIV).

While culpability and harmfulness are crucial to assessments of proportionality, and therefore to desert theory and to aspects of deterrence, they have much less relevance to the pursuit of other purposes. The need for public protection may be influenced by the harmfulness of the offence committed, but culpability factors will be viewed in terms of their significance for the need to protect the public from the offender, and thus in terms of risk rather than responsibility. Mitigating factors that lower culpability may be assigned much less weight if they do not diminish the estimated need for public protection from the offender. On the other hand, reduced culpability and matters of personal mitigation may be highly important if the purpose of sentencing is reform or rehabilitation: where the offence is serious enough to take the starting point above the custody threshold, evidence that drugs were a significant factor in the offence and that the offender is willing to embark on a course of treatment for drug addiction may be sufficient to bring the sentence down to a community penalty. If reparation is a purpose of the sentence, action by the offender to ensure reparation to the victim may be regarded as more important than the relative seriousness of the offence.

One undecided issue is whether there is a strong case for taking account of the impact of a given sentence on a particular offender.

Bentham took the view that this should be taken into account (Bentham 1948 [1789]: ch. VI). Once the appropriate provisional punishment had been set by the judge, it should then be adjusted to reflect the degree of 'sensibility' of the individual offender. Bentham listed thirty-two 'circumstances influencing sensibility', including health, bodily imperfection, pecuniary circumstances and age. His view, then, was that sentences should be adjusted downwards or upwards where that is necessary to ensure the delivery of the same amount of punishment to this individual (given his or her unusual sensibilities) as that prescribed for people in general. The underlying principle, then, is that of equal impact. And for Bentham, since general deterrence was the principal purpose, it would be important that the calculation of the sentence, and the reasons for it, were clearly spelt out to the public.

Are 'circumstances affecting sensibility' relevant to proportionality theory? There should certainly be a place for the principle of equal impact in proportionality theory, most notably in relation to the calculation of fines. Earnings are distributed so unevenly that there ought to be some mechanism, such as 'day fines' or 'unit fines', that is designed to achieve a roughly equal impact for financial penalties. Does it not follow from this that account should also be taken of Bentham's 'circumstances influencing sensibility' when determining the choice between custody and a community sentence, or the length of a custodial sentence? It could be argued that degrees of personal resilience vary no less than earnings, and that custodial sentences should be shorter for the most sensitive and longer for the most resilient offenders (cf. Kolber 2009). Desert theorists are divided and uncertain about this comparison. Easton agrees that equality of impact should be pursued through unit fines, but opposes wider use of the principle of equal impact as 'potentially infringing [retributivism's] core principles of proportionality, equality and agency' and thereby reducing the 'status of formal proportionality' (Easton 2008: 116).

A less uncompromising approach would be to accept that resilience is far more difficult to judge than earnings, and that retributivists should therefore take account only of cases of exceptional vulnerability rather than striving to adjust the sentence in each and every case (compare Ashworth and Player 1998, with von Hirsch and Ashworth 2005: 172–6). That sounds like a pragmatic conclusion, however. Why stop short of taking account of significantly different sensibilities by means of lowering or (more rarely and more controversially) raising the provisional sentence? Desert theorists gauge the severity of sentences by assessing the effect of the sentence on the 'living standard' of ordinary people, but where that assessment is manifestly inapplicable to a particular individual, an adjustment should surely be made. An example of this is the sentencing of young offenders; it is widely recognized that one reason for subjecting them to less severe sentences than adults is that sentences can be expected to have a harsher impact on the young, and the English guidelines adopt this 'sensibilities' approach by providing for the adult starting points to be lowered progressively as the age of the young offender is lower (Sentencing Guidelines Council 2009: 24).

JUSTIFYING EXTRANEOUS MITIGATING FACTORS

Many of the factors listed in the English sentencing guidelines have already been classified above, in the sense that they have a bearing on the elements of harm and culpability that are crucial to the calculation of sentence. Now we need to focus on other factors, which may be termed 'extraneous' in order to distinguish them from factors related to harm or culpability, to see whether they can be classified in any helpful way and then justified. It should be noted that Swedish sentencing law takes a similar approach: most aggravating and mitigating factors affect the seriousness (or 'penal value') of the offence, but there is a list of seven other 'equity factors' that are not related to penal value but which a Swedish court should consider. These will be referred to as and when relevant, since Swedish law does not classify them further (Jareborg 1993; von Hirsch and Ashworth 2005: 166–7).

English sentencing practice yields at least six possible classes or groups of mitigating factors that have no bearing on proportionality. They are:

(i) positive social contributions;
(ii) pursuit of equality policies;
(iii) collateral or consequential effects of conviction and sentence on the offender;
(iv) collateral or consequential effects of the sentence on third parties;
(v) incentives to facilitate the smooth running of the criminal justice system; and
(vi) reparation, remorse and other post-offence matters.

In relation to each of these groups we shall ask two questions. First, if we were designing a sentencing system from scratch, are there persuasive reasons in principle for accepting the factors as a good reason for deviating from the proportionate sentence? Second, given that these factors have been used in practice for many years, which reasons offer the 'best fit' with prevailing practice?

Before starting on that exercise, one preliminary point should be dealt with. A core element of desert theory is that it conveys censure to the offender, to the victim and to wider society. The chosen sentence should express the degree of reprehensibleness of the offender's crime (von Hirsch and Ashworth 2005: 135). Is it not likely that this expressive function will be confused or obscured if other factors, unrelated to proportionality, lead to variations in the sentence imposed? This must be recognized as a possibility: there is a risk that confusion would arise if careful attention were not given to the sentence with which the court started, before making the adjustment. To minimize this would require a much more transparent approach to the explanation of how sentences are calculated. Judges are naturally reluctant to 'spell out the arithmetic', not least because the calculations cannot always be expressed adequately in terms of adding and subtracting individual elements in a complex case. But there has been some movement towards greater transparency in recent years, for example in relation to the reduction for a guilty plea (expressed in percentages) and in relation to the extra increment on sentences passed for racially aggravated offences,[2] and this is a movement that should be encouraged.

We now discuss each of the six groups of mitigating factors in turn:

(i) Positive social contributions

This group of potential mitigating factors includes cases in which an offender has saved another person from drowning while awaiting trial, or has done considerable voluntary service for the community (for examples, see Ashworth 2010a: 182–3). In principle there seems to be no reason why this should have any impact on the imposition of a proportionate sentence. It is a quite separate matter, which is more appropriately marked by some kind of civic award relevant to what has been done.

However, there is a long tradition of courts in various countries regarding this as a ground for mitigation at sentencing. If we are to find the 'best fit' reasoning, it must be that the sentencing process puts the court in the position of being able to choose between recognizing or

[2] The English guideline on sentencing for racially aggravated offences requires the court to state what sentence it would have given for the offence without the element of racial aggravation, and then to add the appropriate increment for the racial aggravation: *R v. Kelly and Donnelly*.

not recognizing this valuable contribution, and that it is regarded as socially fitting to make the recognition by some reduction in sentence. Insofar as that reasoning has some strength, it might be linked with the elusive and controversial concept of public confidence. Some might wish to argue that members of the public would expect a court to give some recognition to the offender's positive contributions when marking the significant negative contribution of the offence committed, and that the failure of the courts to do so would diminish public confidence in sentencing. Others might go further and argue that the courts' failure to recognize positive contributions might be taken symbolically to downgrade those contributions, and to undermine their value.

Even if that is the most plausible 'best fit' reasoning, it does not confront the argument that such matters are separate from the crime and should elicit a response in a different forum rather than being parachuted into the sentencing process. The question is whether the sentencing process is properly expected to incorporate a balance sheet of all the good and bad deeds of the offender in social, family and community circles. The principled answer is that it should not be so expected: a court should take account of previous convictions or absence of convictions, and of aggravating and mitigating factors relevant to harm and culpability, but it is neither appropriate nor always possible for it to attempt this wider exercise in social accounting. So there is a clear divergence between the principled argument and the 'best fit' reasoning.

(ii) The pursuit of equality policies

Sentencing law and practice incorporate various factors that stem from wider social policies. An example in recent English law has been the statutory requirement to aggravate sentence where an offence has been motivated by race, religion, or discrimination on grounds of disability or sexual orientation. Those aggravating factors go to harm and culpability, and so are not discussed in this context. More relevant are the differential effect of sentences on women and the significance of employment. It is widely accepted that imprisonment has a greater effect on women generally, partly because women's prisons are widely scattered and therefore further from their homes, partly because female prisoners can less frequently call on others to look after their family and home, partly because they have a higher rate of self-harming, and so on.

After discussing these findings, the Sentencing Advisory Panel in England recommended that the principle of minimum use of custody 'has a special force in relation to women offenders because of the multiple harms that are likely to result from incarceration' (Sentencing Advisory Panel 2010: 75). Some would regard this as part of the principle of equal impact: if prison has a demonstrably greater negative impact on women, this should be taken into account under the 'sensibility' principle in the second section, above, 'Connecting the factors with the purposes of sentencing'. Easton takes the principled argument further by contending that the proper response is to remove the negative impacts by, for example, relocating women's prisons (Easton 2008: 113–14); but, even then, mitigation of sentence must be the correct approach until the negative impacts are removed. So the argument of principle for this factor is strong; practice is less clear and, although it might be claimed that its 'best fit' is with Easton's argument, it is too variable to be sure.

Distinctly more controversial is the proper approach to employment matters. English courts often say that they are taking account of the fact that an offender would lose employment if given a certain (usually custodial) sentence, as a reason for suspending the sentence or giving a community sentence; the Swedish sentencing statute lists this as an equity-based mitigating factor. Yet no such mitigation is available to someone who is unemployed, often through no fault of his or her own, and in principle such mitigation is therefore discriminatory because unemployed offenders are liable to be sent to prison for the same offence. Indeed, the Minnesota Sentencing Guidelines Commission decided at an early stage that employment and social factors cannot justify a departure from a guideline (Parent 1988: 126–8), and the current guidelines emphasize this by stating that 'it is impossible to reward those employed without, in fact, penalizing those not employed at time of sentence' (Minnesota Sentencing Guidelines Commission 2008, IID101). But the 'best fit' with English court practice is that it is desirable to avoid as many negative consequences of crime and punishment as possible, a benign motivation connected with penal parsimony. The parsimony principle is that, since punishment in general and imprisonment in particular amounts to a significant deprivation of rights, it should be used with great restraint. This is an important liberal principle, but the difficulty of pursuing it in the present context is that it creates inequalities in punishment between employed and unemployed offenders, thus running contrary to the principle of equality before the law. We return to this conflict in the fourth section of the chapter, 'Mitigation, mercy and parsimony'.

(iii) Collateral or consequential effects of conviction and sentence on the offender

This group includes other deprivations resulting from the conviction, such as loss of pension rights and employment prospects; any adverse physical consequences of the offence, such as an injury sustained by the offender; effects flowing from a long delay in prosecution, such as when a person has led a blameless life for many years. One common feature of these examples is that they can usually be said to stem from the offender's fault – the decision to offend.

Another feature common to the first two examples is that they can be said to be part and parcel of the offence: an offender who commits a breach of trust offence ought to realize that it will destroy employment-related benefits, and an offender who climbs over a roof in order to commit burglary, or who drives dangerously, must know that there is a risk of injury to himself. In principle, consequences that can be said to be the offender's own fault do not seem to be strong candidates for mitigation of sentence. But sentencing practice is more equivocal; and, indeed, in Sweden factors of this kind are rationalized as 'natural punishment': the burglar who is injured while committing the offence has inflicted some 'punishment' on himself, and therefore requires less state punishment, and the same might be said of the fraudulent accountant who loses his career and his pension rights. This is a curious concept of punishment, however.

Even if we ignore the argument that the consequence was self-induced and therefore should not redound to the offender's advantage, it cannot properly be regarded as a form of punishment. It is certainly not state punishment. The 'best fit' reasoning here seems to be that the injury or loss of pension rights creates more pain and misery for the offender, and the court should take account of that, either in striving for some kind of wider justice or in reflecting the 'circumstances affecting sensibility' in such a case (see the second section, above, 'Connecting the factors with the purposes of sentencing'). But that reasoning comes into conflict with the equality policy advanced in subsection (ii) above, where it was argued that it is wrong to allow a source of mitigation that is only available to certain offenders who have an advantage that others lack. Moreover, any employment consequences of conviction or sentence may fairly be said to have been brought about by the offender's own fault.

(iv) Collateral or consequential effects of the sentence on third parties

This group of potential mitigating factors includes the effect on a baby or young child of its mother being in prison, the effect on a sick relative of the offender being in prison, and the effect on employees of their employer being in prison. In principle these factors have nothing to do with the appropriate quantum of punishment for the offender. But it is apparent that the sentencing process does afford an opportunity for the court to take one course that would have deleterious effects on third parties and another course that would have markedly fewer deleterious effects. Thus the 'best fit' reasoning is that the state's interest in imposing a proportionate sentence should be overridden by the interest of (innocent) third parties in not being disadvantaged by events over which they had no control. This is a broad and difficult question, long debated in the context of the effect on prisoners' families of having (usually) their breadwinner in prison.

To some extent it is part of the powerful impact of deprivation of liberty that it has these consequences for others as well as the imprisoned offender – that is, it is part of the reason why imprisonment should be used sparingly. Yet in principle that does not indicate that normal sentencing principles should be departed from; there are various social and other measures that can be taken to alleviate the position of the families who would otherwise suffer unfairly (Easton 2008: 113). The same response might be made when a victim's relatives claim that the continued imprisonment of a young man who killed their son is having an adverse emotional effect on them, since the two young men were close friends (see *R* v. *Nunn* 1996); this might be an occasion for counselling rather than for reducing a proportionate sentence.

The same principle could be adopted to deal with cases where an employer is imprisoned and the employees' jobs are then thrown into jeopardy, although this may be more difficult in practice because the necessary social counterbalance would be the intervention of someone capable of continuing to run the business, and it is not clear whether governments have such people available. The principled argument is therefore that the interests of third parties should not normally be treated as sufficient to override the proportionality principle, and that other social measures should be taken in order to deal with the negative consequences of convicting and sentencing the offender. The 'best fit' reasoning would reverse that priority and would favour using the sentencing process to assist third parties.

(v) Incentives to facilitate the smooth running of the criminal justice system

A reduction in sentence for pleading guilty now forms part of many legal systems. The question of principle is whether the state's interests in economy and efficiency are valued so highly as to override the presumption of innocence (see Ashworth 2010a: ch. 5). A similar question arises in relation to sentence reductions for assisting the police or prosecution by giving evidence against other offenders. In England the relevant guideline states that the reduction principle is not 'an aspect of mitigation' but an administrative discount for pleading guilty based on the cost savings in the case, the benefit of allowing other cases to be tried more expeditiously and the benefit to victims and witnesses of knowing that they will not need to give evidence (Sentencing Guidelines Council 2007: para. 2.2). These are wholly pragmatic reasons which have no necessary link with any of the purposes of sentencing. But the pragmatics must be questioned: is there an alternative way of preserving the incentive without altering the sentence? To offer a financial payment would be inappropriate and lead to perverse incentives (committing a crime so as to plead guilty and earn money), whereas at least a sentence reduction uses a token of recognition from within the same criminal justice system. The principled response is that the sentence reduction runs counter to whatever purpose of sentencing is uppermost – it detracts from the proportionate sentence, undermines the calculations on which a deterrent sentence is based, reduces the amount of public protection and so forth.

Some might dispute the first of those claims, on the basis that retributivists are unclear about whether the proportionate sentence is calculated for guilty pleaders or for those convicted after a trial; but, given the attachment of desert theorists to rights such as the presumption of innocence, it would surely be logical to assume that the proportionate sentence is calculated by reference to an offender convicted after a trial. So there is a sharp divide between the 'best fit' reasoning and the principled argument. Most English practitioners accept the inevitability of sentence reduction, because they can only envisage chaos and long waiting times if none were offered. Some may attempt a theoretical justification by claiming that a guilty plea shows remorse which therefore facilitates rehabilitation, but the links in that chain are at best contingent and at worst exaggerated and questionable.

(vi) Reparation, remorse and other post-offence matters

The principled stance that events occurring after the crime are not relevant to sentence would rule out two much-discussed grounds for mitigation. The first is remorse. If we assume that the court is satisfied that the remorse is genuine, it might be relevant to the purposes of rehabilitation or reparation, if either is germane in the particular case. It is difficult to see how it could be relevant to proportionality, unless it is supposed that by some kind of reverse process of absolution it reduces the culpability with which the offence was committed. However, some 'best fit' reasoning may be found in evidence that members of the public are more sympathetic towards offenders who apologize or otherwise show remorse, and Roberts argues that we should recognize the value of an offender publicly denouncing his or her own offending behaviour (Roberts 2008b: 76–7). Such a public self-denunciation should be rewarded in the only coinage available, reduction of sentence. And, although the remorse is self-evidently a post-offence phenomenon, it is at least connected to the offence and its aftermath, and taking it into account therefore cannot be excluded under subsection (i) above as belonging to a wider exercise of balancing an offender's positive and negative social contributions.

A rather different line of argument is relevant to voluntary reparation as a possible mitigating factor. We have noted that reparation is one of the legislative purposes of sentencing, which supplies an additional reason for encouraging it. The problem is that it quickly runs up against the equality principle in (ii) above. Where an offender's ability to make reparation derives from her or his wealth, judicial decisions in England have often repeated the warning that a wealthy offender should not be able to 'buy himself out of prison' (see Ashworth 2010a: 181–2). However, there is another principled argument that points in the opposite direction: that an offender who makes reparation is giving some public recognition of the fact that he has wrongfully injured the victim, which may be termed a 'quasi-retributive' reason because it chimes with the desert rationale's emphasis on offenders reflecting on their crime (von Hirsch and Ashworth 2005: 174–7). Thus one principled argument – that allowing mitigation to offenders who make financial reparation to their victims is discriminatory since it privileges those with wealth over those without financial resources – finds itself in direct conflict with another principled argument as well as with the 'best fit' reasoning, both of which draw on a purpose of sentencing (proportionate punishment, reparation).

MITIGATION, MERCY AND PARSIMONY

In 'Justifying extraneous mitigating factors' we considered six groups of mitigating factors in order to assess whether there are justifications for altering the otherwise appropriate sentence – that is, the proportionate sentence or that required for deterrence, public protection, rehabilitation or reparation. The principled conclusions have been almost entirely negative, supporting only the second class of factors, relating to equality policies. But all the other five classes of mitigating factor have been in common use for many years, and attempts were made above to find the reasoning that offered the 'best fit' with those widely accepted mitigating factors. Much of the reasoning was pragmatic in nature, most obviously in relation to the fifth class – incentives to facilitate the smooth running of the criminal justice system, where sentence reduction was justified as essential to avoid massive delays and costs in the criminal justice system. Pragmatic reasons must be scrutinized in order to ensure that they are pragmatic – that is, that they are based on the best evidence. Other 'best fit' reasoning placed considerable weight on the symbolic effect of court sentences, and the (popular?) belief that sentencers should indulge in a form of social accounting in relation to manifestly pro-social but unrelated behaviour by the defendant, for example.

If the 'best fit' reasoning were adopted, then the classes of mitigating factor in English sentencing law would not change. However, if the principled approach were taken, the range of permissible mitigating factors would be reduced drastically. Female offenders would receive mitigation, at least until the extra negative effects for them of imprisonment are removed. There would be only a small reduction in sentence for pleading guilty ((v)), no reduction on account of collateral consequences ((iii) and (iv)), and no reduction for positive social contributions ((i)). Any such changes in English sentencing would be bound to have a dramatic effect, taking away many long-standing mitigating factors. Two likely consequences would be an increasing resort to the concept of mercy, and concern about parsimony in sentencing, and these are now addressed in turn.

The proper scope of mercy in sentencing depends on the meaning assigned to the term. Tasioulas (2003) adopts a very wide approach to mercy, including frequently raised factors such as provocation, which many people would include within the list of culpability related factors. It is preferable to treat mercy as referring to exceptional situations, so that courts exercise mercy in sentencing only where there is a particularly unusual and compelling factor for which normal principles of mitigation of sentence do not adequately provide. This might extend, for example, to an offender whose mother, through illness, is in the final stages of her life.

Another example is the woman who jumped off the Humber bridge holding her small child, intending to commit suicide and to kill the child. She survived, and also managed to keep the child afloat and alive until rescuers reached them. Her crime was attempted murder and the guideline indicated a high sentence, but the judge took account of her mental disturbance and her efforts to save the child in passing a short custodial sentence, and the Court of Appeal out of 'mercy' substituted a community sentence (*R* v. *Schumann* 2007). This is a case where compassion for the offender was appropriate, and therefore a mitigated sentence based on mercy was in order. A further example was a case in which armed burglars entered a man's house, and the householder (joined by his brother) chased one burglar and gave him a very serious beating. The guideline for wounding with intent indicated a substantial sentence, but the court held that in these circumstances 'the call for a merciful sentence [was] intense' and reduced the sentences well below the relevant guideline (*R* v. *Hussain and Hussain* 2010).

However, there is a practical danger here – that courts might use the concept of mercy as a kind of escape route to avoid following guidelines. In the past, courts have used the concept of mercy in an attempt to avoid setting a precedent; thus, where a prisoner is suffering from a terminal illness or other serious medical condition, the Court of Appeal has stated that it may reduce the sentence as 'an act of mercy . . . rather than by virtue of any general principle' (*R* v. *Bernard* 1997). This is unsatisfactory; there should be a general principle, and courts should not have discretion to decide whether or not to reduce the sentence, when the basis for doing so is established. Thus the importance of being able to mitigate for 'mercy' should not be obscured by suggesting that it can operate outside the realms of principle. The court's stated justification for sentence is particularly important in this type of case.

If the principled conclusions set out above were adopted, one consequence (certainly for the English sentencing system) would be that some traditional mitigating factors would disappear, and one consequence of that might be an overall increase in sentence severity. That would go against the principle of parsimony, or restraint in sentencing, discussed in subsection (ii) above. It seems that, among those who subscribe to the parsimony principle, there are two separate streams. One maintains that parsimony should be pursued at a general level, by reducing overall levels of severity (system parsimony). The other maintains that opportunities for parsimony should be taken as and when they arise, and irrespective of whether this compromises any other value or principle (opportunist parsimony). Opportunists would therefore support the reduction of sentences for people in employment and people who pay compensation to their victims, and in a range of other cases which contravene the equality principle (compare Ashworth 2010a: ch. 7, with Morris and Tonry 1990). This means that opportunists would be disposed in favour of retaining as many grounds of mitigation as possible, holding on to the 'best fit' arguments above. Those who favour system parsimony would oppose the inequalities that would result from opportunist parsimony, and would prefer a more direct and general approach to controlling severity.

CONCLUSIONS

This preliminary examination of the many theoretical problems raised by the role of aggravating and mitigating factors in sentencing has highlighted the difficulty of locating respectable principles in support of many longstanding mitigating factors, and in some instances has revealed a conflict of principles relevant to a particular ground of mitigation. Perhaps the clearest practical example is the broad acceptance of factors such as employment status in English sentencing, compared with the insistence on equality and non-discrimination in systems such as that of Minnesota, discussed in category (ii) above. The questions of priority that this raises cannot be avoided when devising guidance and guidelines on the application of aggravating and mitigating factors. To accept some of the arguments of principle outlined here may require a guidelines authority to go against popular belief or against ingrained judicial practice, or to compromise the principles that seem to have the most powerful appeal. In this sphere as in others, the first step should be to lay bare and to discuss openly the conflicting policies and principles. This chapter seeks to make a modest and provocative contribution to that exercise.

REFERENCES

Ashworth, A. (2010a). *Sentencing and Criminal Justice*, 5th edn. Cambridge University Press.

(2010b). 'Sentencing Guidelines and the Sentencing Council', *Criminal Law Review*: 389–401.

Ashworth, A. and Player, E. (1998). 'Sentencing, Equal Treatment and the Impact of Sanctions', in A. Ashworth and M. Wasik (eds.), *Fundamentals of Sentencing Theory*. Oxford University Press.

Bentham, J. (1948 [1789]). *Principles of Morals and Legislation*, ed. Wilfred Harrison. Oxford: Basil Blackwell.

Easton, S. (2008). 'Dangerous Waters: Taking Account of Impact in Sentencing', *Criminal Law Review*: 105–20.

Jareborg, N. (1993). 'The Role of Aggravating and Mitigating Factors in Sentencing: the New Swedish Sentencing Law', in U. Goranson (ed.), *Modern Legal Issues: An Anglo-Swedish Perspective*. Uppsala: Iustus Forlag.

Kolber, A. (2009). 'The Subjective Experience of Punishment', *Columbia Law Review*, 109: 182–236.

Minnesota Sentencing Guidelines Commission (2008). *Sentencing Guidelines and Commentary*, available at www.leg.state.mn.us/docs/2007/mandated/070551.pdf.

Morris, N. and Tonry, M. (1990). *Between Prison and Probation*. New York: Oxford University Press.

Parent, D. (1988). *Structuring Criminal Sentences: The Evolution of Minnesota's Sentencing Guidelines*. Stoneham, Mass.: Butterworths Legal Publishers.

Roberts, J. (2008a). 'Aggravating and Mitigating Factors at Sentencing: Towards Greater Consistency of Application', *Criminal Law Review*: 264–76.

(2008b). *Punishing Persistent Offenders*. Oxford University Press.

Sentencing Advisory Panel. (2010). *Overarching Principles of Sentencing: Advice*, available at www.sentencingcouncil.org.uk.

Sentencing Guidelines Council (2004). *Overarching Principles: Seriousness*, available at www.sentencingcouncil.org.uk.

(2007). *Reduction in Sentence for a Guilty Plea: Revised Guideline*, available at www.sentencingcouncil.org.uk.

(2008a). *Causing Death by Driving*, available at www.sentencingcouncil.org.uk.

(2008b).*Theft and Burglary in a Building Other than a Dwelling*, available at www.sentencingcouncil.org.uk.

(2009). *Overarching Principles: Sentencing Youths*, available at www.sentencingcouncil.org.uk.

Sentencing Council (2011). *Assault and Other Offences against the Person*. London: Sentencing Council.

Tasioulas, J. (2003). 'Mercy', *Proceedings of the Aristotelian Society*, **CIII**, 101–32.

von Hirsch, A. and Ashworth, A. (2005). *Proportionate Sentencing*. Oxford University Press.

TABLE OF CASES

R *v*.Bernard, (1997) 1 *Criminal Appeal Reports* (Sentencing) 135.
R *v*.Hussain and Hussain, (2010) *Criminal Law Review* 428.
R *v*. Kelly and Donnelly, [2001] 2 Cr. App. R.s (S) 341.
R *v*.Nunn, (1996) 2 *Criminal Appeal Reports* (Sentencing) 136.
R *v*.Schumann, (2007) 2 *Criminal Appeal Reports* (Sentencing) 465.

CHAPTER THREE

THE SEARCH FOR PRINCIPLES OF MITIGATION: INTEGRATING CULTURAL DEMANDS

Allan Manson

Almost all sentencing decisions contain some reference to mitigating or aggravating factors, yet it is extremely rare to come across a judicial discussion of the rationale or scope of these factors. More to the point, there is very little consideration of mitigation and aggravation from a theoretical perspective. As Ashworth notes, these issues 'have tended to attract little close examination or theoretical discussion' (2010: 156). Philosophers have debated some of the issues, but these discussions are, for the most part, limited to arguments about the distinction between mercy and compassion, and their respective relationships with justice. Recently we have also seen efforts by both leading proportionality theorists and their antagonists, the limiting retributivists, to accommodate some sentencing factors in their modes of analysis. While they feel compelled to make this accommodation, neither provides a unified or over-arching theoretical perspective that justifies it. Still, we can learn a lot from their attempts to integrate mitigation and aggravation. The primary lesson is that, from a theoretical perspective, the underlying premises of mitigation and aggravation are elusive.

The courts provide another interesting perspective. Judges seem to know intuitively how to use the factors of mitigation and aggravation to round out their sentencing calculus, although they rarely spend any time discussing these concepts. Questions about underlying rationale,

The author would like to thank his colleagues Andrew Ashworth, Anthony Doob, Julian Roberts and Malcolm Thorburn for their helpful comments while this 'cultural' idea has been percolating in his head.

definition, scope and extent of adjustment remain in play with very little judicial explanation or even attention. Looking at Canadian courts, for example, we can locate their justification of the use of mitigation and aggravation in their abiding concern to characterize sentencing as an individualized process.[1] It is as if this makes it self-evident that some personal characteristics or offence-related factors necessarily influence the quantum and type of sentence. Yet the courts do not explain why or how, beyond references to the larger concepts of proportionality, parity, gravity and culpability.

In some jurisdictions, statutes stipulate mitigating and aggravating factors, albeit without any generalized rationale. In countries with guidelines we see acknowledgment of some accepted factors but these are never intended to be exhaustive. Research on the use by English courts of personal factors in mitigation has recently been published (see Jacobson and Hough 2007). This empirical view of the landscape is enlightening, and even suggests some interesting commonalities, but it does not lead to a theory of mitigation. Indeed, we have a curious situation. It cannot be that the answer to the mitigation and aggravation issue is simply that the concepts are clear and self-evident, requiring no debate and needing no principles. However, a search for principles leaves us with the recognition that there are some accepted factors which fit easily into a typology but others that are difficult to categorize. Accordingly, there is an area that is relatively unconstrained within an unfettered zone of judicial discretion.

In this essay I want to argue that we shall not find a philosophical principle, or principles, that will define mitigating factors adequately. This is because mitigation bears witness to the simple fact that the sentencing process is more than a reasoned response to a problem. Its dimensions are diverse – part punishment and part justice. It is concerned with the public interest in safety and stability, but also with the interests of victims and offenders. The sentencing process employs a complex decision-making matrix that goes beyond normative principles. I start by looking at the adequacy of the two accepted and understandable categories:

(i) Any factor that diminishes the gravity of an offence ought to mitigate the punishment to a commensurate degree.

[1] See numerous Supreme Court of Canada decisions, especially *R v. Angelillo*, at para. 24, *R v. Proulx*; *R v. C.A.M.*

(ii) Factors which diminish culpability ought to have a mitigating effect on the punishment for the offence committed.

However, according to my schematic conception of mitigating factors, there are two other categories. One arises from systemic exigencies:

(iii) Factors which have an intrinsic systemic relation to the effective operation of a criminal justice system can be recognized as mitigating in order to encourage pragmatically their systemic role.

This third category receives little critical attention, but its pragmatic rationale can be easily demonstrated. Its legitimacy is a matter of expedient systemic choice rather than principle. It includes factors like a plea of guilty regardless of sincere remorse, and offering assistance to authorities. In this paper I do not intend to explore this category. My attention here is addressed to a different point, the role that culture plays in mitigation. The above typology leaves out some accepted mitigating factors which cannot be explained by reference to the principles which underlie the three stipulated categories. Ultimately, I shall argue that the elusive fourth category is culturally derived. That is, the culture of a jurisdiction influences what factors ought legitimately to warrant the sympathy of a sentencing judge. This is what I refer to as 'legitimate sympathy'.

As Garland (1990) has shown, sentencing is both a product and an instrument of culture. By the same token that culture provides meaning to community life, it also fills in the subtle meanings of a sentence beyond the demands of other principles and goals. The relationship between culture and sentencing may be broad-based and even opaque in some circumstances, but its impact is clear. Culture influences the attachment to capital punishment in the United States, China, Russia and other countries, but culture also explains why Scandinavian countries have been creative in developing alternatives to imprisonment. I argue below that while philosophy explains the role of gravity and culpability in mitigation and aggravation, culture answers the intriguing residual questions.

DESERT MODELS AND THE OBVIOUS PRINCIPLES

In our effort to accommodate mitigation and aggravation in desert theory, a useful starting point is the very neat encapsulation of proportionality theory provided by Jareborg:

> Proportionate sentencing is a matter of relative, system-internal, proportionality. It can be compared to allotting marks in schools and at universities. There is no given criterion for who is going to be awarded this or that mark. But when it has been decided what criteria to use, and where the borders between different marks are to be, all who are judged to have performed equally well must be awarded the same mark. The fact that it is impossible to say what mark is deserved without intermediation of a system does not exclude that it would be utterly unjust to award different marks for equal performances, or the same mark for performances of a clearly different quality.
>
> (Jareborg 2002: 112)

Any sentencing system that incorporates proportionality as a central determinant of sentencing necessarily relies on certain basic principles to ensure the integrity of the sentencing process. The Jareborg quotation includes two of the principles of justice noted by Hart (1968) as essential to distribution: like cases must be treated alike, and cases of different gravity cannot be treated with equal severity. To complete the principles, Hart would also add the need for some mitigation for those 'who have special difficulties to face in keeping the law' (p. 16). Whether we are speaking of a pure desert model or even limiting retributivism, both approaches accept that any fact that bears on the gravity of the offence or the culpability of the offender needs to be incorporated into the issue of what is proportionate. Regardless of how much work proportionality is expected to do in determining the ultimate punishment, gravity and culpability provide two clear elements which bear on mitigation or aggravation. But culpability and gravity require some examination to understand how much of the turf they can legitimately occupy.

The premise underlying gravity is that the existence of a factor which makes the offence a graver example of its genus is aggravating, while any fact that diminishes gravity ought to mitigate from the proportionate response. Gravity is usually demonstrated by relevant consequential harm, both in terms of harm caused and the level of harm that was intended or ought to have been reasonably foreseen.[2] Certainly, there are some controversies about harm. Proportionality theory has an intrinsic difficulty in finding a mechanism that integrates into a fair and explicable ordinal proportionality calculus different kinds and qualities of harms produced by different offences. Von Hirsch, Ashworth and

[2] See, e.g., Criminal Code, R.S.C. 1985, c. C-46, s.718.1 (Canada); Criminal Justice Act 2003, s. 143.1 and *Overarching Principles*, Sentencing Council (2010).

Jareborg have proposed a 'living-standard gauge' for this purpose (2005: 190). This is an interesting measure which is 'far from perfect' (see discussion in Thorburn and Manson 2007), but for mitigation purposes this is immaterial, because we are not comparing different kinds of offences. Second, there are controversies between jurisdictions as to the scope of harms which can be attributed to the offender. This is usually cast in terms of whether all harm caused by an offence is attributable to the offender or whether some conception of fault limits attributable harm to what was intended, reasonably foreseeable or ought to have been foreseen.[3] However, within each system one can usually find an accepted conception of harm, plus a recognition that both uncharacteristically minimal harm and unusually gross harm are both relevant to the sentencing decision because they affect the assessment of gravity. The third issue is inchoate offences and offences of endangerment where the applicable concept of harm is based on what was intended, or what ought to have been foreseen. In the end, gravity is a principle with limited application, since it deals with only one aspect of potential sentencing facts, the extent of properly attributable harm relevant to the offence.

The culpability of the offender recognizes that there are circumstances and offender-specific personal factors which indicate greater or lesser blameworthiness in relation to the offence.[4] Most of these factors will be personal characteristics that have the effect of reducing culpability due to diminished capacity or judgement.[5] However, there are other motivations which can be viewed as enhancing or diminishing culpability.[6] Some reasons for an action are laudable or generate sympathy, and others are distasteful and abhorrent. Most sentencing regimes provide some room for making these distinctions based on notions of culpability.

An important caveat relates to the role of character. It is common for judges to explain that certain personal or historical facts are relevant to sentencing because they reveal the character of the offender.[7] This may

3 See Sentencing Council (2010) and discussion in Manson (2001: 86–90).

4 See Manson (2001): 105, 145 (discussing the impact of being a 'youthful offender' and having a disadvantaged background, respectively).

5 Ibid., 133–5 (discussing impairment of judgment as a mitigating circumstance); Sentencing Council (2010) s. D, para. 1.22.

6 See Manson (2001: 378–80); Sentencing Council (2010), s. D, para. 1.22.

7 See, e.g., the admissibility of evidence of another as yet unprosecuted offence under the 'character' rubric by the majority in *R v. Angelillo*, para. 17 (relying on *R v. Edwards*); cf. the dissent of Fish J in *Angelillo*, para. 56.

have some relevance to culpability if the goal is to show that the offence was out of character, suggesting the existence of some external influence that ought to mitigate. However, beyond this, it is difficult to see how character, by itself, can have any bearing on proportionality. Judges remind us of the need to learn the 'facts' about the offender. Certainly this is part of what Canadian judges mean when they use the word 'individualization'.[8] But surely the personal facts must be relevant to the sentencing process. Otherwise it is superfluous narrative that creates the potential for irrelevant considerations. So if character matters, it must relate to an instrumental objective such as rehabilitation or incapacitation. Dangerousness increases the prospect of longer incapacitation, while prior success in life may suggest greater rehabilitative prospects. These make sense to utilitarians, but pure desert theory would reject the relevance of both. A proponent of limiting retributivism might be keener to entertain their applicability, but they cannot be understood by resort to gravity or culpability, and an unexplained resort to character is a potential sentencing danger.

The breadth of the seriousness guideline in England and Wales show how much of the mitigation question can be encompassed by these two concepts.[9] But it is still incomplete: there is a residue of mitigating factors often recognized which do not fit neatly within these principles and which do not receive uniform treatment. These are personal factors that seem to generate sympathy but are unrelated to the offence or culpability: collateral consequences, pre-offence praiseworthy lifestyles or achievements and post-offence conduct that reflect remorse, reparation or reintegrative prospects. These receive consideration, but within a theoretical vacuum. We need an answer that treats like cases alike and recognizes differences, and that precludes bias based on status and class.

THE CONTRIBUTION OF PHILOSOPHERS

For decades there has been a rich and interesting debate among philosophers that touches on the basic issues of mitigation through the concepts of justice and mercy. However, from a sentencing perspective it has been an unsatisfactory one. The philosophical debate is an effort to understand how justice can encompass compassion without treading into the extrajudicial territory of mercy. The argument is that justice

[8] See, e.g., *R v. M. (C.A.)*, at para. 70; *R v. Proulx* at para. 92; *R. v. McDonnell*, at paras. 90–92.
[9] See Sentencing Council (2010), section D, 'Assessment of Culpability and Harm'.

and mercy are separate concepts and one needs to determine when justice is implicated as compared with mercy. Philosophers recognize the existence of claims of sympathy in relation to punishment, but they argue about whether justice can always respond to those claims.

While this discourse contains some classic contributions (for example the work of Murphy and Hampton (1988) and Nussbaum (1993)), the philosophical issues are, for the most part, really about definition. Whether a particular matter can be included in the considerations that the system of justice takes into account can be determined simply by adjusting the scope of these relevant factors rather than engaging in a tortuous philosophical argument. Historically, the evolution of the criminal law concepts known as justifications and excuses demonstrates this point. These were first recognized by the exercise of the Royal Prerogative of Mercy before they were incorporated and developed within the common law (Cole and Manson 1990). The sovereign responded to sympathetic claims, some of which found their way into substantive law: self-defence, duress and the partial defence of provocation are examples.

The philosophical debate shows us that there are indeed some personal factors that produce a sympathetic response. To make progress, we need to change the inquiry into one about the concept of 'sympathy' rather than 'mercy'. Sympathy better conveys the emotive and fluid nature of the issue without the baggage that 'mercy' brings to the table. To find appropriate and legitimate sources of sympathy we need to look beyond the philosophical arena.

VON HIRSCH, ASHWORTH AND THE AMERICAN LAW INSTITUTE

Von Hirsch and Ashworth pursue a principled approach to mitigation by using the phrase 'equity factors' (2005: 165). They are correct that neither equality of impact nor the philosophical debate about justice, mercy and compassion can provide an answer (pp. 172–4). The authors do a good job of dealing with age, infirmity and the equality of impact argument, but go astray in searching for what they call a 'quasi-retributivist' solution (pp. 174–5). Regardless of the qualifier 'quasi', they are asking desert to do too much conceptual work. A theorist looks for principle, and a desert theorist looks for a retributivist principle, but does one need artificially to construct a concept like 'quasi-retributivism' to fill the gap that retributivism cannot cross? Like Hart's conclusion that the 'general justifying aim' need not be exactly the same concept that answers the distribution question, a principled response to the problems of mitigation need not be found in 'quasi-retributivism' or any other philosophical concept. Von Hirsch and Ashworth are perhaps looking for apples too high up on the tree; while, slightly hidden and difficult to see, the fruit may be closer to hand.

The American Law Institute in its new draft Model Penal Code (2006) continues the effort to explain mitigation. Limiting retributivists accept the importance of proportionality but also invoke pragmatic concerns about the exigencies of punishment, make substantial room for restraint and accept some evidence-based utilitarian considerations. Accordingly, in the general purpose and principle part of the proposed Model Penal Code we find, right after the statement that sentences need to fall 'within a range of severity proportionate' to gravity, harm and blameworthiness, the second purpose:

> in appropriate cases, to achieve offender rehabilitation, general deterrence, incapacitation, and restoration of crime victims and communities, provided these goals are pursued with the boundaries of sentence severity permitted in subsection (a)(i).
>
> (s. 1.02(2)(a)(ii))

Leaving aside the references to general deterrence and incapacitation, this means that a set of factors can find its way into sentencing because there is a relation to the achievement of future goals such as reintegration, reparation and accountability through remorse. But do these factors operate to encourage a community-based alternative or can they produce a discount? If so, how much of a discount can be provided for these utilitarian goals without undermining proportionality? Is it legitimate to privilege prior status, wealth or professional skills just because they enhance the prospect of future reintegration? In other words, how can we avoid these utilitarian considerations leading to class-based discrimination?

The American Law Institute (ALI) goes further when dealing with how a commission should construct guidelines. First, it stipulates that no weight shall be given to 'race, ethnicity, gender, sexual orientation or identity, national origin, religion or creed, socioeconomic status, and political affiliation or belief' (s. 6B.06 (2)). Second, it expressly addresses a set of mitigating factors that a commission might incorporate:

> the personal characteristics of offenders may be included as considerations within the guidelines *when indicative of circumstances of hardship,*

> *deprivation, vulnerability, or handicap*, but only as grounds to *reduce the severity of sentences* that would otherwise be recommended.
>
> (s. 6B.06(4)(a), emphasis added)

This approach may be attractive but it still leaves residual issues. Not every circumstance that should mitigate is easily included within the 'circumstances of hardship, deprivation, vulnerability, or handicap'. Moreover, some circumstances within these rubrics should not always mitigate.

The work of both the ALI and von Hirsch and Ashworth confirm that there is a need for a sentencing system to accommodate mitigation by addressing some personal characteristics or circumstances, whether we describe them as 'equity factors' or 'circumstances of hardship, deprivation, vulnerability, or handicap'. One might argue that sentencing systems have always done this, but the issue is not whether mitigation plays a role in sentencing but how to make its role a principled one. Beyond providing generic rubrics, the ALI and von Hirsch and Ashworth have not explained comprehensively which factors are encompassed by their conceptions of mitigation, nor how much mitigation may be produced in order not to undermine proportionality and parity. But if we look more carefully at *Proportionate Sentencing* (von Hirsch and Ashworth 2005), there are significant hints about where to find answers.

SUGGESTING THE CULTURAL ANSWER

Von Hirsch and Ashworth (2005) have hit on the right area to survey. The second pillar of their proportionality theory – the one that refines the actual sentencing decision – is known as 'cardinal proportionality'. While 'ordinal proportionality' relies on the sub-requirements of parity, rank-ordering and spacing (pp. 139–40), 'cardinal proportionality' does not deal with the comparative severity of punishment but with determining the 'actual . . . severity levels of at least some crimes' (p. 141). The authors explain, '[w]hen judged in absolute rather than comparative terms, the censure expressed through penal deprivation is in part *a matter of convention*' (p. 142). This assessment derives substantially from 'anchoring points' which are discernible and specific starting points or penalty levels for particular examples of an offence. Over time, 'existing convention' will provide some 'anchoring points' (pp. 141–2). They are like disparate rungs on an incomplete ladder. Ordinal proportionality determines which rung goes above which, as well as their size and the relative spacing between them. But it is the anchoring point that fixes the location of specific rungs. Anchoring points are located by 'existing convention', but the placement of other rungs for other offences is based on adjustments either up or down in accordance with severity levels.[10]

Von Hirsch and Ashworth accept that their approach provides, by itself, only 'a limited degree of guidance on the setting of the penalty system's anchoring points' (p. 143). While precision will evolve over time as more rungs are placed on the ladder, their explanation of 'cardinal proportionality' implicitly accepts a substantial cultural role through the vehicle of convention. Although it is not fully developed by von Hirsch and Ashworth, 'convention' must refer to existing penal practice, namely the product of existing sentencing legislation, judicial interpretation and common law sentencing decisions. Culture is central to these elements, which are produced by institutional actors who are creatures of their own experience and their own context. They are, in varying degrees, influenced by political discourse, pushed by prosecutors and chastised by journalists. Their attitudes will reflect their education, their upbringing, their work experiences, their religious backgrounds and even their local customs. Surely these are all cultural factors although mediated by the deliberative processes of law and politics. While convention may be a euphemism for practice, it is also necessarily a cultural product.

CULTURE, SENTENCING AND DAVID GARLAND

We need to start by looking at what culture is, and what this expansive concept encompasses. Culture produces the array of meanings that give shape and colour to any society's institutions, practices and interactions. It is the diverse and multidimensional product of customs, traditions, folklore and rituals, and is both local and national. It is passed on through generations and disseminated by manners and customs, by oral accounts and narratives, by fiction and non-fiction writing, by festivals and entertainment. Culture has been transmitted in homes, churches, schools, cafes, taverns, workshops, guildhalls and the Women's Institute. More recently, technology has provided

[10] p. 142. The authors argue, invoking an appreciation of the importance of restraint, that only a reduction should be considered, although a dramatic reduction in punitiveness may not be popular, practical or politic.

the pre-eminent avenues of cultural transmission, starting with books, newspapers, radio and television, and moving recently into the expanding era of the Internet, chat rooms, Skype and blogs. Culture is constantly shaped and reshaped by significant events and technological developments, and influenced by prominent individuals. Over time, it develops its own discourses of religion, politics, science, philosophy and literature which produce their own cultural influences. It produces subcultures shared by those in common circumstances, as reflected by the distinct groupings of elites, artisans and underclasses, as well as what is often called popular culture. Orwell and Ma Bell, Google and Gogol, original sin and original intent – these are different forms of cultural engines which have influenced their particular contexts in a variety of ways.

Many writers adopt the anthropological view that culture is 'a system of shared meanings, attitudes and values, and the symbolic forms (performances, artifacts) in which they are embodied' (Thompson 1991: 6). However, it would be wrong to assume that this approach requires consensus or that culture is one-dimensional. Given the breadth and diversity of culture and its sources, and the variety of ways in which it is transmitted and interpreted, there will always be the potential for cultural contradictions and even disputes. This will vary with the extent to which a community is heterogeneous and class-differentiated.

Looking back to custom as the original source of culture, E. P. Thompson (1991) argued that it tended over time to split into various tributaries:

> If, along one path 'custom' carried many of the meanings we assign now to 'culture', along another path custom had close affinities to the common law. This law was derived from the customs, or habitual usages, of the country. Usages which might be reduced to rule and precedents, which in some circumstances were codified and might be enforceable at law.
>
> (pp. 3–4)

This codification goes beyond law and extends to the development of other discourses. The division of custom explains how culture can be both expressive but also instrumental in the ways that it influences the social and material relations within a community. While culture in its broadest sense is always fluid, some cultural norms become entrenched and codified, making them easier to acknowledge, easier to enforce and harder to change.

In *Punishment and Modern Society*, Garland attempts to translate the concept of culture into the field of sentencing. Using the compendious word 'penality' to describe all of punishment, sentencing, penal policy and penal institutions, he starts his cultural analysis by noting that it must be distinctive, 'concentrating upon those elements which most influence punishment and showing how it is that they are expressed in the penal sphere' (p. 194). He dissects culture into two spheres that encompass its cognitive and emotional aspects. These are called 'mentalities' and 'sensibilities'. This is especially significant for our examination of mitigation, even though Garland rarely, and only obliquely, addresses these issues. His description of the two aspects also makes clear the scope of the cultural concept he is examining:

> In its cognitive aspect, culture refers to all those conceptions and values, categories and distinctions, frameworks of ideas and systems of belief which human beings use to construe their world and render it orderly and meaningful. It thus covers the whole range of mental phenomena, high and low, elaborated and inarticulated, so that philosophies, sciences, and theologies are included alongside traditional cosmologies, folk prejudices, and 'plain common sense'. Likewise, normative schemes of taste, fashion, manners, and etiquette are no less a part of culture than are the developed systems of ethics, justice, and morality. These 'mentalities' or ways of thinking are, in turn, closely linked to ways of feeling and sensibilities, so that the cognitive aspects of culture become inseparable from the its affective dimensions.
>
> (1990: 195)

Looking first at 'mentalities', Garland uses a number of examples from history, philosophy and evolving conceptions of justice to show how cultural patterns have influenced the development of penal policy and penal institutions. These include the abandonment of public spectacles of suffering, the movement away from capital punishment and the treatment of young offenders and the mentally ill. Similarly, religious influences played a major role in making character a relevant sentencing factor, although it was originally narrowly defined to ask only how far down the roads to wickedness and dangerousness an offender had travelled.

Garland's sociological analysis relies heavily on Elias's work, particularly *The Civilizing Process* (1994), and he argues that the most 'obvious' example of its application to the penal regime would be with respect to the extension of sympathy to offenders. Here, he refers to the various cultural influences which might be viewed as constituting a 'civilized conscience' and which over time produced 'lowering in the intensity of punishment, the extension of charity to prisoners and offenders, the provision of social welfare measures in the twentieth century, the amelioration of prison conditions in most states and even the legal recognition of prisoners' rights in some of them' (p. 236). Ultimately, Garland concludes in unequivocal terms that penal mechanisms are cultural artefacts:

> penal practices exist within a specific penal culture which is itself supported and made meaningful by wider cultural forms, these, in turn, being grounded in society's patterns of material social life and action. It hardly needs to be said that the major cultural themes which appear in penality – conceptions of justice, of crime, religious forms, attitudes towards age, race, class, gender and so on – did not develop independently there, nor do they stand on their own isolated beliefs. Like all cultural elements they are enmeshed with wider belief-systems and mentalities, deriving their sense and credibility from their ability to resonate with established ways of thinking and understanding.
>
> (p. 211)

This is an important conclusion, but some might suggest that Garland's conclusion applies only on a 'macro' scale to the array of sentencing options and does not extend to the more subtle 'micro' distinctions about individual offenders which the sentencing process often makes.

A closer look indicates that his analysis is also applicable to the more difficult and refined distribution questions posed by mitigation. He makes it clear that culture determines not only 'the contours and outer limits of penality' but also affects the 'shaping of detailed distinctions, hierarchies and categories which operate within the penal field' (p. 196). With respect to sensibilities, he notes that they play a significant role in determining why we sympathize with some people but are indifferent to others. Cultural sensibilities are variable and fluid; sometimes they coincide with the products of particular ideological, political or economic interests and sometimes they actively contradict them. Individuals can experience values and emotions differently, but the bigger question is how these differences should be incorporated into social processes. Culture is not monolithic. Different groups can experience and promote cultural factors in different ways. This is why the residual issues of mitigation ought not to be determined solely by a cultural inquiry. There must also be a question of legitimacy in relation to the sentencing process.

In moving beyond Garland we need to remind ourselves of the true breadth and diversity of culture. Culture is hobbits and hip-hop, Warhol and Willie Nelson, Guernica and Guevara, but it is also football, frisbee, the comics and fish and chips. Along with numerous other elements from the worlds of literature, religion, politics, science, philosophy and popular media, these ingredients integrate, interact, conflict and evolve to comprise culture and produce cultural by-products. It is a multidimensional landscape replete with subtleties and contradictions. Can it be possible to use a diverse concept like culture to locate useful and legitimate sympathetic factors?

There is no 'book of culture' that we can consult to search under 'mitigation' for answers. Culture maps out the shades and complexities of a community's character and tells us about achievement, approval and acceptance, what is essential and what is superficial, what is constant and what is ephemeral, what we prize and what we disdain. These are the indicia of the underlying values of a community which will permit and facilitate a debate about sympathy for sentencing purposes. We accept that sentencing involves censure and usually includes harsh treatment. So the aim of the debate is to identify situations of legitimate sympathy which can be translated into legal norms to transform the modes of censure or reduce the level of harsh treatment. This will engage the arenas of legal, academic, political and public discourse, revealing norms which can be translated into legislation or some other form of articulated guideline, or be assessed by judges. The cultural inquiry will focus on the question of legitimate sympathy and the goal will be the prescription of norms of mitigation that will produce fairness to the individual and reduce unjustified disparity.

The impact of culture becomes clearer when we think back to the 'rich composite of deeply interwoven meanings' (Garland, 1990: 200) encompassed by that social concept. Culture includes the discourses of justice, religions and politics, as well as the specialized discourses of academic, professional and scientific disciplines. Culture also consists of local traditions which necessarily include standards of tolerance and ethics. Cultural influences include individual and collective emotional responses such as compassion and generosity. Culture helps to define the various strata of achievement which are publicly recognized. These factors operate in conjunction to explain who are included in, or excluded from, the mainstream of society. These processes of exclusion or inclusion have their own intermediate processes which determine the treatment of, and respect for, subsets of the community including those defined by gender, race, class, ethnicity and mental or physical disability.

Similarly, culture includes linguistic usage which tells us much about what a community values by understanding phrases which are flattering or unflattering, pejorative or laudatory. In this way language provides keys to social values, as it expresses approval, and disapproval, thereby disclosing local predilections and prejudices. Language can be an unwitting impediment to overcoming hidden prejudice. Look at the historical treatment of the mentally ill. The use of labels like 'lunatics', 'madmen' and 'idiots', and the stigma and ostracism that accompanied it, made it easy to support indefinite confinement but hard to justify leniency. We have witnessed a cultural change from the days of unconstrained civil and criminal confinement, rife with the myth of intrinsic dangerousness. The law has changed and our cultural responses have progressed dramatically. What has happened is the cultural acceptance of autonomy and dignity as pre-eminent considerations, with a dose of compassion for the hardships which the mentally disabled endure.

At the opposite end of the spectrum, language and social practices show us what kinds of achievement or contributions are valued within a given community: who gets the gold medal? Who is paid more? What constitutes wealth? Who is the first to be asked to join a social group, and who is never invited to join? It does not take much imagination to see how all these cultural aspects can find their way into a sentencing matrix. That is, custom can lead to entrenchment.

But what of the elusive factors that regularly arise to support a claim for mitigation but do not fit neatly into gravity and culpability categories? When should claims for sympathy, such as past achievement, post-offence conduct, reparation, collateral consequences and other factors be recognized by a just, fair and compassionate sentencing system? We need to recognize that culture can, and does, generate sources of sympathy. This would explain the factors that the ALI includes as potentially mitigating: vulnerability, hardship, deprivation or handicap, [11] but these categories of factors are not sufficiently precise to be satisfactory. A useful concept of sympathy answers some of the deficiencies of the ALI approach, but we must add a test of legitimacy.

Collateral consequences pose an interesting challenge. The Swedish menu approach encompasses these issues in various ways: whether, as a result of the crime, the accused has suffered severe bodily harm, or will be deported, or has suffered dismissal from employment, or 'will encounter any other obstacle or special difficulty in the pursuit of his occupation or business'.[12] The classical approach to collateral consequences has been

[11] American Law Institute (2006), s. 6B.06(4)(a).
[12] Swedish Penal Code, c. 29, s. 5.

based on the argument that the harm suffered by the offender ought to be considered as part of the punishment already received, like pre-sentence custody (Manson 2001: 136; Ashworth 2010: 184–5), but this claim misses the point that punishment, by definition, is imposed by the state, not by circumstances. As well, one can distinguish between collateral consequences depending on whether the collateral harm suffered is intrinsically linked to the nature of the offence (Manson 2001: 136–7). Consider the example of loss of profession or employment. While recognizing the personal impact, we are not sympathetic when there is a link between the offence and the employment, for example when a surgeon performs an operation while intoxicated and is both prosecuted and struck off, or when a police officer beats up a prisoner and is convicted of assault and fired.[13] Our conclusion would change if the same consequence was applied but after an offence that had no link to job or profession. In these cases, we do have some sympathy for the offender who loses his job or profession.

LEGITIMATE SYMPATHY

One central aspect of culture, as explained by Garland, is what he calls 'sensibilities' as distinguished from 'the cognitive aspects of culture'. He explains:

> All cultures promote certain forms of emotional expression and forbid others, thus contributing to a characteristic structure of affects and a particular sensibility on the part of their members. The range and refinement of the feelings experienced by individuals, their sensitivities and insensitivities, the extent of their emotional capacities, and their characteristic forms of gratification and inhibition show considerable variation across cultures.
>
> (1990: 213).

It is the concept of 'sensibilities' that permits us to ask the threshold question, 'Are we sympathetic?' Sympathy may not always be the route to mitigation but it is a start. Then we can move on to legitimacy.

Sympathy is a normal human response. Tragedy, misfortune, pain and loss elicit sympathy. But sometimes sympathy is truly in the eye of the beholder. This occurs when the sympathy flows from, or is tainted by, a commonality of situation or background. Think of the cliché 'how the mighty have fallen'. This only generates sympathy in

[13] R *v*. Byrne.

someone who resides in a similarly exalted or privileged position. Accordingly, our primary concern is to ensure that natural sympathy on the part of the judge does not create an illegitimate effect on sentencing. However, simply stipulating the removal of sympathy from the sentencing matrix does not remove the potential for sympathy affecting the judge. By making the issue explicit, we not only ensure that sympathy does not play an unexpressed or even subconscious role in decision-making, we also require that it be explained. From a 'rule of law' perspective, it is essential that the reasons for sentence determination be expressed and explained to the offender, the victim, the public and the appellate court.[14]

But we need to add a legitimacy criterion which brings us back to the objectives of sentencing. For mitigation purposes, the most important considerations are rehabilitation and reparation.[15] That is, in some cases we ought to mitigate a sentence to promote the objectives of rehabilitation or reparation, whether by a sentence reduction or by changing the sanction imposed, with or without reduction of penal bite. The question then becomes which sympathetic examples also promote these legitimate objectives.

While sympathy is not enough, the converse is also true: legitimacy is not enough. Some offenders have a real advantage in terms of showing prospects for integration – think of the professional with highly marketable skills, or the child of a wealthy family who can provide many job opportunities. Recognizing these attributes as mitigating would raise serious questions of class distinctions and discrimination.[16] In a sentencing system that subscribes to the principles of parity and fair treatment, it is not acceptable to distinguish between similar offenders based on these characteristics, notwithstanding their potential link to future rehabilitation.

An interesting example is the factor of supportive family. Empirical studies show that judges respond to this factor (see Jacobson and Hough 2007: 13, 15). The scheme which I am advocating would only look to the existence of a supportive family as evidence of rehabilitative prospects after concluding that the individual warrants sympathy. A controversial situation is the solid employment record.[17] Every defence

[14] See, e.g., Ashworth (2010: 370–2); Reitz (2002: 572–4).
[15] See, e.g., Manson (2001: 28).
[16] See, e.g., Ashworth (2010: 250–1). The Model Penal Code: Sentencing, s. 6B06(2)(a), lists 'socioeconomic status' as a ground ineligible for sentencing considerations.
[17] Ashworth (2010: 250–3).

counsel will raise this, but what is the basis for treating it as mitigating? Unless there is reason to be sympathetic, such that the issue of rehabilitative prospects comes onto the table, we ought not to give mitigating effect to 'good employment record'. Otherwise, we are getting perilously close to permitting character to be a sentencing determinant. Outside optimism and the 'out of character' assumption that we tend to apply to first offenders, there can be little room for mitigation based on character. This is antagonistic both to proportionality and to equality of treatment.

A good example of the legitimacy test arises in the context of hardship to other parties, for example the impact of custody on an offender's children.[18] This may give rise to sympathy, although possibly not if there is a record of poor parenting. If one concludes that the imprisonment of a parent and the consequential impounding of the children by the state are unfortunate and unfair for the children, we move to the second aspect of legitimacy: is the hardship sufficient in the context of the particular offence, to be legitimate? That is, will it promote rehabilitation and reform in an acceptable way, or at least not undermine the principle of treating like cases alike? This analysis leads us into the issue of extent of mitigation. Clearly, the only useful response would be to transform the sentence of imprisonment into a community-based sentence, thus providing care for the children. If the co-relative sentence of imprisonment as determined by proportionality is beyond the range to substitute a form of community sentence, then there can be no mitigation. A discount off a long sentence does not answer the problem.

Some factors that do not directly implicate rehabilitation or reparation provide ample grounds for mitigation. They are, indeed, culturally accepted. Two good examples are the aged and the infirm, but there are many analogous groups (von Hirsch and Ashworth 2005: 176; Renaud 2004: 22–34). Here, the issue is legitimacy. This can be addressed by asking whether giving mitigative effect will undermine the important sentencing principle of treating like cases alike. So long as the 'sympathetic' group represents a condition or status that differentiates them for sentencing purposes, then it is a legitimate mitigating factor. Otherwise, parity and the overriding importance of equal treatment are sacrificed. This requires identifying the differentiating feature and determining whether it can be defended. Both normative and cultural considerations come into play to determine whether the ostensible sympathy is explicable and legitimate.

[18] Ruby et al. (2008 : 286–9, discussing the effect on the family as a mitigating circumstance).

CONCLUSION

In this chapter I have outlined a scheme of principles that now looks as follows:

(i) *Principled approach*: does it diminish culpability or gravity (i.e. principles of proportionality)?
(ii) *Systemic rationale*: does the justice system demand recognition of the factor in order to promote its legitimate goals (i.e. penal culture) without creating any unfairness?
(iii) *Sympathy*: does *our culture* make us have sympathy for the offender and, if so, is the sympathy legitimate for mitigation purposes? (i.e. does it either promote rehabilitation or reparations, or at least can it be accommodated without undermining the principle that like cases need to be treated alike?)

The next step is to engage in the debate necessary to identify and define in normative terms the factors to be included in a penal code (as Sweden has done). It should not be considered exhaustive because the code can always be supplemented by a statement of residual sentencing discretion that reflects the principles of the scheme. The important point is to recognize that once we move beyond the basic concepts of gravity and culpability, and the systemic category, there are cases where only a cultural inquiry will properly account for the fine-tuning that determines when a factor leads legitimately to mitigation.

If our goal is to construct legal norms which are useful, practicable and defensible, the cultural analysis encourages a discussion which can promote this objective. In any society, the blatant and subtle influences of culture produce both icons and pariahs, heroes and villains. It is the grand matrix of cultural values that determines whom we admire, exalt, favour and reward and, conversely, whom we shun, condemn, ostracize and mock. Adding the dimension of legitimate sympathy to our understanding of mitigation answers many questions.

REFERENCES

American Law Institute (2006). *Model Penal Code: Sentencing* (discussion draft). Philadelphia: American Law Institute.

Ashworth, A. (2010). *Sentencing and Criminal Justice*, 5th edn. Cambridge University Press.

Cole, D. and A. Manson (1990). *Release from Imprisonment: The Law of Sentencing, Parole and Judicial Review*. Toronto: Carswell.

Elias, N. (1994). *The Civilizing Process*. Oxford: Blackwell.
Garland, D. (1990). *Punishment and Modern Society: A Study in Social Theory*. Oxford: Clarendon Press.
Hart, H. L. A. (1968). *Punishment and Responsibility*. New York: Oxford University Press.
Jacobson, J. and Hough, M. (2007). *Mitigation: The Role of Personal Factors in Sentencing*. London: Prison Reform Trust.
Jareborg, N. (2002). *Scraps of Penal Theory*. Uppsala: Iustus Förlag.
Manson, A. (2001). *The Law of Sentencing*. Toronto: Irwin.
Murphy, J. and Hampton, J. (1988) *Forgiveness and Mercy*. Cambridge University Press.
Nussbaum, M. (1993). 'Equity and Mercy', *Philosophy and Public Affairs*, 22: 83–125.
Reitz, K. (2002). 'American Law Institute: Model Penal Code: Sentencing, Plan for Revision'. *Buffalo Criminal Law Review*, 6: 525–672.
Renaud, G. (2004). *Speaking to Sentence: A Practical Guide*. Toronto: Carswell.
Ruby, C. et al. (2008). *Sentencing*. Toronto: Butterworths.
Sentencing Council (2010). *Overarching Principles: Seriousness*, available at www.sentencingcouncil.org.uk.
Thompson, E. P. (1991). *Customs in Common: Studies in Traditional Popular Culture*. New York: The New Press.
Thorburn, M. and Manson, A. (2007). 'The Sentencing Theory Debate: Convergence in Outcomes, Divergence in Reasoning', review essay on A. von Hirsch and A. Ashworth, *Proportionate Sentencing: Exploring the Principles*, *New Criminal Law Review*, 10: 278–310.
von Hirsch, A. and Ashworth, A. (2005). *Proportionate Sentencing: Exploring the Principles*. Oxford University Press.
von Hirsch, A., Ashworth, A. and Jareborg, N. (2005). 'Gauging Crime Seriousness: A "Living Standard" Conception of Criminal Harm', in A. von Hirsch and A. Ashworth, *Proportionate Sentencing: Exploring the Principles*. Oxford University Press.

TABLE OF CASES

R *v.* Angelillo, 2006 SCC 55, [2006] 2 S.C.R. 728 at para. 24, Charron J [Angelillo].
R *v.* Byrne, 2009 ONCA 134, 245 O.A.C. 370, 2009 Carswell Ont 719.
R *v.* C.A.M., [1996] 1 S.C.R. 500, [1996] S.C.J. No. 28.
R *v.* Edwards (2001), 1555 C.C.C. (3d) 473 Ont.CA.
R *v.* M. (C.A.), [1996] 1 S.C.R. 500.
R *v.* McDonnell, [1997] 1 S.C.R. 948.
R *v.* Proulx, 2000 SCC 5, [2000] 1 S.C.R. 61.

CHAPTER FOUR

PERSONAL MITIGATION AND ASSUMPTIONS ABOUT OFFENDING AND DESISTANCE

Joanna Shapland

When sentencing an offender, sentencers in England and Wales are required to hear any speech in mitigation that the offender or his or her legal representative wishes to make (Shapland 1981). That speech is likely to range widely over all the elements relevant to sentencing for that particular offence and which relate to the legislation governing sentencing. It might include how serious the offence is, whether there are any mitigating or aggravating factors relating to the offence itself and whether the offender should be judged more or less culpable in terms of the part played in the offence. It is also likely to cover personal mitigation, which I shall take as elements relating to the offender and his or her circumstances, history and likely future path. As I shall argue below, little attention has been paid to personal mitigation in official guidance for sentencers. However, for some aims of sentencing – and particularly that of encouraging the offender to commit fewer or no offences in the future (encouraging desistance) – I shall argue that personal mitigation should move from its current obscurity to centre stage.

CHAPTER OVERVIEW

Before turning the spotlight on personal mitigation itself, we need to understand the legislative priorities for sentencers in England and Wales and which of the many possible sentencing philosophies are

The author is very grateful to Julian Roberts and Estella Baker for suggestions in relation to this chapter.

seen as most important. We then need to look at what guidance is currently given. First, we shall look at how sentencers are currently being provided with any pointers to what to do with personal mitigation. We shall then consider the deficiencies of considering only 'harm' and 'culpability' in relation to the aims of sentencing and what is known about reducing crime and helping offenders to desist, as well as how to make reparation. The chapter will conclude by considering what sentencing for desistance (offenders leading a less offending or non-offending life) would mean, and how this would affect the importance of personal mitigation.

PERSONAL MITIGATION AND ITS RELATION TO THE OVERARCHING PRINCIPLES OF SENTENCING

Currently, in England and Wales the key philosophical principle behind the determination of the sentence for offenders is that of the seriousness of the offence they have committed. As *Overarching Principles: Seriousness* of the Sentencing Guidelines Council[1] (2004) states,

> 1.3 The sentence must start by considering the seriousness of the offence, the assessment of which will:
>
> - determine which of the sentencing thresholds has been crossed;
> - indicate whether a custodial, community or other sentence is the most appropriate;
> - be the key factor in deciding the length of a custodial sentence, the onerousness of requirements to be incorporated in a community sentence and the amount of any fine imposed.

As other contributors to this volume have discussed, the seriousness of the offence is then determined by two main parameters, the culpability of the offender and the harm caused or risked being caused by the offence (ibid., para 1.4). Correspondingly, the guidance to sentencers and the work of the appeal courts have focused on seriousness, and hence on the seriousness of different offences (which generally relates to harm), different ways in which the offender was involved in the offence (as principal, as lookout, as minor player etc., all of which relate

[1] The Sentencing Guidelines Council and the Sentencing Advisory Panel were set up to provide authoritative guidance to sentencers. They have now been superseded by the Sentencing Council for England and Wales. The new Council is required to prepare sentencing guidelines, but, at the time of writing, had not yet published any. The emphasis on the seriousness of the offence remains in the Coroners and Justice Act 2009 (e.g. s. 121(2)).

to culpability), and on the intention or recklessness of the offender (again, mostly relating to culpability).

However, retribution and punishment, as shown by the seriousness of the offence, are not the only, or even sometimes the most applicable, sentencing philosophies. The Criminal Justice Act 2003 states:

> Any court dealing with an offender in respect of his offence must have regard to the following purposes of sentencing–
>
> (a) the punishment of offenders,
> (b) the reduction of crime (including its reduction by deterrence),
> (c) the reform and rehabilitation of offenders,
> (d) the protection of the public, and
> (e) the making of reparation by offenders to persons affected by their offences. (s. 142(1)).

This considerable widening of the scope for sentencers brings in its train a potentially much wider scope for mitigation and aggravation. Indeed, as the Criminal Justice Act 2003, s. 166, says,

> Nothing in [list of previous sections re imposing custodial and community sentences etc.] prevents a court from mitigating an offender's sentence by taking into account any such matters as, in the opinion of the court, are relevant in mitigation of sentence.

This is possibly slightly tautologous phrasing, but it does show the importance placed by the Act, which is the key framework for sentencing in England and Wales, on the freedom which sentencers have to consider all the aspects around the offence and the offender.

It is strange, therefore, that, compared with the attention paid to offences and seriousness in guidance stemming from official sources, very much less attention has been paid to personal mitigation. Personal mitigation can be relevant to seriousness, as we shall see, but it is also clearly relevant to the reduction of reoffending, rehabilitation, the protection of the public and reparation. It is very difficult even to find an official definition of personal mitigation, which tends to be at the end of lists of important elements, along the lines of 'everything else which might be relevant'. So, for example, the *Overarching Principles: Seriousness* state:

> (iii) Personal mitigation
>
> 1.26 Section 166(1) Criminal Justice Act 2003 makes provision for a sentencer to take account of any matters that 'in the opinion of the court, are relevant in mitigation of sentence'.

> 1.27 When the court has formed an initial assessment of the seriousness of the offence, then it should consider any offender mitigation. The issue of remorse should be taken into account at this point along with other mitigating features such as admissions to the police in interview. (Sentencing Guidelines Council 2004: 7)

'Offender mitigation' is clearly, for the Council, 'personal mitigation', but no further elucidation is given. 'Offender mitigation' is also to be seen as separate from the lists of 'Aggravating factors' and 'Mitigating factors', which appear above this paragraph at (i) and (ii) respectively (2004: 10–11). This is a little confusing, because 'Aggravating factors' include some pertaining to the offender and his or her relation to the offence, which seems to stray a little way from direct culpability or intention (such as 'Offenders operating in groups or gangs', '"Professional" offending' and 'Abuse of a position of trust').

Similarly 'Mitigating factors' include a (much shorter) list which clearly describe the offender, not the offence at all – such as 'mental illness or disability', and 'youth or age, where it affects the responsibility of the individual defendant'. Mental illness, for example, may be entirely unrelated to the offence – some thieves are mentally disordered, some are not, but, apart from sometimes leading to more incompetent commission of the offence, there is little relationship between the disorder and the offence, except with the rare disorder of kleptomania. One is left with the feeling that there is a rather unclear dividing line between the mitigating and aggravating factors listed and 'personal mitigation'; and that this dividing line may have more to do with the prevalence with which these factors have been mentioned in sentencing than with any logical connection with seriousness (culpability or harm) which led to the listing of those included in aggravating or mitigating factors.

Having a residual category of 'personal mitigation' is not surprising. As Lord Justice Rose says in the introduction to the 'Guideline judgments case compendium',

> Sentencing is a complex and difficult exercise. It can never be a rigid, mechanistic or scientific process. Consistency of approach by sentencers is essential to maintain public confidence. But perfect consistency in outcome is impossible to achieve because of the infinite variety of circumstances with which, even in relation to one kind of offence, the courts are presented. (Sentencing Guidelines Council 2005: i)

In other words, no list of principles or factors can ever be exhaustive. Sentencers need to try to look at similar situations in a similar fashion – but if they expect any guidance to be able to lead them blindly to the right sentence, without sentencers themselves thinking hard about the particular offence and offender, they will not only be sadly mistaken but also liable to create injustice.

These points about personal mitigation seem to me to be key, not only to understanding personal mitigation, but to sentencing as well. England and Wales have, in the Criminal Justice Acts of 1991 and 2003, elevated seriousness to the key place among philosophies of punishment. However, the idea of a sentencing system which depends *only* on a consideration of seriousness (culpability and harm) is inconceivable – it would presumably seek to deal with all offenders, whoever they are and in whatever circumstances they find themselves, in an identical way. That would affront ideas of 'justice' for both sentencers and the general public. Moreover, I shall argue that lists of factors which try to enumerate what is seen as aggravating or mitigating are doomed to failure in terms of being comprehensive – even when they stray away from seriousness and also start including personal mitigation. Sentencing is just more complex than following lists.

GUIDANCE ON PERSONAL MITIGATION IN ENGLAND AND WALES

Sentencing in magistrates' courts

The vast majority of offenders in England and Wales are sentenced at the magistrates' court, where the key guidance is provided by the *Magistrates' Court Sentencing Guidelines*, again published by the Sentencing Guidelines Council (2008). The guidelines themselves are all in the same format, with usually one page per legal offence, arranged alphabetically. So, for example, the guidelines start with 'Alcohol sale offences' and proceed to 'Alcohol/tobacco, fraudulently evade duty' and then to 'Animal cruelty'.

If we take a common offence which has considerable scope for personal mitigation, such as 'Assault occasioning actual bodily harm & racially or religiously aggravated assault occasioning actual bodily harm – factors to take into consideration' (pp. 26–7), the general format of the guideline is similar to that for all other offences. It starts with a discussion of offence seriousness (culpability and harm), which instructs sentencers first to identify the appropriate starting point on what is clearly seen as a tariff of penalties by severity. The starting point will depend on the nature of the 'activity' (i.e. the offence). The sentence should then consider the effect of aggravating or mitigating factors, identified in a pull-out card (discussed below). The sentencer should then form a preliminary view of the appropriate sentence (increased if the offence was racially or religiously motivated) and then consider offender mitigation, which is again the subject of a pull-out card (discussed below). Finally, the sentence should consider a reduction for a guilty plea and any ancillary orders such as compensation, before deciding on sentence and giving reasons for the sentence.

The key guidance on personal mitigation (offender mitigation) is obviously the pull-out card at the back. This last page of the guidance contains a list of, first, 'Aggravating factors' (some indicating 'higher culpability', some 'a more than usually serious degree of harm'), then a smaller list of 'Mitigating factors', all of which indicate 'lower culpability', then a three-point list of 'Offender mitigation', which simply says:

Offender mitigation

- Genuine remorse
- Admissions to police in interview
- Ready co-operation with authorities

This is hardly in-depth guidance to offender mitigation. Moreover, it is not about aspects of the offender or his or her social or personal background which the phrase 'personal mitigation' might lead the reader to expect. The sentencer who might, for example, want to know the relevance of the offender experiencing extreme poverty, just having found a new job after a prolonged period of unemployment, falling in with the wrong people or having a problematic drug habit is doomed to disappointment.

The specific guidance to 'Assault occasioning actual bodily harm' and a few other offences does, indeed, recognize that 'matters of offender mitigation are often highly relevant to sentencing for this offence and may justify a non-custodial sentence, particularly in the case of a first time offender' (p. 26). However, what is then discussed does not relate to offender mitigation, but to the use of a weapon (increasing culpability and harm) and premeditation (increasing culpability).

Sentencing at the Crown Court

If we turn to the Crown Court, the key sentencing guidance here includes the Sentencing Guideline Council's publication *Overarching Principles: Seriousness* (2004), and their *Guideline Judgments Case Compendium*

(2005 and updates), as well as the individual pronouncements of the Court of Appeal on sentencing cases. It is notable that there is no Council publication dealing with personal mitigation and no detailed guidance. Although courts can of course strike out on their own where there is no guidance, the extent to which they are enjoined to follow guidelines,[2] even though not slavishly,[3] will, I suspect, make at least the higher courts wary of developing significant jurisprudence on personal mitigation. This is possibly not helped by the cases suggesting that draft or consultation guidance is to be approached with extreme caution.[4]

Magistrates and judges are clearly being enjoined by the official bodies to follow a route stressing culpability and harm, in which a starting position on a scale which corresponds to the severity of sentencing is affected by individual characteristics. This must leave them with a number of difficulties:

- How should they deal with cases where they have decided that a key purpose of sentencing is not just deserts or retribution but reducing reoffending (encouraging desistance) or reparation?
- What kinds of factor are relevant in terms of offender mitigation in relation to just deserts?
- What kinds of factor should they see as likely to promote desistance or reparation?
- How should they think about the offender before them – as a list of factors or as a whole person in whom different factors interact and are given meaning by the person him- or herself?
- Where do they properly obtain information about offender mitigation?

If we take the last question first, sentencers may turn to the other personnel at court who can provide them with information. They may, however, be looking in vain. It is my contention that the provision of information to sentencers has not been developed such that they can have reliable information on personal mitigation. The contribution by

[2] For example the Criminal Justice Act 2003, s. 172(1): 'Every court must (a) in sentencing an offender, have regard to any guidelines which are relevant to the offender's case, and (b) in exercising any other function relating to the sentencing of offenders, have regard to any guidelines which are relevant to the exercise of the function.'

[3] Attorney General's References (Nos. 14 and 15 of 2006) (*R v. French and Webster* [2007]; *R v. Wilson (Daniel Rushton)* [2008]).

[4] For example, *R* v. *Abbas* [2009], in which it was said that draft guidance was not a guideline 'to which it is appropriate for this court to have any reference at all'.

the prosecution tends to be limited to a description of the circumstances of the offence, together with information about previous convictions. It has changed little since observations in court in the 1970s,[5] except for the significant addition of the victim personal statement and more details about possible compensation. These changes will help the sentencer in relation to reparation, but not necessarily in relation to offender mitigation.

The probation service, in providing pre-sentence reports, is a potential provider of information on personal mitigation where such reports are requested[6] – except that the current key role of pre-sentence reports is to give the sentencer information on risk of reoffending, and 'managing the risk of harm posed by offenders and protecting of the public [*sic*] is always paramount' (Ministry of Justice 2007). The National Offender Management Model categorizes offenders according to the risk of their causing serious harm, and both court reports and proposals for managing offenders are subject to this overall categorization. This may help in terms of aiding desistance (although see below), but does not mean that the court report will necessarily mention personal mitigation. Unless the offender is assessed as very high risk, for example, no home visit by the person preparing the pre-sentence report is necessary, and the whole initial assessment and outline plan for the court may be conducted face to face in a probation office, in prison or over a video link to the prison.

When looking for information on personal mitigation, the sentencer may well be forced to rely on the speech in mitigation given by the defendant's legal representative or, increasingly, given the decline in legal assistance in England and Wales, by the defendant. There have been few empirical studies of the content and purpose of mitigation speeches recently. The important study of personal mitigation in the Crown Court by Jacobson and Hough (2007; and this volume) is in fact a study of sentencers' spoken reasons for sentence (or homilies), not of mitigation speeches, although these researchers then tried to ascertain which of the reasons came from the mitigation speech or any reports presented to the court. The list of mitigating factors in Table 2.2 from that study does include a much wider range than those in the magistrates' guidelines, examples being in relation to wider circumstances at the time of the offence:

[5] Compare, for example, the description of what was said by the prosecution in Shapland (1981), which was based on observation in the magistrates' courts and Crown Court in London, with that of youth courts in the 1990s in several parts of England and Wales, in Shapland et al. (2003).

[6] Almost certainly in a minority of cases at the magistrates' courts.

- youth
- pressing personal or family need
- vulnerable/immature/naïve
- psychiatric illness/problems

as well as, in relation to the defendant's past,

- good character or limited/irrelevant/gap in previous offending
- has led a productive/worthwhile life
- has shown a general improvement in behaviour
- offence uncharacteristic/'let yourself down'
- difficult/deprived background

and, in relation to the defendant's present and future,

- can address/is addressing drug problems
- has family responsibilities
- supportive family/partner
- currently in work/training or prospects of work/training
- can address/is addressing alcohol problems
- can or may make amends for offending behaviour
- age (older)
- physical illness/disability.

It is interesting that sentencers are in practice using a wider range of factors than those set out in the guidance. Clearly there is an accepted tradition of common law practice in sentencing which can be drawn on by sentencers to deal with the case before them, and many of the texts for legal practitioners reflect this. However, there are dangers where the 'official' guidance is less comprehensive than practice, particularly when the official guidance to courts is so strongly reinforced through statute: for example, the Coroners and Justice Act 2009 states that '(1) Every court . . . must, in sentencing an offender, follow any sentencing guidelines which are relevant to the offender's case' (s. 125). Sentencers are likely to concentrate on those factors which are officially endorsed, while others will be more sporadically and inconsistently applied.

Of the factors which Jacobson and Hough found cited by Crown Court judges in their study, several are relevant to encouraging desistance (reducing reoffending) as well as to reparation and retribution. Unfortunately, we do not know in what way these were cited by sentencers or how they supported the sentence given, nor from which source they were obtained. As has been found in previous studies of reasons given for sentence and homilies, the judiciary are not always terribly helpful in saying what weight is attached to each factor or how it was useful – as Jacobson and Hough say, factors can be referred to 'to signal to the court and any appellate bodies that the decision had been properly taken' (2007: 12).[7] However, we do know that the sentencers said that personal mitigation had had an impact in around half of all cases – quite an astonishing extent, given the lack of guidance provided.

Jacobson and Hough (2007) were looking at sentencing in the Crown Court, where mitigation is normally still provided by the defendant's legal representative. Legal representation is much rarer in the magistrates' court. Previous research in the 1970s indicated that mitigation by unrepresented defendants was much briefer and less rich than that by legal representatives (Shapland 1981). This is hardly surprising: it is difficult for someone both to apologize (which was the main content of unrepresented defendants' mitigation) and to set out personal mitigating circumstances. Apologies are complex societal communications, in which the offender is normally apologizing both to the direct victim and to the judge, representing society (for having committed a proscribed act and to show that the offender knows and respects the moral boundaries of that society; Shapland et al. 2011; 2006; Shapland 1981).

Trying in addition to provide personal mitigation – to portray oneself as being in an unfortunate personal situation – begins to become too complex a web to weave in terms of self-identity: the defendant has simultaneously to be a person who has done wrong but whose actions were atypical of their conduct; a person who knows what is right and is now in mainstream society; and a person who is set apart from most in society by being in a difficult social situation. It is extremely difficult to sustain all these in a single speech. It means that defendants may be able to indicate that they have imminent prospects of improvement (e.g. an offer of employment or accommodation, going to take up drug treatment, a supportive family or probation officer), but find it difficult to mention excuses based in the past. This may be the theoretical background behind the remarkable dearth of mentions of personal mitigation from unrepresented defendants in the magistrates' court in Shapland (1981).

[7] See also Shapland (1981), in which it is argued that, in the spoken reasons given, judges tend to have at least as much of an eye on the appellate courts as on those present at court.

THE EFFECT OF A LIST OF FACTORS

As we have seen, mention of 'mitigation' in sentencing guidance has tended to occur through a list of mitigating factors. Another example is to be found in *Archbold*, the key handbook for counsel in the Crown Court, which provides a list of 'selected mitigating factors' (Ch. 5, section III(E)(3)) drawn from specific mention of mitigation in cases at the Court of Appeal. This is almost as minimal a list as those described above. It comprises a plea of guilty, age, assistance to law enforcement authorities, entrapment, particular meritorious conduct unrelated to offence and attitude of offender's family (in reporting the offence to the police). I have already criticized the paucity of these lists of personal mitigation. One may ask also, though, why mitigation is referred to as a list of disembodied factors.

The creation of a list of factors (with a similar list for aggravation of sentence) may be related to the way in which sentencing in England and Wales – and other common law countries – has developed and knowledge about it has been disseminated.[8] On the one hand, appellate courts have sought to restrain the discretion of the courts of first instance, so that sentencing is not delegitimized by appearing to be a lottery or at the whim of the judge. On the other hand, it has clearly been impossible to set out how to approach every possible circumstance or defendant who might appear before a court in the future. The task is different from that involved in specifying what is illegal – that is, guiding the courts on the substantive criminal law.

Substantive criminal law is set by Parliament through statutes and is only refined by the appellate courts; the key for the appellate courts is to be specific, bald and precise as to exactly what is criminal. Sentencing guidance, however, tries to be inclusive of possible future circumstances rather than precise about today's offence. Moreover, it only rarely has the benefit of an overarching structure given by statute. Instead, sentencing guidance until very recently has had to be developed through case law, with statutes confined to the introduction or modification of types of penalty, not their application to cases. Initially the Court of Appeal picked particular appeals as occasions for setting out to

[8] It may also be due to some sentencing legislation using the term 'factors', for example, the Criminal Justice Act 2003, s. 156(1), which mandates courts to 'take into account all such information as is available to it about the circumstances of the offence or (as the case may be) of the offence and the offence or offences associated with it, including any aggravating or mitigating factors'.

sentencers how to approach particular classes of offence or types of offender, and these became known as 'guideline cases'. Case law is good for refining ever more precisely one particular line of legal reasoning as a case is distinguished from previous cases, but it tends to be very bad at starting a new line of reasoning. If guidance on personal mitigation was underdeveloped in the 1970s – as it was – then it is not surprising that it remained underdeveloped in 2003, before the advent of the guidelines.

What, then, about the opportunity afforded by the move to guidelines, rather than the restrictions necessarily embedded in having guideline cases, such as the guidance having to be related at least tangentially to the particular circumstances of that case? It would have been possible to have constructed guidelines rather like statutes, which started from philosophical principles of punishment to guide sentencers in their application. That would probably have produced guidance looking rather like a broad-brush road map, as opposed to a list of factors. It can only be a matter of speculation as to why guidance has taken the form it has, but I suspect that three elements played a part in the reasons for there being little development: a wish not to depart too far from the type of guidance offered by the previous guideline cases; the particular principles embodied in the Criminal Justice Act 1991 and its successor, the Criminal Justice Act 2003; and the dominance in criminology and criminal justice of the developmental criminology of adolescence and cognitive behavioural programmes.

The first merely embodies the innate conservatism of the criminal law (and a strong wish not to be enmeshed in the grid-like categorizations of the approach of some US states to sentencing). In relation to the second, the Criminal Justice Act 1991 made just deserts pre-eminent among sentencing philosophies: the seriousness of the offence became the most important strand in sentencing. If one considers seriousness, then one needs to be specific about which offence. One rapidly ends up with a list of many offence-related factors, some of which apply to some types of offence, some to others – together with a much more limited list of offender-related elements linked to culpability (i.e. moral judgements on the decisions that offenders, making rational choices, are supposed to have made about whether and how to offend). Culpability decisions are judgements about offenders at the individual level of the person who ends up in the dock. Because they are time limited between the decision and the point of commission of the act, they can, and do, ignore the societal elements which may have been acting to propel the offender towards offending in general, or which might intervene to reduce reoffending. Although events after 1991 combined to push other philosophies of sentencing forward (including the more punitive deterrence, as well as the more societally based rehabilitation and reparation), as we saw above, seriousness and just deserts managed to hold on to their top perch in the 2003 Act. The result is, then, inexorably, the creation of a list of ways in which offences and the culpability of offenders should be seen as more or less serious and so punished more or less.

The third element which may have influenced this list-like tendency is the dominance in the 1990s and 2000s of the idea of risk or protective 'factors' which propel offenders into crime, or help to keep them from it. Life-course criminology, concentrating on the move *into* delinquency in adolescence, has developed a long list of attributes of the individual and their social position which predict which young people might offend more (Farrington 2002). The risk-based instruments being used by the probation service for pre-sentence reports, such as OASyS,[9] derive directly from this tradition. Within the tradition, because of the methods of quantitative analysis used, offenders tend to be seen as collections of factors, some risky, some protective, which predict their criminality. The development of cognitive behaviour programmes for the treatment of offenders has drawn from the same traditions: offenders are seen as needing to participate in programmes, each of which deals with one need (stemming from one risk factor).[10] It is not surprising that sentencing guidance, which needed to fit with these developments in sentence plans and corrections, also took up the idea of factors to adjust the level of severity of the sentence.

What, though, is wrong about the idea of dissecting offenders into lists of factors (apart from its intrinsic de-humanizing nature)? The key difficulty comes from the fact that such lists contain factors which are not independent either of each other or of the person concerned. Risk-based sentencing necessarily predicts on the basis of what a population of offenders might do, not what that particular individual in the dock will do. Even someone at the highest, most criminogenic level of a scale of

[9] OASyS is an assessment tool used by probation staff to assess the risks and needs posed by offenders when preparing pre-sentence reports or at the beginning of a custodial or community sentence. It includes both static elements (e.g. previous criminal convictions), which the offender cannot change, and so-called dynamic elements which, potentially through supervision, could be changed, such as employment, attitudes to offending etc.

[10] Examples are anger management programmes, drug treatment programmes, programmes which encourage offenders to 'Think First'.

likelihood of reconviction (such as OGRS2, the Offender Group Reconviction Scale), however good that scale is, can, and occasionally does, decide to desist and stops offending.[11] Worse, the factors that predict the onset and amplification of criminality during adolescence do not seem to be the same as those which predict desistance in late adolescence and on into people's 20s and 30s (Stouthamer-Loeber et al. 2004; Laub and Sampson 2003). It seems that the person inside the factors might have something to do with desistance.

WHY MIGHT PERSONAL MITIGATION MATTER?

If sentencing is purely about seriousness and about just deserts, it is unsurprising that guidance to sentencers looks like a list of mitigating and aggravating factors – and that most of these will relate to the offence, not the offender. The offender will not be entirely absent – our moral construction of the person and the ways in which it is permitted for that person to come to decisions may also allow some factors related to the offender and his or her culpability to be taken into account, such as those that impair mental capacity to take decisions (youth, mental disorder, some drugs, some provocation). However, as we have seen, sentencing is not now supposed to be solely about just deserts. It is also supposed to consider public protection (which relies on incapacitation, deterrence or desistance), preventing reoffending (encouraging desistance) and reparation. Lists of factors, though, as we shall see, cannot describe decisions taken by individual offenders to change their lives or any need felt by communities or victims that offenders should recompense those who have been hurt for the hurt they have caused.

Let us consider first the sentencing purpose of 'the reform and rehabilitation of offenders' (Criminal Justice Act 2003, s. 142(1)(c)). Reform and rehabilitation are directed towards the reduction or cessation of offending (desistance), which would also of course serve 'the protection of the public' (subsection (d)) as well as 'the reduction in crime' (subsection (b)). More recent work on developmental or life-course criminality has shown the importance of looking at both the individual and the individual's social context in considering

[11] In Bottoms and Shapland's longitudinal study of persistent offenders in their early 20s (2011), some of those with the highest OGRS2 score desisted (although they were few). OGRS2 score was not the best predictor of desistance.

both the path into crime and the path out of crime (Wikstrom 2006). In terms of desistance, both the individual's own decisions (agency) and the social situation in which the individual is living are crucial (Maruna 2000; Farrall and Calverley 2006; Bottoms and Shapland (2011); Laub and Sampson 2003). Indeed, Bottoms and Shapland (2011) demonstrate that, for their sample of recidivist young adult offenders, decisions to desist predicted subsequent self-reported criminality.

Yet it will be extremely difficult for individual offenders to create a new, non-offending life for themselves through their own efforts, however strong their desire and resolve to do so. Actually desisting requires that income through offending is replaced by legitimately earned income, the thrills of offending are replaced by the quieter but safer joys of family life, accommodation is found and kept, jobs are obtained and so forth (Bottoms and Shapland 2011). Particularly in difficult economic times, these are a challenge for all young people. They are extremely difficult for offenders, who usually have few qualifications, little job experience and blank spaces on their curricula vitae due to spells in prison on remand or as sentenced prisoners.

Nor do offenders, especially persistent offenders, tend to have many resources to tackle the route to desistance once decisions have been made. Their friends tend also to be delinquent (Wikstrom 2006; Bottoms and Shapland 2011): people to be kept away from, rather than sought out, if the offender is trying to desist. National social and economic policies may help or hinder the offender trying to rehabilitate. I have argued elsewhere that in England and Wales policies on education and housing have been difficult in this regard (Farrall et al. 2010). One can also argue that views of offenders towards desistance have been negative – offenders in England and Wales have tended not to be seen as citizens who have gone astray but are welcomed back into mainstream society when they desist, but as sub-citizens, who will be regarded as continuing to be inferior until they prove otherwise. So, for example, the right to vote during incarceration is still resisted by the government, those initially on benefits are portrayed as 'slackers' and the categorization of people into 'risk' categories is negative towards changing one's self-identity away from 'offender' towards 'citizen'. Societal mores in England and Wales, we have suggested, are currently oriented, not towards the reintegration of offenders, but to policing the boundaries carefully so that outcasts find it difficult to get back into the mainstream.

The current position as regards personal mitigation is, in my view, in tune with these trends against desistance. Far from emphasizing what would encourage desistance, sentencing guidance is silent. Sentencing practice (as shown by Jacobson and Hough 2007) is actually rather more forward-looking, in that the aspects of employment, training, education and housing are being considered in Crown Court practice. So, for example, the collection of mitigating factors cited by sentencers as affecting sentence includes sixty-three instances, the largest category overall, relating to the defendant's present and future. They are a very mixed bag, but include addressing drug problems (fourteen instances), prospects of work (five instances) and addressing alcohol problems (five instances). All these are key 'obstacles' which, if relevant to the individual offender, will need to be addressed during desistance (Bottoms and Shapland 2011). The way in which these are phrased by Jacobson and Hough suggests that they are also being used in a desistance-oriented way – that they are mitigating because the offenders have stressed that they wish to pursue these avenues, rather than that they would be applied to the offenders.

This is the critical difference between sentencing which follows a rehabilitative principle and sentencing which aims to support and increase desistance. Rehabilitation has in the past been seen primarily as being directed by and applied by professionals, in particular the probation service, to offenders. In the R-N-R paradigm[12] which lies behind cognitive behavioural therapy, offenders are assessed to see what criminogenic needs they have and what requirements there would have to be for those needs to be addressed.[13] Although the R-N-R theoretical paradigm stresses the need to work with the offender, it is still the case that assessment is something done to, rather than with, the offender. The same is true of the use of standard assessment instruments (such as OASyS) in probation practice in England and Wales today. The rehabilitative paradigm essentially puts the professional in the driving seat – it is the professional who assesses the offender, decides which requirements are best in sentence and tries to ensure that the offender undertakes these.

[12] The R-N-R (risks – needs – responsivity) paradigm suggests that the key elements in promoting behavioural change in offenders are assessing risks (related to reoffending) and criminogenic needs (problematic aspects of the offender's life, such as having no job, which are related to criminality), and addressing these through using the appropriate programmes and supervisory elements appropriate to that offender (responsivity) – see Dowden and Andrews (2004).

[13] Criminogenic needs are those areas of the offender's life which are promoting further involvement in crime. They may be the need to change attitudes towards offending, or more practical problems (Bonta et al. 2008).

A desistance paradigm, in contrast, would stress the need for the offender to show agency – to move towards wishing to change their life. The offender may not know how to achieve this and, for persistent offenders, it is very much a struggle. Help, ideas and support from professionals are likely to be key to successful desistance (actually managing to reduce or stop criminal behaviour: Farrall and Calverley 2006). But input from the offender is also vital. This makes personal mitigation essential for sentencing which aims at desistance. The need is not just remorse, because that is essentially backwards-looking to the offence, but a drive to change one's life in the future. Personal mitigation, as set out in sentencing guidance in England and Wales, does not seem to have made this link. It is almost as though the past is the responsibility of the offender, but the future is the responsibility of the sentencer and other professionals. I would urge, therefore, that wish to change and evidence that action is beginning to be taken to change be separated from remorse in discussions of mitigation.

Some evidence of action being taken to change is, indeed, currently used to bolster judgements as to how much remorse the offender is showing. Writing letters of apology to the victim or making financial reparation is seen as positive evidence of taking responsibility and of remorse. Indeed, the mitigatory effect of making financial reparation before sentence is underlined to sentencers in the Council of Europe guidance to member states (1999) and the European Union Council framework decision (2001).

An interesting adjunct to the mitigating effects of trying to change one's life is shown in the reactions of victims of serious offences to offenders' apologies. For very serious offences, empirical evidence suggests that, although victims appreciate apologies from offenders, a purely verbal apology is not seen as sufficient really to indicate remorse – 'it's easy to just say sorry' (Shapland et al. 2006; 2011). Victims looked for, and were far more impressed with, offenders starting to take action to turn round their lives and to start to change. Victims in England and Wales were in general not very interested in financial or material reparation, but were enthusiastic about offenders trying to tackle those parts of their lives which were leading them to offend (Shapland et al. 2011; 2007). We have called this 'symbolic reparation' – it is not a direct payment to, or work for, the victim, but is seen, by both victims and offenders, as working to ensure that such victimization does not reoccur. In relation to mitigation, this means that, at least for serious offences, a reparative purpose of sentencing also needs to focus on personal mitigation and on decisions by the offender. The idea of 'symbolic reparation', which is a key part of restorative justice, has echoes of rehabilitation and of reparation – but it is crucially highly offender-focused, in that the desire to achieve it comes from the offender and it is something offered by the offender to the victim and to society.

FINDING THE PERSON IN PERSONAL MITIGATION

What, then, would a mitigation which emphasizes movement towards desistance or reparation look like? It would emphasize remorse and decisions towards desistance, which combine to create offers of symbolic reparation, all of which I would see as important individual-level factors which should be emphasized in a new personal mitigation of desistance. However, it would also acknowledge the necessary interaction between these and societal support for desistance (social capital, particularly bridging capital[14]). The desistance literature is clear that only the rare offender can accomplish the path to desistance without help. So, offers of employment, agreement to participate in substance abuse programmes, skills training (particularly learning to drive – a driving licence seems currently to be the key to less skilled employment for men), seeking out help, participating in debt advice and family support would all be recognized as mitigating elements in guidance, not just in judicial practice. The pre-sentence report would become less of an exercise in risk prediction, more of a proposal to build on desistance decisions – although only of course if the offender wished to desist.[15] Above all, the list of factors would be replaced by guidance that a package needs to be in place which combines individual elements and decisions with social support. That social support could come from families or from criminal justice or social agencies. Sentencers would be provided with information, both generally and in individual cases, on what has been found to be more effective for different obstacles to

[14] The social capital on which someone can draw includes all their contacts, acquaintances, friends and family. Bridging capital encompasses those people and settings to which the individual belongs which link him or her to societal institutions which can help – so, for example, a probation officer may provide bridging capital to housing associations which could help with providing accommodation, or a friend of the family may know a private landlord who could do the same.

[15] Having no desire to desist would clearly not be mitigating, just as showing no remorse or being proud of offending is currently not seen as mitigating – and may be seen as aggravating.

desistance – how best to turn from unemployment to obtaining and keeping work, what life skills and work skills are needed and so on.

How does this differ from current ideas about personal mitigation? One element is that it brings together and brings to the fore forward-facing philosophies of sentencing, such as rehabilitation and deterrence, without neglecting the need to pay proper respect to the past and the seriousness of the offence, through the offender taking responsibility for the offence and through reparation to the victim. There is no intrinsic difficulty in sentencing under such a desistance paradigm being, overall, proportional to the seriousness of the offence – neither offender nor victim will see anything else as fair. However, this desistance paradigm for sentencing would not find a bare retributivist perspective – one which merely measures the offence and culpability for the offence – helpful. A desistance paradigm for sentencing would have the offender as central in its sights and the offender's decisions would also be important. Such a paradigm would also make personal mitigation key – and the person which such personal mitigation would reveal would be a rounded person, rather than a collection of mitigating factors.

The current paradigm for sentencing and the current limited role for a small number of aspects of personal mitigation has made sentencing a relatively mechanical process, as the magistrates' court guidelines indicate. This has advantages in potentially promoting consistency of process and in curtailing the discretion of sentencers. The problem is that it does not really serve the overall interests of society, which lie in protection from further offending, reparation for victims and creating change in offenders' lives. To achieve those ends, I would argue, we need to move towards a sentencing process which has desistance, reparation and protection as its key goals, and a mitigation which sees the offender as a person, with corresponding prominence given to personal mitigation.

REFERENCES

Bonta, J., Rugge, T., Scott, T. L., Bourgon, G. and Yessine, A. (2008). 'Exploring the Black Box of Community Supervision', *Journal of Offender Rehabilitation*, 47 (3): 248–70.

Bottoms, A. E., and Shapland, J. (2011). 'Steps towards Desistance among Male Young Adult Recidivists', in S. Farrall, M. Hough, S. Maruna and R. Sparks (eds.), *Escape Routes: Contemporary Perspectives on Life after Punishment*. London: Routledge.

Council of Europe. (1999). *Mediation in Penal Matters: Recommendation No. R(99)19 and Explanatory Memorandum*. Strasbourg: Council of Europe.

Dowden, C. and Andrews, D. (2004). 'The Importance of Staff Practice in Delivering Effective Correctional Treatment: A Meta-analytic Review of Core Correctional Practice', *International Journal of Offender Therapy and Comparative Criminology*, 48 (2): 203–14.

European Union (2001). *Council Framework Decision 2001/220/JHA of 15 March 2001 on the Standing of Victims in Criminal Proceedings* (OJ 2001 L82/1).

Farrall, S. and Calverley, A. (2006). *Understanding Desistance from Crime: Emerging Theoretical Directions in Resettlement and Rehabilitation*. Maidenhead: Open University Press.

Farrall, S., Bottoms, A. E. and Shapland, J. (2010). 'Social Structures and Desistance from Crime', *European Journal of Criminology*, 7: 546–70.

Farrington, D. P. (2002). 'Developmental Criminology and Risk-Focused Prevention', in M. Maguire, R. Morgan and R. Reiner (eds.), *The Oxford Handbook of Criminology*, 3rd edn. Oxford University Press.

Jacobson, J. and Hough, M. (2007). *Mitigation: The Role of Personal Factors in Sentencing*. London: Prison Reform Trust.

Laub, J. H. and Sampson, R. J. (2003). *Shared Beginnings, Divergent Lives*. Cambridge, Mass.: Harvard University Press.

Maruna, S. (2000). *Making Good*. Washington, DC: American Psychological Association.

Ministry of Justice (2007). *National Standards for the Management of Offenders, Standards and Implementation Guidance 2007*. London: NOMS, available at http://noms.justice.gov.uk/news-publications-events/publications/guidance/OM_National_Standards_0907?view=Binary.

Sentencing Guidelines Council (2004). *Overarching Principles: Seriousness*. London: Sentencing Guidelines Council, available at www.sentencing-council.org.uk/.

(2005). *Guideline Judgments Case Compendium*. London: Sentencing Guidelines Council, available at http://webarchive.nationalarchives.gov.uk/20100519200657/www.sentencing-guidelines.gov.uk/docs/complete_compendium.pdf

(2008). *Magistrates' Court Sentencing Guidelines: Definitive Guideline*. London: Sentencing Guidelines Council, available at www.sentencing council.org.uk.

Shapland, J. (1981). *Between Conviction and Sentence*. London: Routledge & Kegan Paul.

Shapland, J., Atkinson, A., Atkinson, H., Chapman, B., Colledge, E., Dignan, J., Howes, M., Johnstone, J., Robinson, G. and Sorsby, A. (2006). 'Situating Restorative Justice within Criminal Justice', *Theoretical Criminology*, 10 (4): 505–32.

Shapland, J., Atkinson, A., Atkinson, H., Chapman, B., Dignan, J., Howes, M., Johnstone, J., Robinson, G. and Sorsby, A. (2007). *Restorative Justice: The Views of Victims and Offenders*, Ministry of Justice Research Series 3/07. London: Ministry of Justice, available at www.justice.gov.uk/docs/Restorative-Justice.pdf.

Shapland, J., Johnstone, J., Sorsby, A., Stubbing, T., Hibbert, J., Howes, M., Jackson, J. and Colledge, E. (2003). *Evaluation of Statutory Time Limit Pilot Schemes in the Youth Court*. London: Home Office, available at www.homeoffice.gov.uk/rds/pdfs2/rdsolr2103.pdf.

Shapland, J., Robinson, G. and Sorsby, A. (2011). *Restorative Justice in Practice*. London: Routledge.

Stouthamer-Loeber, M., Wei, E., Loeber, R. and Master, A. S. (2004). 'Desistance from Persistent Serious Delinquency in the Transition to Adulthood', *Development and Psychopathology*, 16 (4): 897–918.

Wikstrom, P. O. (2006). 'Individuals, Settings and Acts of Crime: Situational Mechanisms and the Explanation of Crime', in P. O. Wikstrom and R. Sampson (eds.), *The Explanation of Crime: Context, Mechanisms and Development*. Cambridge University Press.

TABLE OF CASES

R *v*. Abbas, [2009] R.T.R. 3.
R *v*. French and Webster, [2007] 1 Cr App R (S) 1.
R *v*. Wilson (Daniel Rushton), [2008] 1 Cr App R (S) 90.

CHAPTER FIVE

INTOXICATION AS A SENTENCING FACTOR: MITIGATION OR AGGRAVATION?

Nicola Padfield

The criminogenic effect of alcohol is well known; in a significant proportion of offences, particularly those involving violence, the accused was intoxicated at the time of the offence. Should the fact that he or she was drunk be taken into account and, if so, how? There are three possible positions: intoxication could either mitigate or aggravate the 'deserved' penalty, or the offender's lack of sobriety might be immaterial to sentencing.

CHAPTER OVERVIEW

This chapter explores this common circumstance which has such important consequences for sentencing across offences and jurisdictions. In the conclusion of his book *Alcohol and Crime* (2006), Dingwall writes:

> Given the large number of defendants who raise intoxication as a mitigating factor at the sentencing stage, the paucity both of a guiding approach and of academic attention to the issue is alarming.
> (p. 170)

He identifies a pressing need for a proper consideration of how intoxication should affect sentencing, arguing that in general it should not be treated as a mitigating factor unless the offender had never previously offended while intoxicated. This chapter seeks to contribute to the debate he starts, but by adopting a less 'unashamedly retributive' (p.171) approach. The argument here is that, although Parliament, the higher courts (and, to a lesser extent, academics) have largely ignored the problem, sentencing courts do in fact seek to help 'suitable' offenders with less punitive and more rehabilitative sentences. This chapter tentatively encourages such an approach.

If Dingwall's approach – that drunkenness is not to be taken as a mitigating factor unless the offender has previously never offended while intoxicated – were taken seriously, it is suggested here that sentence levels would rise. In practice, sentencers who believe both that an offender may be ready to change his or her ways, and that treatment is available, may well impose a lenient sentence. Particularly in the case of less serious offences, they may well recognize the human weakness which resulted in the offence and seek to impose a sentence which 'helps' the offender to go straight or at least mend his or her ways. More evidence is clearly needed, but this chapter seeks to urge caution to those who argue that guidelines on aggravating and mitigating factors should be more prescriptive (see Roberts (2008) for a discussion of the arguments for more structured judicial discretion regarding sentencing factors). Here it is argued that, if the aim of the penal system is to reduce reoffending, intoxication should be taken into consideration by sentencers. Of course, identifying suitable candidates for what might be considered 'lenient' sentences needs to be done as fairly as possible. Reasons must always be given. Further non-binding guidance on the precise role of intoxication on sentence decisions would be helpful. It is also important to recognize that the hopelessly inadequate provision of alcohol abuse treatment programmes, both in prison and in the community, is a significant barrier to effective sentencing.

The scope of the problem of alcohol and crime

Alcohol consumption levels in Britain are far higher than they were fifty years ago. There was a 24 per cent increase in the number of 'dependent drinkers' between 2000 and 2007, with the current figure now standing at 1.6 million dependent drinkers in England (Ward et al., 2010). The social problem of 'binge drinking' (sometimes defined as drinking in order to get drunk) is a subject of widespread debate, perhaps rightly: 69 per cent of male binge-drinkers and 45 per cent of female binge-drinkers reported at least one violent incident in the previous year, compared with 34 per cent of regular male drinkers and 18 per cent of regular female drinkers.[1] Alcohol-related crime costs the UK billions of pounds a year (in terms of policing, prevention services, processing

[1] See fact sheets, available at www.alcoholconcern.org.uk.

offenders through the criminal justice system and the human costs incurred by the victims of crime).

According to one survey, nearly two-thirds of sentenced male prisoners (63%) and two-fifths of female sentenced prisoners (39%) admitted to hazardous drinking which carries the risk of physical or mental harm (Prison Reform Trust, 2004). Of those, about half had a severe alcohol dependency. In 2008/9, 19 per cent of prisoners surveyed for HM Inspectorate of Prisons reported having an alcohol problem when they entered prison. The rate of prisoners reporting alcohol problems was even higher among young adults (30%) and women (29%). As that report states, 'these figures almost certainly underestimate the scale of the problem, as many of those with alcohol problems will fail to recognize or acknowledge them' (HM Chief Inspector of Prisons for England and Wales 2010 : 5). The report is deeply troubling: it found that a considerable number of prisons had no alcohol strategy. Where strategies existed, inspections often found them inadequate. Community provision for alcohol treatment is equally poor (Ward et al. 2010).

The role of intoxication at sentencing

What impact – if any – should these facts have on sentencing policy, guidelines and on individual sentencing decisions? Newspaper and formal law reports constantly discuss drunk offenders. The impact of intoxication on criminal liability has been explored at great length, and academics have explored in depth and at length the rules which should operate in order fairly to convict those who 'should' be convicted and to acquit those who 'should' be acquitted.[2] However, Dingwall is clearly right that judges and academics have given much less thought to the impact of alcohol as a mitigating or aggravating factor in sentencing (although notable contributions include Shapland 1981; Rumgay 1998; Dingwall and Koffman 2008; these will be explored later in this chapter).

In practice, intoxication can be either a mitigating or an aggravating factor. With additional empirical research, it may be possible to identify more reliably when drunkenness currently aggravates a sentence, and when it may mitigate. This chapter will seek to show that whilst greater clarity in the analysis of different types of 'drunk offender' might lead to greater clarity of guidance to sentencers, this may not be helpful or appropriate to translate into rigid guidelines. The complex impact that

[2] Though the solution (adopted by the House of Lords in *Majewski*) remains controversial: see for example Law Commission of England and Wales (2009).

an offender's intoxication rightly has on a sentencer reveals the realities of sentencing practice and the danger with formulaic sentencing. While offenders should never be punished disproportionately, a sentence should be tailored to the individual offender. A recognition that judges inevitably (and rightly) make 'informed guesses' leads to the conclusion that sentencing should not be seen as a one-off event, but as a continuing process. Given the severe underfunding of alcohol treatment programmes for offenders, it is hardly surprising that there is scepticism about 'what works'. But this might be a reason to involve judges in the management of sentences.

THE LAW

There is little statutory guidance on the impact that intoxication should have on sentencing decisions, and only a little to be gleaned from the Sentencing Guideline Council's guidelines and from decisions of the Court of Appeal. We start with a brief exploration of parliamentary involvement in this area.

Legislation

Given the fact that Parliament has been encouraged to pass an enormous amount of sentencing law in recent years, and that there are specific offences (being drunk and disorderly, or drunken driving being obvious examples) and specific sentences for drunk offenders (a variety of banning orders), it is perhaps surprising that there is no general law on the impact of intoxication on offence seriousness. There has been a proliferation of punitive measures designed to protect the public, often from those who offend when drunk: as well as driving disqualifications these include drink banning orders (under the Violent Crime Reduction Act 2006, ss. 1–14, brought into force in August 2009) and football banning orders (governed by the Football Spectators Act 1989, s. 14A, which has already been amended a number of times in its short history). But apart from specific offences and specific protective punitive measures, there is no general legislative guidance on sentencing the drunk offender. We know that in considering the seriousness of an offence 'the court must consider the offender's culpability in committing the offence and any harm which the offence caused, was intended to cause or might forseeably have caused' (Criminal Justice Act 2003, s. 143). But to what extent is culpability aggravated or mitigated by intoxication?

Sentencing guidelines in England and Wales

The Sentencing Guidelines Council (SGC) was created by the Criminal Justice Act 2003 and ceased to exist on 1 April 2010, when its role was taken over by the Sentencing Council of England and Wales. The new Council has some different and some expanded powers and duties (Coroners and Justice Act 2009, ss. 118–136).[3] The existing guidelines continue to apply, however. The relevant provision is to be found in section 125(1) of the Coroners and Justice Act 2009: 'Every court must, in sentencing an offender, follow any sentencing guidelines which are relevant to the offender's case.'

The SGC's recommended decision-making process was that the sentencer should identify the appropriate 'starting point' for any offence, following published guidelines, before considering, first, relevant aggravating factors, both general and specific to the type of offence, then mitigating factors and finally matters of personal mitigation. In its first guidance published, *Overarching Principles: Seriousness* (2004), the SGC identified 'commission of an offence while under the influence of alcohol or drugs' as one of twenty-two possible 'factors indicating higher culpability', but no detail was added to develop this direction. Intoxication (unsurprisingly) was not mentioned as one of the four 'factors indicating significantly lower culpability', and on personal mitigation the only specific examples given are of remorse and admissions to the police.

Many individual guidelines reproduce the general factors listed in the overarching principles, and sometimes others are added. For example, the *Magistrates' Court Sentencing Guidelines* provide that 'an obvious state of intoxication' is an aggravating factor, or a factor 'indicating higher culpability' for the offence of failing to provide a specimen contrary to section 7(6) of the Road Traffic Act 1988, and 'evidence of alcohol or drugs' is an aggravating factor in the offence of aggravated vehicle taking contrary to the Theft Act 1968, sections 12A(2)(c) and (d). It is thus clear that intoxication can be an aggravating factor at sentencing.

What about intoxication as a mitigating factor? It would appear that the SGC did not believe that intoxication ever diminishes the seriousness of an offence. It may play a role in choice of sentence, but not as a mitigating factor. Thus they comment on suitable punishments for offenders with various dependencies in their guidance on sentencing offenders for *Theft and Burglary Other than a Dwelling*, published in December 2008:

[3] For further information see Ashworth (2010b) and www.sentencing.council.co.uk.

> Many offenders convicted of acquisitive crimes are motivated by an addiction, often to drugs, alcohol or gambling. This does not mitigate the seriousness of the offence, but an offender's dependency may properly influence the type of sentence imposed. In particular, it may sometimes be appropriate to impose a drug rehabilitation requirement or an alcohol treatment requirement as part of a community order or a suspended sentence order in an attempt to break the cycle of addiction and offending, even if an immediate custodial sentence would otherwise be warranted. (p. 5, para. 16)

Breaking the cycle of offending – we shall return to this when looking at the aims that sentencers must bear in mind.

Court of Appeal guidance

The Court of Appeal has long had the roles of advising sentencers and of encouraging a consistent approach to sentencing. Walker (1999) suggests that before the nineteenth century drunkenness was no excuse, but that in the nineteenth and twentieth centuries case law made 'step-by-step concessions' (p. 108). He gives examples of intoxication exceptionally being accepted as mitigation. Yet the overwhelming message remained clear: drunkenness is never an excuse. Hence the strong words of Lawton LJ in *Kirkland* (1975) and Widgery CJ in *Bradley* (1980), making it clear that even out-of-character, first-time drunken behaviour can never be condoned. Nor does the Court of Appeal give any support to the idea that committing an offence to get money to support an addiction might be a mitigating factor. For example, in *Lawrence* (1988) Simon Brown J wrote:

> It is no mitigation whatever that a crime is committed to feed an addiction, whether that addiction be drugs, drink, gambling, sex, fast cars or anything else. If anyone hitherto has been labouring under the misapprehension that it was mitigation, then the sooner and more firmly they are disabused of it the better.

However, it is difficult to draw clear guidance from recent case law, as, perhaps surprisingly, intoxication gets little discussion. Other issues usually appear more relevant to the Court of Appeal, and appear to 'trump' the intoxication factor. Intoxication can be, as the English guidelines suggest, an aggravating factor, but the case law would suggest that it can also serve either as a mitigating factor (reducing the seriousness of the offence) or at least as offender mitigation. Finding clear general guidance is very difficult; the words used by a court do not always match the eventual sentence imposed.

Exploring intoxication as a source of mitigation

Let us start with the most serious offence, murder. Some people who kill when drunk will be convicted of murder, as an intent to kill formed by a person who is drunk is still an intent in law. But what is the impact of intoxication in determining their sentence? All those convicted of murder face a mandatory sentence of life imprisonment, with a lengthy minimum term (see Schedule 21 of the Criminal Justice Act 2003). Although many offenders convicted of murder had been drinking when they committed the offence, the role of alcohol in fixing the minimum term is often ignored. An obvious opportunity to clarify the issue was missed in *Holmes* (2010), who was convicted of the murder of his father. Clearly Holmes had been drinking heavily, and psychiatrists noted that this would have had a disinhibiting effect. But when the Court of Appeal reduced the minimum term of the mandatory life sentence from nineteen to seventeen years, they avoided any discussion of the role of intoxication in the sentence calculation. Other cases could have been selected to illustrate the same point: when aggravating and mitigating factors are discussed, the role of alcohol is notable by its absence.

Many alcoholics or drunken people who kill are convicted of manslaughter rather than murder. Either the jury is not satisfied that they intended to kill or cause serious harm, or one of the complex partial defences to murder will apply, reducing the conviction from murder to manslaughter. A useful starting point is *Kehoe* (2008). Kehoe was a 43-year-old woman with significant alcohol and mental health problems who killed a fellow resident in the sheltered housing where she lived. Both she and the victim had severe problems with alcohol. The Court of Appeal reduced the life sentence imposed on her to an indefinite sentence of imprisonment for public protection (IPP) with a three-year minimum term. The Court was obviously somewhat sympathetic to her case: the 'unpremeditated killing of one drunk by another, at a time when her responsibility was diminished, and after she had been provoked, could not be said to be so grave that a life sentence was required or even justified' (at para. 17). Yet there is no discussion of what role was played by her intoxication in the decision to fix the minimum term at only three years. The emphasis is simply on the substantial degree of provocation.[4]

How does one reconcile the decision in *Kehoe* with the much tougher line taken by the Lord Chief Justice in *Wood* (2009)? This is an important case, where the Court chose to sit as a bench of five judges.

[4] A related question to that addressed in this chapter is the impact on sentence when the victim was drunk and in some manner contributed to or caused the offence: see *Conn*.

Wood's murder conviction was reduced to manslaughter by diminished responsibility. But the key question was not simply was his responsibility reduced, but to what extent did alcohol dependency syndrome reduce his liability for the killing? In *Wood*, the Court says that his responsibility, although diminished, remained high. Unlike *Kehoe*, which they say was at the 'lowest level of seriousness', this case was at the highest level: a prolonged murderous attack of the utmost ferocity. A very substantial element of mental responsibility remained. It seems that the Court justifies the life sentence with a thirteen-year minimum term by reference to the culpability of the offender. But, again, the impact of his alcoholism on the actual sentence is not clear. It is interesting to note that the Court is also making guesses for the future, a point to which we will return later:

> While in custody he is not able to obtain alcohol but there is no basis on which we can be satisfied that the alcohol dependency syndrome from which he suffered at the date of his crimes is now permanently cured, and that if and when released, he would not return to his excessive and dangerous drinking habits. (at para. 19)

Intoxication and driving offences

One area which has provoked much controversy is the sentencing of offenders who cause death or injury when driving under the influence of drink or drugs. The Criminal Justice Act 2003 (s. 285) increased the penalties for driving-related offences. Thus the maximum sentence for causing death by dangerous driving and causing death by careless driving when under the influence of drink or drugs was increased to fourteen years. In *Richardson* (2006), the Court of Appeal reconsidered the previous guideline case of *Cooksley* (2003) in the light of this change in the law:

> where death arises from a road traffic accident caused when the driver has voluntarily consumed excess alcohol, in culpability terms this is and should be equated with causing death by dangerous driving. The consumption of alcohol is deliberate. Everyone knows, or should know, that the consumption of even small quantities of alcohol undermines the ability of any driver to apply his full concentration to the road. Where the consumption is high, it is effectively extinguished. Alcohol makes a driver personally unfit to drive, and the car of which he is in control becomes as dangerous with him at the wheel as if it were subject to a serious known, potentially fatal, mechanical defect. Looking at the matter broadly, there is never any acceptable excuse for driving a vehicle

> when the ability to do so properly is impaired by alcohol or drugs. That is the critical ingredient of this offence. (at para. 22)

So driving drunk is no excuse. Perhaps this is unsurprising. It would be fascinating to look in more detail at all sentencing decisions involving drunk drivers. It would seem obvious that being drunk would never be a mitigating factor for this offence, yet even here drunk drivers have very different stories and backgrounds.[5] It is possible that sentencers are in fact making important judgements on culpability in the way in which they impose specific conditions within a sentence.

As we move down the ladder of offence seriousness, even where it would appear by their words that the Court is identifying alcohol as an aggravating factor, it is often not clear how this works on the facts of the individual case. For example, in *Willoughby* (2010), the 25-year-old defendant pleaded guilty to threatening to damage property. When the staff at a petrol station refused to sell him alcohol because he was drunk, he threatened the staff, took a petrol nozzle, spilt some petrol and threatened to set fire to it with his cigarette lighter if they did not sell him alcohol. The Court was in no doubt that the appellant's behaviour 'was influenced by his state of intoxication, as it had clearly been on previous occasions which had brought him before the courts' (at para. 4). His long list of previous convictions, going back to when he was aged 14, included ten offences of assaulting members of the public, five of obstructing or assaulting police officers, five of using threatening or abusive words or behaviour, two of being drunk and disorderly, four of criminal damage, eight of theft and two of robbery. The Court noted that his record revealed a pattern of offences of escalating seriousness. Despite this, the Court reduced his sentence from two years' imprisonment to sixteen months. Why? The Court gives little explanation.

Even where the Court notes that intoxication is an aggravating factor, it may appear actually to work to reduce the sentence. Thus, for example, in *Blazys* (2008) the Court of Appeal said that the judge 'understandably treated the consumption of alcohol and the disinhibiting effect it had had upon the appellant as an aggravating rather than a mitigating feature of the offending' (para. 7). Yet it reduced the sentence for a man of previous good character from twelve months to eight months'

[5] For example, contrasting levels of culpability could turn on the offender's prior history with alcohol. The previously abstemious offender who naively drives after a rare drinking session to celebrate some event may be contrasted with another who drinks regularly, and has full awareness of the incapacitating effects of alcohol as well as his own tendency to drink.

imprisonment. This case involved a common scenario: a group of four drunk men had approached a lone woman at a bus stop and then attacked a man who came to her support. In a not dissimilar 'disgraceful street incident', in *Bell* (2010) the Court of Appeal upheld a sentence of twelve months for affray after a guilty plea. The Court, in distinguishing *Blazys*, discusses his good character but not the question of intoxication.

Occasionally intoxication does appear as mitigation, particularly if the Court is convinced that the offender was acting out of character. In *Trace* a 19-year-old student pleaded guilty to robbery and to damaging property, offences committed on an Asian takeaway delivery driver when he was drunk and dressed as a Mexican bandit. 'What gives us some cause for thought is that this was an offence which would appear to have been out of character' (at para. 11). The Court of Appeal quashed a custodial sentence of twelve months in a young offender institution, and substituted a twelve-month suspended sentence (in fact thirty-two weeks, in view of time already served). Interestingly, the Court was also critical of the university concerned for its toleration of a drinking culture. The wider social context of offending is rarely so explicitly considered.

It is not only the offender who is acting out of character who may exceptionally be successful in using their intoxication as some kind of mitigating factor. In *Birkett* (2009), where an alcoholic had set fire to his flat, the Court imposed a fixed three-year term of imprisonment, removing the much harsher indeterminate IPP with a minimum term of two years. Having noted that the offender was drunk, the Court of Appeal notes that the offence could have been viewed as a cry for help.[6] Is this simply an example of the Court being lenient or merciful (on which see Walker 1999: ch. 14)?

Despite examples of leniency, much the most common scenario is a drunk offender, whose drunkenness passes almost without comment. Thus in *Bunch* (2010), where a pharmacist's assistant used the keys he possessed to let himself into the pharmacy early one morning to steal a small quantity of Diazepam, the Court of Appeal carefully identified the breach of trust, and the need to protect vulnerable members of public, but did not discuss the fact that he was drunk. And in *Jeffcoate* (2010) the Court of Appeal had to consider whether the trial judge was entitled to consider that a 67-year-old arsonist, a lonely individual who led an impoverished and solitary life, was 'dangerous' when a psychiatric report

[6] Another recent drunken 'cry for help' case was *Judd*.

concluded otherwise. The Court focused on his history of offending to agree with the sentencing judge that the appellant was dangerous. There is no discussion of the fact that he was drunk when he committed the offence.

It was noted above that new sentencing options include measures, such as banning orders, designed to protect society from drunken offenders. There is already significant case law on football banning orders, but, interestingly, the issues on appeal have not turned on questions or levels of intoxication. Thus in *R (White) v. Blackfriars Crown Court* (2008) it was made very clear that was no need for clear evidence of repeat hooliganism: the aim of a football banning order can simply be to deter other potential hooligans. With the emphasis on the deterrent effect of the order, it is perhaps unsurprising that courts have not been interested in considering the relevance of intoxication.

To summarize, this brief review of recent and Court of Appeal case law illustrates that while alcohol plays an enormous role in criminal activity, it is a topic on which the Court rarely focuses in appeals against sentence. Frequently a factor in criminal activity, it is rarely discussed. It is time to turn to the empirical evidence and to legal theory.

EMPIRICAL EVIDENCE AND THEORETICAL DEBATES

The starting point here, too, is the absence of analysis. There is very little empirical research into the reality of sentence decision-making: data are not routinely collected which permit ready analysis. In recognition of the need for such data, a major project designed to help in understanding the reasons behind individual sentence decisions was launched in 2007/8. But it was very disappointingly abandoned in 2009 because crucial data were simply unavailable (see Dhami and Souza 2009).

There has been some relevant research. Shapland (1981), some thirty years ago, looked at the impact of intoxication in her detailed study of the process of mitigation. Her categorization of mitigating factors in pleas in mitigation (reasons for the offence, descriptions of the gravity of the offence, attitudes of the offender to the offence, present personal circumstances of the offender, past personal circumstances of the offender, future personal circumstances of the offender, factors concerned with the probation service, factors concerned with court processes, and 'others') reveals how difficult it is to identify the role that intoxication should play. Her hypothetical example was a burglar, Mr Smith, who had drunk five pints of beer before the burglary. Where does this fit in as mitigation? Only eight out of thirty barristers interviewed mentioned the beer as a mitigating factor:

> Some barristers commented during the interview that any mention of drink to the court would need to be carefully done, as some benches regarded this almost as an aggravating factor, particularly in an unemployed person. Others considered that the amount drunk had affected by Mr Smith's judgement or mood to some extent and so might be considered a reason for the offence. (pp. 116–17)

Jacobson and Hough's much more recent (2007; see also this volume) study of mitigation in practice again reveals the vital importance of personal mitigation in actual sentencing decisions, a factor which is all too often ignored. The study was carried out across five Crown Court centres, and involved the observation of 132 cases involving 162 defendants and 52 sentencers, as well as interviews with 40 sentencers. The study developed a six-fold categorization of factors that can play a part:

- factors relating to the criminal act, including harm caused to any victim(s);
- factors relating to the immediate circumstances of the offence;
- factors relating to the defendant's wider circumstances at the time of the offence;
- factors relating to the defendant's responses to the offence and prosecution;
- factors relating to the defendant's past; and
- factors relating to the defendant's present and future.

These authors acknowledge the difficulty of 'forcing' intoxication into these categories:

> It is difficult to determine where to place factors relating to drug and alcohol misuse in our six-fold categorization. A sentencer may regard as aggravating the fact that an offence was committed when the offender was intoxicated (Category 2) . . . Where acquisitive crime is committed in order to fund a drug habit, this might be treated as a mitigating or aggravating (within Category 3), depending on whether the sentencer views this as a manifestation of diminished or increased culpability. It seems that the most crucial point considered by sentencers with respect to both alcohol and drug misuse is whether there are prospects of effective treatment of dependency. If this is deemed to be the case, the sentence

> may be passed with reference to the offender's present/future (Category 6), and the prospects of treatment will mitigate in the sense that a rehabilitative rather than punitive sentence is passed. Conversely, evident lack of willingness to address a drug or alcohol problem may be an aggravating factor within the same category. (p. 10)

Perhaps this is the key: whether the sentencer believes that the defendant can address his or her alcohol problems. Two lay magistrates recently explored five hypothetical case studies of young people involved in alcohol-related offences in order to support the introduction of the youth rehabilitation order's intoxicating substance treatment requirements (Bache and Fassenfelt 2010). Their argument is one which suggests that magistrates do indeed want to help offenders who are ready to be helped. Interestingly, Shapland (1981) pointed out that offenders and sentencers may see the purposes of sentencing very differently. For her, both have a role to play. The offender can excuse, apologize, justify or compensate, thus restoring the balance in social relations and so allow the sentencer to be more lenient. This process of 'dialogue' is an important aspect of sentencing, to which we will return.

Rumgay (1998) explored what she calls the versatility, the power and the popularity of the intoxication excuse by studying sentencing hearings in a city magistrates' court and interviewing magistrates in 1990 (before the important legislative changes of the Criminal Justice Act 1991). In accessing culpability, magistrates were keen to identify 'defendant's capacities for moral self-control in particular situations' (p. 164). Intoxication was frequently raised in mitigation, and often used to account for the offender's moral failings. Commenting on the situation in 1998, Rumgay found that 'sentencing was paralysed by the inaccessibility of treatment' (p. 165). She was clearly struck by the display of magisterial humanity (p. 208). Magistrates 'took a paternalistic and consensual approach to sentencing; they were receptive to the notion of alternatives to custody' (p. 207).

What can one conclude from this evidence? First, that we need a lot more empirical research into the realities of sentencing. Second, that judges and magistrates are faced with difficult human decisions. Sentencers may well be more likely to see intoxication as mitigation when the offence is more minor (Harrell 1981). As well as the sentencer, the defendant and the defence advocate, there is also the important role of the probation officer to be considered. Do probation officers see alcohol use as a mitigating or aggravating factor? The shape, content and recommendations of pre-sentence reports have changed enormously over the years (the latest guidance is in Probation Circular 12/2007: *Pre-sentence Reports*).

The changing role of the probation officer has been subject to wide-ranging analysis beyond the scope of this chapter (see Gelsthorpe and Morgan 2007). Clearly, risk assessment tools such as OASys[7] identify use of alcohol as a factor to predict risk, and the fact that someone has even a conviction for being 'drunk and disorderly' on their record may be relevant to assessing risk.[8] But there has been little research into probation officers' perceptions of the impact that intoxication should have on sentencing. A key is likely to be a probation officer's subjective assessment of an offender's probable success while on probation in dealing with his problem drinking (see Harrell (1980), although research carried out in Canada in the late 1970s may have little relevance to England today).

Public views

What does 'the public' think about the fact that an offender was drunk at the time of the offence? Roberts et al. (2009) report findings from a study involving a representative sample of the British public. These researchers found that there was clearly ambivalence among members of the public about the issue of intoxication: in answer to a question whether they thought the fact that the offender was drunk made the crime more serious, 24 per cent of respondents thought that it always increases seriousness, 26 per cent that it often increases seriousness, 20 per cent that it sometimes increases seriousness and 29 per cent that it makes no difference (p. 776). Perhaps this ambivalence simply reflects public awareness that sentencing is not straightforward.

Purposes of sentencing

Let us turn now to the purposes of sentencing. Section 142(1) of the Criminal Justice Act 2003 provides:

[7] OASys (the Offender Assessment System), developed in the late 1990s by the Home Office Probation Unit and HM Prison Service for use in England and Wales, is very often used in post-conviction, pre-sentence reports. It uses static factors (such as age, previous offending) as well as dynamic (social, economic and personal) factors to assess the risk of reconviction.

[8] See *Parker*.

(1) Any court dealing with an offender in respect of his offence must have regard to the following purposes of sentencing –
  (a) the punishment of offenders,
  (b) the reduction of crime (including its reduction by deterrence),
  (c) the reform and rehabilitation of offenders,
  (d) the protection of the public, and
  (e) the making of reparation by offenders to persons affected by their offences.

This provision is often criticized as inviting inconsistency, with the implication that it appears 'to embody the worst of "pick and mix" sentencing' (Ashworth 2010a: 77). Yet, looking at cases of drunken offenders, one can perhaps provide support for 'pick and mix' sentencing, or at least support for recognizing in law the fact that sentencers may indeed be faced with sentencing options which are at the same time both realistic, and inconsistent and contradictory. Can penal theory help? At the risk of over-simplification, with its focus on justice and proportionality, modern desert theory appeared in the late twentieth century to have supplanted the utilitarian and consequentialist justifications for punishments (von Hirsch 1993). The message was clear: it is unjust to give differential sentences based on the likelihood of successful reform or rehabilitation; sentences should be proportionate to culpability and harm caused.

How should intoxication affect a sentence under a desert-based model? This is the question addressed by Dingwall and Koffman (2008), who conclude that it is difficult to find a persuasive retributive justification for intoxication as an aggravating factor (contrary to the guidance of the SGC (2004)). But given that 'central to a retributivist response is the idea of an offender deserving punishment as a consequence of choosing to offend' (p. 346), they conclude that in a desert-based sentencing framework 'the repeat intoxicated offender forfeits the right to mitigation'. Their paper follows Dingwall's wide-ranging book *Alcohol and Crime* (2006), wherein the author appears, like Ashworth, to regret the enactment of conflicting sentencing aims without further guidance on priorities. He argues that they do little to aid a consistency of approach. He criticizes, too, section 143(2) of the 2003 Act, which provides that, generally, previous convictions should be treated as an aggravating factor, for the way in which the sentencer's attention is removed from the instant offence to the offender's record. Yet, intriguingly, he readily admits that both incapacitation and rehabilitation have a useful role to play in sentencing those who offend while drunk: 'it makes sense . . . to choose the options most likely to help the offender and potentially to remove him from areas where he has offended' (p. 158).

Again at the risk of over-simplification, just deserts and retributivist aims of punishment may now be, in Dingwall's words, 'in retreat' (Dingwall 2006: 151). Although we do not know nearly enough about the reality of sentencing practice in this country at this time, it may well be that utilitarian aims, such as the reduction of offending and the rehabilitation and reintegration of offenders into mainstream society, never went entirely out of fashion and, indeed, remained uppermost in the minds of many of those who actually sentence. These aims are certainly in the minds of politicians. Although much of the recent political discourse on sentencing has focused on public protection, encouraging longer than commensurate sentences for dangerous people, politicians are starting to acknowledge that the public can be given greater protection by focusing more explicitly on the causes of offending behaviour and on the reintegration of offenders. Indeed, there is currently talk of a 'rehabilitation revolution' (Cabinet Office, 2010). There is renewed interest in 'problem-solving courts', such as the North Liverpool Community Justice Court (see McKenna 2007). No one should encourage disproportionate sentences, but a fixation on seeking to identify aggravating and mitigating factors in order to fix 'offence seriousness' may lead to an unduly blinkered approach. Desert should certainly fix the upper limits of a sentence, but not necessarily its precise details.

A paradox often overlooked is that sentencing, a hugely difficult process, is, in this country at any rate, seen as a one-off event, conducted very swiftly. Jacobson and Hough (2007) discuss the difference between sentencers who take decisions rapidly and those for whom the process is much slower and more painstaking (although this difference partly reflected differences in court workloads). Several sentencers in the Jacobson and Hough research talked of having days when they are faced with too many cases – with the figure for 'too many' ranging from over three to over twenty. Some pointed out that this was problematic not just because they had insufficient time to give proper consideration to each case, but also because, as one said, it did not allow justice 'to be seen to be done as well as done'.

Several respondents stressed that the number of cases they can manage comfortably depends on whether they get the papers the night before, allowing time for preparation or – as happens far too often – the papers arrive on the day of the case. 'The process of sentencing was characterized by a kind of rolling chaos, whereby cases were frequently adjourned for a wide variety of reasons' (p. 50). Jacobson and Hough 'were left with a strong sense that sentencers genuinely needed appropriate discretion to allow them to do justice to the complexity – and indeed, the sheer quirkiness – of cases coming before them, even if the price that has to be paid for this discretion is a degree of sentencing disparity' (p. 57).

This complexity is well reflected if one concentrates on drunken offenders. For example Shapland (1981) and Jacobson and Hough (2007) had difficulty categorizing drunk offenders. How is the court meant to distinguish remorseful drunks from dangerous drunks, one-off drunks from alcoholics, those who get drunk in order to commit their offences from those who did not know they were drunk? Can guidelines ever be sufficiently and specifically detailed to be applicable in practice? Faced with an offender with a real drink problem who says the time has come for him to sort it out, there are strong arguments for encouraging the sentencer to follow a carefully considered and well explained 'hunch'. As Lord Woolf says in his foreword to the report by Jacobson and Hough (2007), 'justice and the public can in some cases be best served by lenience'. Leniency and indeed mercy have a part to play (see also Walker 1999).

The danger with rigid guidelines is that they may exclude the humanitarian concerns which sentencers rightly have for those who appear before them to be sentenced. It may well be that the step-by-step route to decision-making advocated by the SGC is actually unhelpful if taken too rigidly: identifying offence seriousness (a mixture of culpability and harm caused or potentially caused), and then finding additional aggravating and mitigating factors. Culpability itself is 'an elastic concept which potentially encompasses a range of personal mitigating and aggravating factors' (Jacobson and Hough 2007: 39). Should the new Sentencing Council focus on helping sentencers to tailor their sentence more precisely to the needs of the individual offender, developing a more structured way of harnessing their human desire to have a humanitarian (paternalistic?) dialogue with offenders?

The difficulties in distinguishing between different categories of drunken offender may be an argument, not simply for stricter guidelines, but for sentence review courts. It has already been noted that judges and magistrates are inevitably guessing when they make their decisions. Of course sentencers are left to guess: what is this defendant's real motivation? What is his likely future behaviour? This is not necessarily inappropriate, but it does mean that when their assumptions are proved wrong, they should be reviewed. A suspended sentence may become activated; a tough penalty may be softened. Reviews may have positive as well as negative outcomes (see Maruna (2011) on the potential impact that courts might have in providing 'rituals of reintegration'). Desistance from crime, especially for those with an alcohol problem, is not a one-off event, and sentencers should be able to recognize this.

We turn now to the elephant in the room noted at the beginning of this chapter, the extraordinary shortage of prison and community alcohol support and treatment programmes: see Fowles and Wilson (2010), who document and explore the huge barriers to successful treatments; and McSweeney et al. (2009), who identify the improvements which are required in relation to alcohol screening and specialist assessment processes, the accessibility of specialist alcohol treatment services, and the level of training for probation staff on delivering brief interventions, specifically, and alcohol issues more generally. They urge that continuing uncertainty and inconsistency around funding should be dealt with as a matter of urgency. Perhaps the most formidable barrier remains what Ward et al. (2010) argues is 'the single biggest gap in local alcohol treatment systems': the 'lack of an adequate pathway from prison into community treatment'. Despite the creation of the National Offender Management Service (NOMS)[9] some five years ago, the penal system remains disappointingly fragmented.

Many difficult questions remain: whether sentencers should take resource issues into account, and whether offenders should in effect be penalized for the lack of suitable provision, for example. I would argue that it is the role of the sentencer to shout loudly about the inadequate provision: sentencing is not just about the offence, but also about the wider social context of the offending and the offender. But that is beyond the scope of this chapter.

[9] The Government announced the creation of NOMS in 2005 to bring together HM Prison Service and the Probation Service in order to enable a more 'effective' delivery of their services. It is responsible for commissioning and delivering offender management services in custody and in the community, and oversees the contracts of privately run prisons, managing probation performance and creating probation trusts. Situated within the Ministry of Justice, its precise constitutional position, as well as its effectiveness, remains somewhat disputed.

CONCLUSION

The chapter began by showing that little help is given to sentencers by appellate case law or indeed by the Sentencing Guidelines Council. Roberts (2008) argues that this is regrettable, that current guidelines do not give adequate direction when it comes to the consideration of both mitigating and aggravating factors. When it comes to intoxication in particular, he suggests that some guidance for sentencers would be helpful. This chapter urges great caution before going down this route. The Sentencing Guidelines Council was hugely successful in developing very useful general guidelines, but the Sentencing Council should be wary of going much further. In reality, sentencing decisions are fact-specific, and individual offences and offender are infinitely complicated. Sentencers may well be right to choose between those offenders 'ready to change' and those who are not. It is unsurprising that judges and magistrates, as humans, want to help. Despite the undoubted attractions of a firmer framework for aggravating and mitigating factors, a sentencer should be allowed to take certain risks in sentencing in order to help an offender break their cycle of offending. What would certainly be useful is more empirical evidence on how sentencers work in practice, and wider consideration of regular sentence reviews.

REFERENCES

Ashworth, A. (2010a). *Sentencing and Criminal Justice*, 5th edn. Cambridge University Press.

(2010b). 'Sentencing Guidelines and the Sentencing Council', *Criminal Law Review*: 389–401.

Bache, J. and Fassenfelt, J. (2010). 'Committed in Drink', *Magistrate*, 66: 10–11.

Cabinet Office, *The Coalition: Our Programme for Government*, 2010, available at http://programmeforgovernment.hmg.gov.uk/justice/.

Dhami, M. and Souza, K. (2009). *The Study of Sentencing and its Outcomes: A Pilot Report*, Ministry of Justice Research Series 2/09. London: Ministry of Justice.

Dingwall, G. (2006). *Alcohol and Crime*. Cullompton: Willan Publishing.

Dingwall, G. and Koffman, L. (2008). 'Determining the Impact of Intoxication in a Desert-Based Sentencing Framework', *Criminology and Criminal Justice*, 8: 335–348.

Fowles, T. and Wilson, D. (2010). 'The National Probation Service's Work with Alcohol-Misusing Offenders', *Howard Journal*, 49: 182–4.

Gelsthorpe L. and Morgan, R. (2007). *Handbook of Probation*. Cullompton: Willan.

Harrell, W. A. (1980). 'Alcohol Misuse and Prior Alcohol-Related Convictions as Predictors of Probation Officer Perceptions and Sentencing', *Substance Use and Abuse*, 15: 1271.

(1981). 'Effects of alcohol use and offenders' remorsefulness on sentencing decisions', *Journal of Applied Social Psychology*, 11: 83–91.

HM Chief Inspector of Prisons for England and Wales. (2010). *Alcohol Services in Prisons: An Unmet Need*. London: HMIP.

Jacobson, J. and Hough, M. (2007). *Mitigation: The Role of Personal Factors in Sentencing*. London: Prison Reform Trust.

Law Commission of England and Wales (2009). *Intoxication and Criminal Liability*. Report No 134. London: Parliament, Cm 7526.

McKenna, K. (2007). *Evaluation of the North Liverpool Community Justice Centre*, Ministry of Justice Research Series 12/07. London: Ministry of Justice.

McSweeney, T., Webster, R., Turnbull, P. and Duffy, M. (2009). 'Evidence-Based practice? The National Probation Service's Work with Alcohol-Misusing Offenders', Ministry of Justice Research Series 13/09.

Maruna, S. (2011). 'Re-entry as a Rite of Passage', *Punishment and Society*, 13: 3–28.

Prison Reform Trust (2004). *Alcohol and Reoffending: Who Cares?* London: Prison Reform Trust.

Roberts, J. (2008). 'Aggravating and Mitigating Factors at Sentencing: Towards Greater Consistency of Application', *Criminal Law Review*: 264–76.

Roberts, J., Hough, M., Jacobson, J. and Moon, N. (2009). 'Public Attitudes to Sentencing Purposes and Sentencing Factors: An Empirical Analysis', *Criminal Law Review*: 771–82.

Rumgay, J. (1998). *Crime, Punishment and the Drinking Offender*. Basingstoke: Macmillan.

Sentencing Guidelines Council (2004). *Overarching Principles: Seriousness*, available at www.sentencing.council.co.uk.

Shapland, J. (1981). *Between Conviction and Sentence: The Process of Mitigation*. London: Routledge.

Thomas, D. A. (2010). *Current Sentencing Practice*, London: Sweet & Maxwell.

von Hirsch, A. (1993). *Censure and Sanctions*, Oxford: Clarendon Press.

Walker, N. (1999). *Aggravation, Mitigation and Mercy in English Criminal Justice*. London: Blackstone.

Ward, M. et al. (2010). 'Investing in Alcohol Treatment – Reducing Costs and Improving Lives: Alcohol Concern's Learning from 10 Years of Consultancy and Training', available at, www.alcoholconcern.org.uk.

TABLE OF CASES

Bell [2010] Crim 1138.
Birkett [2009] EWCA Crim 2302.

Blazys [2008] EWCA Crim 904.
Bradley (1980) 2 Cr App R (S) 12.
Bunch [2010] EWCA Crim 952.
Conn [2010] EWCA Crim 933.
Cooksley [2003] EWCA Crim 996
Holmes [2010] EWCA Crim 896.
Jeffcoate [2010] EWCA Crim 1079.
Judd [2010] EWCA Crim 1444.
Kehoe [2008] EWCA Crim 819.
Kirkland (1975, unreported, but cited in Thomas (2010).
Lawrence (1988) 10 Cr App R (S) 463.
Majewski [1977] AC 443.
Parker [2010] EWCA Crim 1141.
R (White) *v.* Blackfriars Crown Court, [2008] EWHC 510 (Admin); [2008] 2 Cr App R (S) 97.
Richardson [2006] EWCA Crim 3186.
Trace [2010] EWCA Crim 879.
Willoughby [2010] EWCA Crim 950.
Wood [2009] EWCA Crim 651.

CHAPTER SIX

BEYOND THE PARTIAL EXCUSE: AUSTRALASIAN APPROACHES TO PROVOCATION AS A SENTENCING FACTOR

Arie Freiberg and Felicity Stewart

Most mitigating factors will be relevant only at sentence – for example, good character, remorse, a plea of guilty, stress or personal crisis, or assistance to law enforcement authorities. Some factors, however, are more substantial and may be relevant for both the determination of guilt and for sentence because they relate to the offender's responsibility or culpability for the offence. Thus a factor such as self-defence may result in a complete acquittal or a conviction for a lesser offence such as manslaughter on a charge of murder,[1] or it may be a mitigating factor at sentencing. Mental disorder is another factor with multiple applications.[2] Youth is generally recognized as a mitigating factor, but is also formally recognized in almost every jurisdiction by a separate sentencing regime that applies different sentencing principles and sanctions from those available in the adult courts.

Of the hundreds of sentencing factors, provocation has been among the most controversial, problematic and variable in its treatment by the law. It is a factor that has been dealt with at all stages of the criminal process and with various consequences. In some jurisdictions it is treated

This chapter draws on Stewart and Freiberg (2008a; 2008b). Our thanks to Jenny Morgan, Ian Leader-Elliott, John McLoughlin, Stephen Farrow and Gavin Silbert for their comments on earlier drafts of this chapter and to Donald Ritchie, Tal Karp and Catherine Jeffreys for their assistance.

[1] For example, in Victoria the offence of defensive homicide applies where a person kills another believing that their conduct is necessary to defend themselves or another person from the infliction of death or really serious injury but had no reasonable grounds for that belief (Crimes Act 1958 (Vic), s. 9AD).

[2] Mental disorder, if sufficiently severe, may result in a successful plea of insanity or, in some jurisdictions, a plea of diminished responsibility to a charge of murder resulting in a verdict of manslaughter. It may also be taken into account in sentencing.

as a partial defence to the crime of murder, reducing it to manslaughter; in others it is now relevant only to sentencing in murder cases. For some non-fatal offences against the person, provocation is a complete defence (resulting in acquittal) in some jurisdictions, while in others it is a mitigating factor to be considered in sentencing.

In recent years the partial defence of provocation has undergone the most radical transformation in the antipodes. Tasmania (in 2003),[3] Victoria (2005),[4] Western Australia (2008)[5] and New Zealand (2009)[6] have all abolished the partial defence and moved consideration of provocation in homicide cases from the substantive part of the criminal law to the sentencing stage. In comparison with the relatively modest reforms introduced in England and Wales in 2009[7] and the negligible changes in the United States (Ramsey 2010), these bold (or, in the view of some, misguided) reforms provide an opportunity to reconsider the relationship between partial defences and the role of sentencing factors in the criminal justice process.

CHAPTER OVERVIEW

In this chapter we examine the reasons for abolishing the partial defence of provocation in some Australasian jurisdictions and discuss some of the sentencing policy issues raised by such reform. We briefly examine the nature of provocation and its role as a partial defence to murder, discuss some of the considerations relevant to deciding whether it should be part of the substantive criminal law or a sentencing factor, query the manner in which provocation should be approached when raised as a sentencing factor in homicide cases, and ask whether the same approach should apply to other offences. Finally, we outline our proposals for a coherent theoretical approach to provocation as a factor to be taken into account in sentencing.

PROVOCATION AS A PARTIAL DEFENCE

The long history of the partial defence has been well documented (Ashworth 1976; Coss 1991; 2007; Horder 1992; Leader-Elliott 1996;

[3] Criminal Code Amendment (Abolition of Defence of Provocation) Act 2003 (Tas).
[4] Crimes (Homicide) Act 2005 (Vic).
[5] Criminal Law Amendment (Homicide) Act 2008 (WA).
[6] Crimes (Provocation Repeal) Amendment Act 2009 (NZ).
[7] Coroners and Justice Act 2009 (UK).

1997; 2010; Morgan 1997; 2002; Stewart and Freiberg 2008a: 5–7; VLRC 2004: paras. 2.3–7; Wasik 1982). While the original conception of provocation focused on the wrongfulness of the victim's conduct as a basis for reducing the defendant's culpability, under its later conception the defendant's own loss of self-control was viewed as a reason to view him or her as less morally culpable than a 'cold-blooded' killer (Law Reform Commission (Ireland) 2003: paras. 1.22–4; VLRC 2004: paras 2.6–7).

THE ASSAULT ON THE DOCTRINE

Australia and New Zealand

The first serious antipodean attack on the doctrine of provocation came in 1976 in the form of the New Zealand Criminal Law Reform Committee's *Report on Culpable Homicide*, which recommended abolishing both the partial defence and the mandatory penalty for murder (Criminal Law Reform Committee (NZ) 1976: paras. 6, 16; see also Wasik 1982: 530–1). The Committee argued that the use of provocation as a partial defence to murder was an anomaly compared with its use as a mitigating factor for other offences. With the abolition of the death penalty, the original reason for its existence had 'almost evaporated' (Criminal Law Reform Committee (NZ) 1976, para. 8). The Committee also criticized the legal definition of provocation and suggested that transferring it to the sentencing stage would allow the judge to determine the issue 'untrammelled by artificial legal rules and definitions' (para. 27). This trenchant attack on the law of provocation did not bear fruit until 2009, when the law was finally changed.

In Australia, the partial defence continued to flourish in the twentieth century[8] until Tasmania, in a little-heralded move in 2003, became the first jurisdiction to abolish it[9] due to concerns about gender bias and male aggression, the fact that provoked killers had an intention to kill, the absence of a mandatory sentence for murder and the concept of loss of self-control.[10]

It was the Victorian Law Reform Commission (VLRC 2004) in its 2001–4 review of *Defences to Homicide* that provided the most comprehensive and cogent critique of the doctrine in Australia. The

[8] See, e.g., *Masciantonio v. The Queen* (1995).

[9] Criminal Code Amendment (Abolition of Defence of Provocation) Act 2003 (Tas), s. 4.

[10] Tasmania, *Parliamentary Debates*, House of Assembly, 20 March 2003, 59–60 (Judy Jackson, Minister for Justice and Industrial Relations).

Commission argued that the continued existence of provocation as a partial defence to killings committed in anger was no longer morally acceptable, and that contemporary community standards require people to control their anger and not to kill, even where they may have been provoked (VLRC 2004, para. 2.95).

The VLRC identified gender bias in the application of provocation, particularly in relation to intimate relationship homicides (2004: xxv, paras. 2.18–2.25). For example, allegations of infidelity or 'sexual taunt' provocation by men who had killed their intimate partner often masked the fact that the victim had been attempting to end the relationship or otherwise assert her personal freedom, and her death was the final act in a series of violent or controlling behaviour. The need to address these issues was a significant factor in the VLRC's recommendation to abolish provocation as a partial defence and in the government's acceptance of that recommendation.[11] The abolition of the partial defence of provocation in Victoria took effect from 23 November 2005. Western Australia and New Zealand followed suit, for similar reasons.[12]

England and Wales

In England and Wales reform of the law of homicide has had a long and tortuous history, significantly influenced by successive governments' resolute determination to retain the mandatory sentence of life imprisonment for murder. The Law Commission for England and Wales reviewed the law of provocation twice in quick succession, first in 2004 and then again in 2006. Constrained by the mandatory life sentence, the Commission recommended reforming, rather than abolishing, the partial defence (Law Commission 2006: paras. 5.8–5.10). In both reviews, the Commission criticized the requirement for a loss of self-control and recommended against including it in the reformulated test (Law Commission 2004: para. 3.28; 2006: paras. 5.17–5.20). Instead, the Commission proposed a test that focused on whether the defendant had acted in response to gross provocation 'which caused the defendant to have a justifiable sense of being seriously wronged' or in response to fear of serious violence or to a combination of both (Law Commission 2004, para. 3.66; 2006, para. 5.11).

[11] See further VLRC 2004: paras. 2.22–3, 7.5; Victoria, *Parliamentary Debates*, Legislative Assembly, 6 October 2005, 1349 (Rob Hulls, Attorney General).

[12] Criminal Law Amendment (Homicide) Act 2008 (WA); Crimes (Provocation Repeal) Amendment Act 2009 (NZ).

The Coroners and Justice Act 2009 (UK) implemented some of the Law Commission's recommendations, but it did not abolish the requirement for a loss of self-control as recommended by the Commission; on the contrary, it rebranded the partial defence as the partial defence of 'loss of self-control'.[13] The limitations on the reform process created by the mandatory penalty for murder and the ultimate retention of the requirement for a loss of self-control represent a disappointing ending to a lengthy and considered law reform process (Miles 2009: 6).

PROVOCATION: DEFENCE OR SENTENCING FACTOR?

Does it matter whether provocation is a sentencing factor or a substantive defence, if it is ultimately a *relevant* factor? And is it just a question of a lack of will on the part of legislators who wish to change the law but do not? The answers to these questions are not only dependent on the substance of the law of provocation (and its deficiencies), but are also strongly influenced by:

- a jurisdiction's sentencing structure;
- perceptions of the meaning of the term 'murder';
- the appropriate responsibilities placed on judges and juries; and
- the onus and burden of proof placed on the prosecution and defence.

Sentencing structure

The debate over the substance and status of the defence of provocation is intimately connected with the structure of sentencing. Historically, provocation was a life or death matter, not just for the victim, but also for the defendant. When capital punishment was in force, the difference between a verdict of murder and a verdict of manslaughter was the difference between a mandatory death sentence, which might or might not have been executed, and a discretionary sentence of imprisonment.[14] Even following the abolition of capital punishment, the existence of mandatory sentences of life imprisonment has been a major factor in the retention of the partial defence and in inhibiting its reform.

[13] The Act specified the need for the loss of self-control to have a 'qualifying trigger' – which was defined as a fear of violence, or words or conduct that 'constituted circumstances of an extremely grave character' and caused the defendant to have a 'justifiable sense of being seriously wronged'. A number of exclusions attempted to limit the successful use of the partial defence in sexual jealousy intimate homicide cases.

[14] See *John Royley's case* (1612); *R v. Mawgridge* (1707).

Neither Tasmania nor Victoria has a mandatory sentence for murder, while in New Zealand and Western Australia the sentence of life imprisonment for murder was changed from mandatory to presumptive, which facilitated the abolition of the partial defence of provocation.[15] In the United Kingdom, life imprisonment remains the mandatory sentence for murder, while in the United States, the toxic variations of capital punishment, life without parole provisions, three strikes laws, mandatory and presumptive minima and strict guideline regimes have greatly inhibited reform of the law. If provocation were to be abolished without concomitant reform of sentencing, a larger number of killers would be exposed to significantly more severe (and mandatory) penalties (Ramsey 2010: 89). While one object of provocation reform is to ensure that some killers do indeed serve a more severe sentence, the lack of judicial discretion for those who are deserving of mercy is a barrier to reform. Sentencing reform is thus an essential prerequisite to reforming the law of provocation.

The nature of 'murder'

A second factor in considering whether provocation should be retained as a partial defence is that the partial defence operates to reduce a charge of murder to a conviction for manslaughter. Arguments against abolition include the critique that a wider range of offenders would face the stigma of a murder conviction (Wasik 1982: 531). Conversely, it is argued that abolition would undermine the stigmatizing effect of a murder conviction because the concept of 'murder' would become too broad, eroding the public's apprehension of what has been described as a widely understood crime 'carrying the strongest possible overtones of moral condemnation'.[16] The response to the first argument is that the historical conceptions of the law of provocation improperly exclude certain killers from the ambit of the law of murder (VLRC 2004, para. 2.97). The response to the second is that communal conceptions of murder constantly evolve and it is legitimate for legislators to attempt to shape public opinion where there are compelling public policy reasons for so doing.

[15] Criminal Law Amendment (Homicide) Act 2008 (WA), s. 10; Sentencing Act 2002 (NZ), s. 102.

[16] New South Wales, *Parliamentary Debates*, House of Assembly, 11 March 1982, 2483 (Frank Walker, Attorney General, Minister of Justice and Minister for Aboriginal Affairs; cited in Brown et al. (1990: 670).

The role of the jury

Another factor that must be considered in deciding whether provocation should be a partial defence or a sentencing factor is the role of the jury. Where provocation is a partial defence to murder, the jury has the responsibility to decide the issue of guilt, including whether the defendant was provoked. Where provocation is a sentencing factor, it is for the judge alone to decide whether, how and to what extent to take it into account (Wasik 1983: 454). Those who believe that the jury plays an important and fundamental role in the criminal justice system argue that it is vital that the jury retain the power to judge the legal and moral responsibility of an alleged offender and that 'it is the jury's decision that sets the parameters of just punishment, particularly the upper limits of punishment that may be imposed in any particular case' (Potas 1982: 62). The converse view is that if there is a discretionary sentence for murder, why should murder continue to be treated differently from all other crimes, for which provocation is simply a sentencing question (VLRC 2004: 33, 57)? Those who support abolition argue that provocation is not different from other mitigating circumstances which are determined by judges.

The modern reality is that, even in respect of indictable offences, the majority of cases are resolved by a guilty plea, placing the real loci of power with the prosecution, the defence and, most importantly, the sentencing judge, who, many believe, is capable of making (and giving) sensible, defensible and transparent reasons relating to the moral and legal responsibility of the offender (VLRC 2004: 57). Unlike the jury, a sentencing judge must give reasons for sentence and is subject to appeal. Furthermore, sentencing judges regularly determine matters that are relevant to the offender's culpability, including whether offenders sentenced for non-fatal offences against the person were provoked and, if so, whether the provocation was sufficient to reduce the offender's culpability and thus mitigate his or her sentence (for examples of the consideration of provocation in sentencing for non-fatal offences see Stewart and Freiberg 2008a).

Evidentiary considerations

Finally, shifting provocation from the trial stage to the sentencing phase has implications for the application of the rules of evidence. In a traditional murder trial in Australia, the issue of provocation had to be left to the jury if 'on the version of events most favourable to the accused which is suggested by material in the evidence, a jury acting reasonably might fail to be satisfied beyond reasonable doubt that the killing was unprovoked in the relevant sense'.[17] In contrast, when it comes to sentencing, the sentencing judge is required to determine the facts that will form the basis of sentence. There is no general requirement that the sentencing judge must sentence an offender on a view of the facts most favourable to the offender.[18] Provocation is likely to be raised by the defence as a factor in mitigation of the offender's sentence, in which case the defence will have the onus of proving, on the balance of probabilities, that the offender was provoked.[19]

We agree with both the Victorian Law Reform Commission and the Western Australian Law Reform Commission (WLRC) that differences in degrees of culpability generally should be dealt with through the sentencing process, rather than through the existence of partial excuses (VLRC (2004): 56–8; see also discussion: xxvii, paras. 1.29, 2.31–2.33, 2.93–2.102, 7.2; WLRC 2007: 220–1; Neave 2005: 33). As the WLRC has written,

> The Commission believes that the sentencing process is uniquely suited to identifying those cases of provocation that call for leniency and those that do not. This is because the sentencing process is flexible and is accustomed to taking into account both aggravating and mitigating factors ... Unlike the substantive criminal law, sentencing is a flexible process – it can accommodate the wide variety of circumstances that arise in homicide cases. Dealing with issues affecting culpability during sentencing allows those issues to be considered at the same time as other relevant sentencing factors [citations omitted].
>
> (Law Reform Commission of Western Australia 2007: 220–1, 309)

BURYING THE GHOSTS OF THE PAST?

When considering in 1982 the possibility of transforming provocation from a partial excuse to a sentencing factor, Wasik argued that such a strategy would solve nothing because the issue would simply reappear at the sentencing stage (1982: 530–1). Certainly, if nothing were done by the courts to recognize the reasons for change nothing would have been achieved. Anticipating this possibility in Victoria following the abolition of the partial defence, the authors, under the aegis of the Victorian

17 *Stingel v. The Queen* (1990). This raised some controversy, particularly in the context of intimate partner homicides; see further Stewart and Freiberg 2008a: paras. 5.3.3–5.3.6; 8.10.62–8.10.72.
18 *R v. Mokbel.*
19 *Tyne v. Tasmania*, per Blow J. See further Stewart and Freiberg 2008a, paras. 5.3.1–5.3.11.

Sentencing Advisory Council, proposed a new normative framework for considering provocation in sentencing under the new regime. This approach, discussed further below, was also intended to create a consistent approach to provocation in sentencing fatal and non-fatal offences against the person (Stewart and Freiberg 2008a; 2008b).

Since the new law came into operation in Victoria in November 2005, only a handful of cases have arisen in which provocation has been directly considered as a factor in murder sentencing,[20] and similarly there have been few cases in Tasmania since the law has changed.[21] In some of these cases the sentencing judge was satisfied that the offender's culpability was reduced by the victim's conduct (such as a false confession to molesting the offender's eleven-month-old daughter in one case, or conduct by the offender's wife (the victim) including deliberately harming their children and attempting to conceal this behaviour (she had suffered from Munchausen by Proxy syndrome), and in another case a statement that the offender would never see his children again).[22]

Other offenders who have pleaded guilty to, or been convicted of, murder have been less successful at establishing mitigating provocation, such as in cases in which the defendant murdered a female partner who was trying to exercise equality rights (such as ending the relationship, forming a new friendship or wanting to participate in English classes) or where the defendant unsuccessfully submitted that he had been provoked by an unwanted sexual advance by the victim.[23]

The fact that there have been relatively few cases that directly raise provocation as a mitigating factor in sentencing for murder may be due, in part, to the changed burden of proof. Or it could be that in the types of case that led to the abolition of provocation (such as cases in which men kill intimate partners out of control or jealousy or anger at their attempt to end the relationship), trial practice is so transformed that counsel rarely make submissions in relation to provocation in the knowledge that, if the provocation is insufficient to reduce the offender's culpability, they will not succeed. However, we doubt that such a major cultural change has been effected in such a short time. Rather, it appears that other forces operate that relate to the manner in which this long-recognized, emotionally powerful and culturally entrenched mitigating factor continues to influence prosecutorial, defence and judicial practices.

[20] See, e.g., *R v. Maddox*; *R v. Johnstone*; *DPP v. Tran*; *DPP v. Lam*.
[21] See, e.g., *R v. Tyne*. [22] *R v. Maddox*; *R v. Tyne*].
[23] See, e.g., *DPP v. Lam*]; *R v. Johnstone* (at the time of writing this decision was subject to appeal).

Abolishing the partial defence of provocation in Victoria did not mean that complex dynamics of homicide prosecutions would necessarily become simpler.

Law reform is a contingent process. The partial defence of provocation did not operate in a vacuum. Prior to its abolition in Victoria, the number of provocation manslaughter cases was low in proportion to other homicides.[24] Murder cases raising provocation were likely also to raise other issues, such as whether there had been an intention to kill, whether the defendant had been acting in self-defence or had been culpably negligent or committed an unlawful and dangerous act. In a number of cases more than one category of manslaughter was open to the jury and it was for the trial judge to infer the ground on which the jury had returned a verdict of 'manslaughter'.

With the abolition of the partial defence there was a possibility that there would be an increased reliance on other defences. There was no expectation that 'provoked killers' would automatically face a murder conviction under the new law; rather, a variety of possible outcomes was anticipated:

> It is likely that some of these offenders will be found guilty of murder under the new law and face the higher maximum penalty and sentencing range that applies to this offence. Others may be acquitted altogether on the grounds of self-defence, or instead be found guilty of defensive homicide, particularly in cases involving family violence by the victim towards the offender. Yet others may be convicted of other types of manslaughter, such as unlawful and dangerous act manslaughter or negligent manslaughter. (Stewart and Freiberg 2008a, para. 10.1.16)

It appears that in Victoria this is what has eventuated. In some cases, it would seem that the change in the law has achieved its goal. Some defendants who might have once raised the partial defence of provocation may instead be pleading guilty to murder and raising provocation in mitigation of sentence. Other defendants, such as those who were subjected to family violence by the victim, have other avenues of mitigation such as self-defence (leading to full acquittal if successful) or a verdict of defensive homicide on the basis that the defendant's belief

[24] For example, from 1998–99 to 2006–07 in Victoria, 266 people were sentenced for murder and 175 people were sentenced for manslaughter. Of the 175 manslaughter sentences, 20 were provocation manslaughter and 155 were other categories of manslaughter (including 140 that were unlawful and dangerous act (UDA) manslaughter and 11 that were negligent manslaughter) (Stewart and Freiberg 2008a: 117).

that their conduct was necessary was not based on reasonable grounds.[25] The new offence of 'defensive homicide' was an 'exception' to the guiding principle in the VLRC report that 'differences in degrees of culpability should generally be dealt with through the sentencing process, rather than through the continued existence of partial defences' (VLRC 2004: xx), as it gives the jury the substantive decision-making power to decide whether a homicide will be murder or defensive homicide (Neave 2005: 33).

A key reason for abolishing the partial defence in Victoria was to remove it as a means of avoiding a murder conviction for violent, jealous or controlling people (usually men) who intentionally killed their intimate partner who was attempting to end the relationship (VLRC 2004: 29–30). While some defendants charged with killing their intimate partners since the new law took effect have pleaded guilty to (or been found guilty of) murder, others have pleaded guilty to (or been found guilty of) negligent manslaughter, unlawful and dangerous act manslaughter or defensive homicide.[26]

In the murder cases in which provocation has been raised in mitigation of sentence under the new law, there has not been a consistent approach to its consideration. In some murder cases, provocation has been assessed by reference to the old test; in others, the provocation has been assessed less formally, akin to its assessment in relation to non-fatal offences against the person. The law is still evolving.

In the following section we outline some of the salient differences between the previous law of provocation and how we believe a transformed law ought to operate in the sentencing arena.

PROVOCATION, CULPABILITY AND MITIGATION OF SENTENCE

In our view, provocation should only have mitigatory effect, in relation both to homicide and to non-fatal offences, where the person who was provoked is legally and morally less culpable than one who is not provoked. Culpability, or blameworthiness, reflects the extent to which an offender should be held accountable for his or her actions by assessing

[25] Aside from *R v. Middendorp* (in which there was conflicting evidence about the extent and instigator of past family violence between the victim and the defendant) we have not identified any defensive homicide cases in which the defendant had been subjected to family violence by the victim.

[26] See, e.g., *R v. Middendorp*; *DPP v. Sherna*; *R v. Jagroop*.

the circumstances including his or her intention, awareness and motivation in committing the crime, such as

> whether the act was done with knowledge of its consequences or only in negligent disregard of them, or whether, and to what extent, the actor's criminal conduct was provoked by the victim's own misconduct.
> (von Hirsch 1983: 214).

Culpability in relation to provocation in homicide cases did not relate to the absence of an intention to kill the victim or cause serious injury, but to some other factor, which was traditionally described as a loss of self-control, but sometimes regarded as some form of justifiable response by the defendant to an act of the victim.

Loss of self-control

A number of broad theoretical approaches have been identified which attempt to justify or explain why provocation should reduce an offender's culpability. Three of these are (1) character theory, (2) objective capacity theory, and (3) the reasons-based approach. The first two are linked to the notion of loss self-control.

Character theory proposes that the actions of a person who has lost his or her self-control are partially excused on the basis that those actions were uncharacteristic or atypical of the person and therefore unlikely to be repeated. On this rationale, sentencing purposes such as specific deterrence may be viewed as less important because the offender is unlikely to repeat the behaviour. This theory presupposes that a person's character is 'settled' (otherwise it is difficult to argue that behaviour was 'out of character'). It is problematic in situations such as where a perpetrator of family violence who ultimately kills his victim appeared 'in control' and of good character to workmates and others, who testify that the killing was 'out of character'. If the victim could speak, she might advance a different view as to whether the final, terrible act of violence and control was 'out of character' (Stewart and Freiberg 2008a, para. 8.4.8).

The objective capacity theory (Horder 2004: 123) holds a person less culpable if the person did not have the capacity to exercise self-control and avoid criminal behaviour in the light of the provocation that he or she faced, and if others in a like position could also have been unable to control their behaviour. This theory provides a foundation for the question in the test for provocation whether the defendant lost self-control and an ordinary person might also have done so. Critics query whether this is actually 'a *failure* to exercise self-control or an *inability* to exercise self-control', pointing out that 'those who give vent to anger by "losing self-control" to the point of killing another person generally do so in circumstances in which they can afford to do so' (Law Commission (UK) 2004, para. 3.28 (emphasis added)).

Both theories explain provocation on the basis that the offender is less responsible for his or her actions, because of the loss of self-control. They marked a change from provocation as a partial justification (viewing people acting under provocation as acting rationally in response to being wronged), to provocation as a partial excuse (placing greater emphasis on the defendant's emotional response to that provocation, and whether an ordinary person faced with provocation of similar gravity might have reacted as the defendant did).

Our proposed normative framework rejects both of these theoretical approaches to provocation and the significance placed on whether the offender was found to have lost self-control. Our rejection is based on the work of the Law Commission for England and Wales and the VLRC which argued that the requirement of a loss of self-control in the test for substantive provocation added to the gender bias in its operation (Victorian Law Reform Commission 2004, paras. 2.18–2.25; Law Commission 2004, para. 3.28). Our approach (and that of the VLRC) is more consistent with the earlier conception of provocation which focused on the gravity of the victim's conduct and the reasons behind the defendant's response, rather than on whether or not it caused the defendant to lose self-control.

Reasons for being provoked: a justifiable sense of being wronged

In its review, the VLRC considered looking beyond the act to reasons and emotions that drove the defendant's actions. This 'reasons-based' approach was intended to provide a framework for considering the moral or social dimensions of culpability. The VLRC argued that changing provocation from a partial defence to a sentencing consideration would have the advantage of

> readily allow[ing] reasons to be taken into account along with the specific contexts and individual circumstances ... Reasons-based sentencing could then evaluate a defendant's reasons for killing along with their life circumstances to arrive at an appropriate sentencing outcome.
>
> (VLRC 2003, para. 7.37)

The defendant's culpability is reduced only when the reasons for being frightened, angry or resentful are good reasons – such as serious provocation. This approach, which marks a return to provocation's original rationale (Stewart and Freiberg 2008a, paras. 8.4.14–8.4.22), is consistent with the approach taken in the sentencing guideline *Manslaughter by Reason of Provocation* in England and Wales. The factors influencing sentence set out in the guideline include assessing the offender's culpability by reference to what emotions and reasons motivated the offender's actions in responding to the provocation (Sentencing Guidelines Council 2005, para. 3.2).

The foundation of the reasons-based approach is the idea of justifiability. In its 2004 report on partial defences to murder, the Law Commission of England and Wales attempted to articulate the rationale for provocation and its relationship to culpability:

> Putting it in broad and simple terms, we think that the moral blameworthiness of homicide may be significantly lessened where the defendant acts in response to gross provocation in the sense of words or conduct (or a combination) giving the defendant a justified sense of being severely wronged.
>
> (Law Commission 2004, para. 3.63)

In our view, the Law Commission's broad conception of 'gross provocation' can hold equally well as the basis of mitigation of sentence and is consistent with the reasons-based approach advocated by the VLRC. With provocation in the sentencing arena, we suggest that the key to whether a reduction in the offender's culpability is warranted is the *justifiability* of the offender's grievance in the light of the degree of provocation – that is, were there words or conduct that caused the offender to have a justifiable sense of being wronged?

Relevant to this consideration will be the nature and gravity of the provocation (to which we turn next). The result of conceptualizing provocation as having some legal force when a defendant is *justifiably aggrieved* by the provocation is that the question of whether the defendant lost self-control will not be of special importance in sentencing. This approach is consistent with the approach to provocation in sentencing guidelines in a number of US jurisdictions (Stewart and Freiberg 2008a, para. 8.6.4) which emphasise the nature and gravity of the provocation.

Gravity of provocation: public policy and protecting prevailing values
The next question is, what type and degree of provocation will give the offender a justifiable sense of having been wronged? A number of jurisdictions have emphasized the logical relationship between the nature and degree of provocation and the degree to which a reduction in the offender's culpability is warranted. For example, the Sentencing Advisory Panel for England and Wales thought that 'an assessment of the *degree* of the provocation as shown by its nature and duration is the critical factor in the sentencing decision' in provocation manslaughter cases (Sentencing Advisory Panel 2005, para. 30 (emphasis in original).

However, in some circumstances, courts have considered that an offender's criminal behaviour in causing death or injury did not warrant mitigation of sentence, even if the person maintained that he or she had been acting under the influence of what he or she considered to be gross provocation. They have done so where public policy reasons outweigh individual considerations that may tend to mitigation. We considered two approaches for assessing the nature and degree of provocation to determine whether it reduced an offender's culpability: the ordinary person test and an equality analysis.

THE 'ORDINARY PERSON' TEST OR AN EQUALITY ANALYSIS?

In the past, some sentencers have referred to the 'ordinary person test' while assessing provocation at sentencing in order to decide whether a reduction in the offender's culpability was warranted by the provocation.[27] While some judges have continued to approach sentencing provocation in this way since the 2005 changes to the law, in our view the changes leave open the question whether there remains a place for the ordinary person in assessing provocation in sentencing or whether there is a better normative approach in the light of the public policy reasons for abolishing the partial defence.

In its review, the VLRC explored incorporating an equality analysis into the test for substantive provocation to 'attempt to ensure that legal rules operate without reinforcing systemic or historically discriminatory

[27] We do not wish to dwell in this chapter on the complex doctrinal issues which bedevil the law of provocation, such as the meaning of an 'ordinary person' and so on. These issues are discussed in Stewart and Freiberg (2008a, paras. 8.6.15–8.6.20).

perspectives' (VLRC 2003, para. 3.163, see further paras. 3.164–3.168). The VLRC described this as modifying the law 'to ensure that it is compatible with the right to equality' (VLRC 2003, para. 3.163). Leader-Elliott (2010: 43) has proposed that the equality test could be framed in a way that anything done in the exercise of one or more of the fundamental rights included in the Universal Declaration of Human Rights could not be put forward as a provocative act.

Under our proposed normative framework this test would be a mechanism for delineating categories of conduct by the victim that should *not* be sufficient to justify an offender's sense of grievance and thus warrant a finding of reduced culpability. An equality analysis of potentially mitigating provocation would disqualify behaviour that arose out of the victim exercising his or her equality rights, such as the right to personal autonomy (including conduct associated with leaving an intimate relationship, forming new social or intimate relationships, choosing to work or gain an education, or other assertions of independence).

We argue that assessing provocation at sentencing does not require the application of the ordinary person test. Although it is clearly necessary to assess provocation by reference to social norms and values to determine whether the provocation justifies reducing the offender's culpability, we believe that assessing the victim's conduct according to equality principles is a better approach than attempting to determine what an ordinary person might have done.

THE OFFENDER'S PERSONAL CHARACTERISTICS

Even if an equality-based approach is accepted, the question nevertheless remains as to what relevance the personal characteristics of the offender should have to assessing the provocation. There is some authority for the view that in assessing the extent to which the provocation contributed to the offence and the weight, if any, to be given to it in sentencing, the relevant personal characteristics of the offender should be taken into account by the sentencing judge.[28]

In the context of both substantive and sentencing provocation, the issue of culture or race often arose through a suggestion that due to considerations of the offender's race or culture – in particular the culture's attitude to women – his intimate partner's behaviour such as

[28] *Pearce v. The Queen*: 150; *R v. Tuimauga*; *R v. Khan*).

trying to end the relationship, forming a new friendship or relationship, joining the workforce or seeking education was elevated to mitigating provocation. Under our suggested approach, the victim's enjoyment of equality rights should not be found to justify any reduction in an offender's culpability for a responsive act of violence or other offence against the victim, regardless of whether the offender submits that his or her personal characteristics such as race or culture 'caused' him or her to be provoked by the behaviour.

A proposed approach to provocation in sentencing

In our view, in considering provocation at sentencing, the central issues to determining whether, and to what extent, an offender's culpability for the offence is reduced by the provocation should be:

1. The degree of provocation – that is, whether, in all the circumstances of the case, the provocation caused the offender to have a justifiable sense of being wronged, considering:
   (a) the nature and context of the provocation, including whether it consisted of the victim exercising his or her equality rights and whether it was induced by the offender; and
   (b) the duration of the provocation.
2. The degree to which the offender's response was disproportionate to the provocation: the greater the disproportionality the lower the reduction in the offender's culpability. For the most serious examples of offences against the person, only serious provocation is likely to warrant a reduction in the offender's culpability.
3. Whether the provocation was an operative cause of the offence, and remained an operative cause throughout the duration of the offence.

In homicide cases and the most serious non-fatal offences against the person, it is likely that only serious provocation will be capable of reducing an offender's culpability under our approach. For less serious non-fatal offences, moderate provocation may be sufficient to trigger some mitigation. Where a reduction in culpability is warranted, the extent of the reduction will depend on the gravity of the provocation and the degree to which the offence was disproportionate. Trivial provocation is unlikely to justify an offender's grievance no matter how minor the responsive offence is deemed to be.

One of the strongest impetuses for bringing provocation into the sentencing arena was the gender-biased way in which it was said to operate in relation to intimate partner homicides. We looked at this in great detail in our larger paper, concluding that if our approach is applied to the sentencing of offences committed in the context of intimate and family relationships:

- Actual or threatened violence by the victim against the offender (or, in some circumstances, to another person) is likely to be viewed as serious provocation, capable of reducing the offender's culpability for a responsive offence. Factors relevant to considering family violence include its context (including past violence by the victim towards the offender or other family members); the danger presented or reasonably perceived by the offender (taking into account the victim's reputation for violence); the balance of power between the victim and the offender; and the relative size and strength of the victim and the offender and other relevant physical characteristics.
- It is unlikely that an offender will be able to establish that he or she had a justifiable sense of being wronged by the exercising of equality rights by an intimate partner, child or other family member (such as ending an intimate relationship, engaging in an intimate relationship, forming social relationships, seeking an education and choosing to work). Such conduct is unlikely to reduce an offender's culpability, regardless of whether his or her personal characteristics contributed towards his or her sense of grievance at this conduct or whether the offender is found to have lost his or her self-control as a result of it (see further Stewart and Freiberg 2008a, paras. 8.10.1–8.10.91).

SENTENCING PRACTICES

The abolition of the partial defence raises two possibilities in terms of the effect on sentencing provoked killers. One is that it could be expected to result in more severe sentences for killers found guilty of murder who might once have been convicted of provocation manslaughter (Stewart and Freiberg 2008a, paras. 7.1.1–7.3.10). In Victoria, for example, between 1998–99 and 2006–07, the median sentence for murder was around nineteen years with a fourteen-and-a-half-year non-parole period, while the median sentence for manslaughter was around seven years with a non-parole period of around four years. The average sentence for provocation manslaughter was around eight years with a six-year non-parole period (Stewart and Freiberg 2008a, para. 7.3.4, Appendix 3).[29] The sentencing range was much greater for murder than it was for manslaughter and there was little overlap between the two.

A second possible effect is that if provocation was seen to be so mitigating that a lower range should apply to provocation murder cases this would result in the low end of the range for murder being dragged downwards to encompass provoked murder cases. This argument was advanced (and rejected) in the Tasmanian case of *R* v. *Tyne*. Although this issue has not been expressly raised in Victoria, the approach in the Victorian case of *R* v. *Maddox* indicates that Victorian judges are likely to take a similar view to their counterparts across the Bass Strait. As yet it is too early to determine whether there have been major changes to murder sentencing patterns, but the indications are that offenders convicted of murder are being sentenced within the range applicable to that offence even where mitigating provocation is established.

CONCLUSIONS

Few of the aggravating or mitigating factors at sentencing have aroused as much controversy, engendered such passion, produced as much literature and created as many legal responses as provocation. This is not only because it resulted in life and death decisions but because it is a deeply emotive issue which strikes at the heart of human relationships. Emotions such as anger, jealousy and fear are deep and powerful, and in many cases in which provocation is relevant it concerns the dynamics of sexual and gender relationships. Provocation is as much a political as it is a legal issue and emotions are highly influential in the development of public policy (Freiberg and Carson 2010). As has been the experience with the long history of the reform of the law relating to sexual assault offences, changing professional and lay behaviour and attitudes is not easy. Stereotypes die hard. Reform is not just about changing the words on a page.

In this chapter we have examined some of the recent changes to the law of provocation in some Australasian jurisdictions and have found that, in some, merely abolishing the partial defence has not necessarily eliminated all the problems that numerous law reform bodies have identified. These have now re-emerged in different guises, particularly through the various forms of manslaughter and a new offence of defensive homicide. Changing charging and plea-bargaining practices may

[29] Appendix 4 in the 2009 reprint.

now reflect a belief that conviction for murder where provocation may exist may be difficult to obtain and that a plea to manslaughter, on whatever grounds remain, may be a safer option for both prosecution and defence.

It is still too early to determine the direction of sentencing theory and practice in the post-abolition era. The number of cases is small, the grounds of mitigation are still uncertain and some courts remain under the influence of the old law. In previous publications we have argued for a new approach to sentencing where provocation is advanced as a mitigating factor, an approach that is divorced from the foundations of the partial defence. Although we believe that it provides a more principled, coherent, contemporary and fair approach, we are realistic enough to know that these attributes alone are rarely sufficient to bring about change in such a vexed and controversial area.

REFERENCES

Ashworth, A. J. (1976). 'The Doctrine of Provocation', *Cambridge Law Journal*, 35 (2): 292–320.

Brown, D., Farrier, D., Egger, S., McNamara, L. and Steel, A. (1990). *Criminal Laws: Materials and Commentary on Criminal Law and Process in New South Wales*. Sydney: Federation Press.

Coss, G. (1991). '"God is a Righteous Judge, Strong and Patient: and God is Provoked Every Day": A Brief History of the Doctrine of Provocation in England', *Sydney Law Review*, 13 (4): 570–604.

(2007). 'The Defence of Provocation: An Acrimonious Divorce from Reality', *Current Issues in Criminal Justice*, 18 (1): 51–78.

Criminal Law Reform Committee [New Zealand] (1976). *Report on Culpable Homicide*, available at http://132.181.2.68/Data/Library4/law_reports/criminlaw_71041.pdf.

Freiberg, A. and W. G. Carson (2010). 'The Limits to Evidence-Based Policy: Evidence, Emotion and Criminal Justice', *Australian Journal of Public Administration*, 69 (2): 152–64.

Horder, J. (1992). *Provocation and Responsibility*. Oxford: Clarendon Press.

(2004). *Excusing Crime*. Oxford: Oxford University Press.

Law Commission [England and Wales] (2004). *Partial Defences to Murder*, final report, available at www.lawcom.gov.uk/docs/lc290(2).pdf.

(2006). *Murder, Manslaughter and Infanticide*, Law Com No. 304, available at www.lawcom.gov.uk/docs/lc304.pdf.

Law Reform Commission [Ireland] (2003). *Consultation Paper on Homicide: The Plea of Provocation*, LRC CP 27–2003, available at www.lawreform.

ie/_fileupload/CPS%202004%20and%20older/CPhomocideProvocation.pdf.

Law Reform Commission of Western Australia (WLRC) (2007). *Review of the Law of Homicide: Final Report*, Project 97, available at www.lrc.justice.wa.gov.au/2publications/reports/homicide/P97-Forepages.pdf.

Leader-Elliott, I. (1996). 'Sex, Race and Provocation: In Defence of *Stingel*', *Criminal Law Journal*, 20 (2): 72–96.

(1997). 'Passion and Insurrection in the Law of Sexual Provocation', in N. Naffine and R. Owens (eds.), *Sexing the Subject of Law*. New South Wales: LBC Information Services.

(2010). *Revising the Law of Murder in the Indian Penal Code: A Macaulayan Reconstruction of Provocation and Sudden Fight*, Research Paper No. 2010–002, available at http://ssrn.com/abstract=1538643.

Miles, J. (2009). 'The Coroners and Justice Act 2009: A 'Dog's Breakfast' of Homicide Reform'. *Archbold News*, 10 (10): 6.

Morgan, J. (1997). 'Provocation Law and Facts: Dead Women Tell No Tales, Tales are Told about Them', *Melbourne University Law Review*, 21: 237–56.

(2002). *Who Kills Whom and Why: Looking Beyond Legal Categories*, Victorian Law Reform Commission Occasional Paper, available at www.lawreform.vic.gov.au/CA256902000FE154/Lookup/Homicide/$file/Occasional_Paper.pdf

Neave, M. (2005). 'Homicide Sentences: Taking Culpability into Account', *Reform*, 86: 33–35.

Potas, I. (1982). *Just Deserts for the Mad*. Australia: Australian Institute of Criminology.

Ramsey, C. (2010). 'Provoking Change: Comparative Insights on Feminist Homicide Law Reform', *Journal of Criminal Law and Criminology*, 100 (1): 33–108.

Sentencing Advisory Panel for England and Wales (2005). *Manslaughter by Reason of Provocation: The Panel's Advice to the Sentencing Guidelines Council*, available at www.sentencingcouncil.org.uk.

Sentencing Guidelines Council for England and Wales (2005). *Manslaughter by Reason of Provocation: Guideline*, available at www.sentencingcouncil.org.uk.

Stewart, F. and Freiberg, A. (2008a). *Provocation in Sentencing: Research Paper*. Melbourne: Sentencing Advisory Council.

(2008b). 'Provocation in Sentencing: A Culpability-Based Framework', *Current Issues in Criminal Justice*, 19 (3): 283–308.

Victorian Law Reform Commission (VLRC) (2003). *Defences to Homicide: Options Paper*.

(2004). *Defences to Homicide: Final Report*, available at www.lawreform.vic.gov.au/wps/wcm/connect/b151a200404a0e8e9c86fff5f2791d4a/FinalReport.pdf?MOD=AJPERES.

von Hirsch, A. (1983). 'Commensurability and Crime Prevention: Evaluating Formal Sentencing Structures and Their Rationale', *Journal of Criminal Law and Criminology*, 74 (1): 209–48.
Wasik, M. (1982). 'Partial Excuses in the Criminal Law', *Modern Law Review*, 45 (5): 516–33.
(1983). 'Excuses at the Sentencing Stage', *Criminal Law Review*: 450–65.

TABLE OF CASES

DPP *v*. Lam [2007] VSC 307.
DPP *v*. Tran [2006] VSC 394.
DPP *v*. Sherna [2009] VSC 526.
John Royley (1612) Cro Jac 296; 79 ER 254.
Masciantonio *v*. The Queen (1995) 183 CLR 58.
Pearce *v*. The Queen (1983) 9 A Crim R 146 (CCA Vic).
R *v*. Jagroop [2009] VSCA 46.
R *v*. Johnstone [2008] VSC 584.
R *v*. Khan (1996) 86 A Crim R 552, 556–8.
R *v*. Maddox [2009] VSC 447.
R *v*. Mawgridge (1707) 84 ER 1107.
R *v*. Middendorp [2010] VSC 202.
R *v*. Mokbel [2006] VSC 119, para. 24.
R *v*. Tuimauga [2003] VSCA 218, paras. 12–14.
R *v*. Tyne [2005] (unreported, Supreme Court of Tasmania, Crawford J).
Stingel *v*. The Queen (1990) 171 CLR 312, 334.
Tyne *v*. Tasmania (2005) 15 Tas R 221, 229 [27].

CHAPTER SEVEN

EQUALITY BEFORE THE LAW: RACIAL AND SOCIAL BACKGROUND FACTORS AS SOURCES OF MITIGATION AT SENTENCING

Kate Warner

Some sentencing factors are offence-specific, while others cut across all forms of offending. One of the most important – and contested – examples of the latter is the offender's social background. Are offenders who present for sentencing with a socially disadvantaged background – or who belong to a minority group which historically has been associated with high rates of imprisonment – entitled to some mitigation on this basis?

CHAPTER OVERVIEW

This chapter explores how courts in Australia and Canada have dealt with the relevance of race and cultural and social background factors, and it considers these sources of mitigation in the light of the principle of equality before the law. It begins with a short discussion of the principles of equality followed by a sketch of the over-representation of Aboriginal people in prisons in the Western world, before focusing on the way in which Australian and Canadian jurisdictions have dealt with the relevance of factors associated with Aboriginality. Analysis of the position in Australian jurisdictions suggests that, in recent years, courts have moved from a position which accepted that a more lenient approach to Aboriginal offenders was justified to one which emphasizes the need to denounce and deter violence. While this appears to be a reaction to a legitimate concern with problems of violence in Aboriginal communities, the criticisms of this approach are outlined. The Canadian Supreme Court's decision in *Gladue* is then discussed, together with the arguments of its critics and advocates and its extension to other socially and economically disadvantaged offenders.

The chapter then seeks to identify the unique differences which are claimed to justify giving mitigatory weight to Aboriginality in these countries. It is argued that factors associated with Aboriginality, such as adverse social background and broader considerations of dispossession and separation, can be taken into account without offending equality principles. In short, substantive as opposed to formal equality requires devoting proper attention to culpability and the impact of sanctions.

INTRODUCTION

The social background of the offender is invariably referred to in sentencing submissions and sentencing remarks. Pre-sentence reports recount in some detail the family background, race or ethnicity of the offender, their social advantages or disadvantages, and educational and employment status. In Canada, so-called '*Gladue*' reports detail the systemic and background factors courts are mandated to consider in sentencing Canadian Aboriginal offenders. And yet the weight that should be given to these factors is by no means clear. Courts in Australia and Canada have developed principles addressing the relevance of social and economic disadvantage in the context of sentencing indigenous offenders and the broader relevance of Aboriginality to the sentencing task. However, this exercise has not been without controversy.

Apart from the principle of equality before the law, there is a second equality principle against which indigenous factors can be judged, namely the principle of equal impact. This requires that sentences should be so calculated as to impose an equal impact on the offenders subjected to them. In other words, we should strive for equal impact of sanctions on different offenders and different groups of offenders. These two principles have similarities with the principle of proportionality, which requires that sentences be proportionate to the seriousness of the offence and the culpability of the offender, a principle which also seeks to ensure that sentencing outcomes are fair and just. In the sentencing context proportionality is regarded as fundamental by sentencing courts and it also plays a part in most contemporary theories of punishment.

The relevance of race and cultural and social background should also be tested against different sentencing rationales, but given the hybrid approach to sentencing aims in Australia, Canada and the United Kingdom, equality before the law is arguably a more appropriate foundational principle. It also has the attraction of public appeal. Whatever misgivings academics may have about speaking of just sentences in an unjust world (Ashworth 2010: 99, 258), it seems that proportional sentencing outcomes are highly valued by the public (Roberts and Hough 2005).

EQUALITY PRINCIPLES

Human rights instruments and constitutional documents commonly enact a principle of equality or non-discrimination. For example, the International Convention on the Civil and Political Rights, Article 26, provides that: 'All persons are equal before the law and are entitled without any discrimination to the equal protection of the law.'

Similarly the Victorian Charter of Human Rights and Responsibilities, section 8(3), provides:

> Every person is equal before the law and is entitled to the equal protection of the law without discrimination and has the right to equal and effective protection against discrimination.

Similar provisions exist in the Australian Capital Territory Human Rights Act, in the Canadian Charter of Rights and Freedoms and in the South African Constitution. The Human Rights Act 1998 (UK) is more restrictive and, like Article 14 of the European Convention, forbids discrimination in relation to rights contained elsewhere in the Act rather than enacting a free-standing equality and discrimination right. Aside from human rights and constitutional documents, common law recognizes a general principle of equality as fundamental to the rule of law (Dicey 1959: 202). At common law the principle of equality meant that everyone from prime minister to police constable was subject to the law. Only more recently has it been interpreted as a non-discrimination right. For example, the Privy Council in *Matadeen* v. *Pointu* asserted, 'Equality before the law requires that persons should be uniformly treated, unless there is some valid reason to treat them differently.' It described the principle as 'one of the building blocks of democracy' (at p. 109).

Equality of impact

The principle of equal impact also derives from the general principle of equality, but is separate from the principle of equality in its non-discrimination sense (see discussion in von Hirsch et al. 2009). The principle of equal impact was recognized by Bentham, who, despite his emphasis on general deterrence, argued for a rule which takes into account individual sensibilities in calculating punishment (Bentham 1970: 169; Ashworth and Player 1998: 255). In its application to sentencing, the general principle of equality before the law means that no person should be sentenced differently because of their race, national or ethnic origin, religion, gender, sexual orientation, mental or physical disability or similar characteristics. The equal impact aspect of the general principle means that no sentence should be imposed that may be expected to have a more severe impact on an offender because of the offender's race, national or ethnic origin and so on.

In the sentencing context the equality principle is sometimes called the principle of parity. The Canadian Criminal Code, for example, provides in section 718.2(b) that 'a sentence should be similar to sentences imposed on similar offenders for similar offences committed in similar circumstances'. In Australia, the High Court has pronounced that 'Equal justice requires that like should be treated alike but that, if there are relevant differences, due allowance should be made for them' (*Postiglione*: 301). The principle raises the question of the extent to which it mandates equal treatment. Does taking into account as a mitigating factor such circumstances as adverse social background or membership of a socially and economically deprived minority group infringe the principle? This chapter disputes this. It is argued that just as equals must be treated equally, unequals must be treated unequally. And while there is 'no universally accepted standard of what kinds of difference constitute a relevant form of inequality, so as to justify different treatment' (Spigelman 2008:1), the fact that social and economic deprivation and disadvantage affects an offender's culpability for the offence provides a justification for treating it as relevant. Other factors associated with racial and social background may also qualify as relevant differences.

THE OVER-REPRESENTATION IN PRISONS OF RACIAL AND DISADVANTAGED MINORITIES

It is well known that visible minorities and offenders from disadvantaged backgrounds are over-represented in prison statistics relative to their numbers in the general population. In Australia, the age-standardized imprisonment rate was fourteen times higher for indigenous people than non-indigenous people in 2009, and the increase in imprisonment rates for indigenous people was eight times that of non-indigenous people between 2000 and 2009 (Australian Bureau of Statistics 2009: 47).

In New Zealand and Canada indigenous offenders are also over-represented in the sentenced population and in the prison population. For example, in 2007/08, Aboriginals accounted for only 3 per cent of the general population but 22 per cent of all admissions to custody (Statistics Canada 2009; for trends see Roberts and Melchers 2003). And in the United States, black Americans are incarcerated at nearly six times the rate of whites (Mauer and King 2007). In England and Wales the proportion of black prisoners relative to the general population was recently reported to be five times higher than for whites (Riley et al. 2009: 171).

Putting to one side the issue of whether or not over-representation is a result of direct or indirect discrimination, such over-representation raises the question of whether adverse social background and other indigenous factors as causes of offending and over-representation should be taken into account as mitigating factors and if to do so violates the principle of equal treatment.

SOCIO-ECONOMIC DISADVANTAGE AND INDIGENOUS SENTENCING FACTORS

Australia

A disadvantaged social background can be regarded as a mitigating factor in Australian courts, particularly if there is a causal link between such a background and the offending behaviour (*Chambers*: 22–4; *B* v. *DPP*, [28]; Edney and Bagaric 2007: 170–5). In the case of indigenous offenders the issue of the relevance of socio-economic disadvantage to sentence has been widely canvassed in case law and by law reform bodies and similar organizations. The following discussion is necessarily somewhat selective; decisions are not always consistent and divergences exist within and across the eight separate Australian jurisdictions. However, it does appear that in the last decade or so, courts have tended to resile from the approach of the 1970s to the late 1990s, which accepted that the history of colonization and the socio-economic disadvantage suffered by Aboriginal Australians justified imposing more lenient sentences on indigenous offenders. Instead, courts have emphasized the need to denounce and deter violence against Aboriginal women and children in particular. It has been argued that the change has been such that membership of a dysfunctional indigenous community is now aggravating rather than mitigating. The discussion that follows will survey these developments.

Building on the High Court decision in *Neal*,[1] Wood J, of the New South Wales Court of Criminal Appeal in *Fernando* laid down eight propositions which covered the relevance of alcohol abuse, the particular hardship suffered by indigenous offenders in prison, especially offenders from remote communities and the limited utility of long prison sentences in such cases. Alcohol abuse, while not normally an excuse, was said to be mitigating in the case of indigenous offenders in 'recognition by the court of the endemic presence of alcohol within Aboriginal communities, and the grave social difficulties faced by those communities where poor self image, absence of education and work opportunity and other demoralizing factors have placed heavy stresses on them, reinforcing their resort to alcohol and compounding its worse effects' (pp. 62–3).

While New South Wales courts continue to apply the *Fernando* principles,[2] a number of recent decisions of the New South Wales Court of Criminal Appeal have been characterized as a 'retreat' from *Fernando* because they suggest that the principles have little or no application to indigenous offenders in urban communities, to offenders who are 'part Aboriginal' or to Aboriginal offenders who have not been brought up within a wholly dysfunctional community dominated by substance abuse, or whose disadvantage is unexceptional (Edney and Bagaric 2007: 256–9). This approach has been criticized because it denies that the indigenous experience of criminal justice is unique and different from other disadvantaged groups (ibid.; Anthony 2008: 14–16).

The focus in *Fernando* was on social and economic disadvantage suffered by indigenous offenders by reason of their Aboriginality, an approach criticized for its failure to link disadvantage with a loss of culture and dispossession (Nicholson 1999). Following the Human Rights and Equal Opportunity Commission's report *Bringing Them Home* (1997), a number of Victorian decisions, exemplified by the judgment of Eames J in *Fuller-Cust* demonstrate a broader understanding of disadvantage to include complex aspects of childhood development, colonialism and cultural identity and its nexus with offending. For Eames J, the fact that because of his Aboriginality the offender was removed by the state from his natural parents was pivotal to understanding

1 In *Neal* the mitigation lay not so much in socio-economic disadvantage and membership of a dysfunctional community as in the paternalistic and racist environment of the reserve and the resulting tensions.

2 See, e.g., *Waters* (2007), [39].

the subjective circumstances of the offender and his offending. Not to consider them would be to sentence him as 'someone other than himself' (at p. 520). In this case it was 'emotional stress' rather than economic disadvantage and lack of educational opportunities which diminished culpability for his offending. This was directly related to the offender's fears of rejection which were in turn closely related to the separation from his mother and the impact of that on his life, a history replicated in many cases reported by the Royal Commission into Aboriginal Deaths in Custody (1991).[3] However, in *Fuller-Cust*, Eames J was in dissent. In contrast with his judgment, the majority gave little weight to the principles in *Neal* and *Fernando*, in part because the offender was well educated and was an urban rather than a tribal Aborigine. Despite this decision, the Victorian Court of Appeal has recently described Eames J's judgment as 'seminal' and affirmed that different outcomes may result for Aboriginal offenders if it is shown that mitigating factors in their background had a particular impact because of their Aboriginality (*DPP* v. *Terrick*, [45]–[46]).

South Australian courts have applied the *Fernando* principles and have also specifically adverted to the problem of petrol sniffing and its relationship to socio-economic disadvantage and offending (*Scobie*, Gray J at [70]; *Peters* v. *Police*).[4]

In the Northern Territory, the jurisdiction with the highest proportion of indigenous prisoners – 82 per cent in 2009 (Australian Bureau of Statistics 2009: 47) – the courts have not relied on the *Fernando* principles. However, decisions in the 1970s and 1980s had a similar focus: widespread alcohol abuse arising out of despair and dislocation and the unlikelihood of prison operating as an effective deterrent (Anthony 2010: 3). Northern Territory courts also demonstrated a willingness to take account of indigenous customary law, community expectations and the need to restore the offender and the community (Anthony 2008: 11–13).

However, in *Wurramara* (1999), in which the Court of Criminal Appeal gave what has been referred to as 'a guideline judgment for sentencing Aboriginal offenders for violent offences' (Eames 2008: 24), the emphasis changed to sending the 'correct message' that Aboriginal women, children and 'the weak' will be protected against

[3] The report made 339 recommendations directed at reducing the rate of imprisonment of indigenous people and preventing the deaths of those imprisoned.

[4] Cf. *Bux* v. *Police* (2009), where evidence of petrol sniffing and its link with offending was absent (at [29]).

personal violence including violence fuelled by excessive alcohol consumption. Sending 'the correct message' means that in cases of violent offences at least, historical disadvantage and membership of a dysfunctional community is no longer regarded as a significant mitigating factor and, as a result, sentences appear to have increased in the Territory for violent crimes since *Wurramara* was decided (Anthony 2010: 3).

Aboriginal over-representation is currently higher in Western Australia than in any other state (Australian Bureau of Statistics 2009: 7). The Western Australian Law Reform Commission's review of the relevance of indigenous factors in sentencing shows that such factors extend beyond socio-economic disadvantage to a recognition of the impact of colonialism, loss of culture and removal (2006: 171–2). However, *Richards* (2008), a recent decision of the Western Australian Court of Appeal, narrowly circumscribes the relevance of Aboriginality. In contrast with the Canadian *Gladue* approach (discussed later in the chapter), the Court dismisses any role for the courts in reducing Aboriginal over-representation and characterized the problem as one for social policy rather than for the courts. In the words of Martin CJ,

> It is impossible to overstate the importance of these issues to the development of social policy. However, it is equally important to emphasize that these things provide no justification whatever for adopting any different approach in the sentencing of Aboriginal offenders. There is only one law of Western Australia, and it applies equally and without differentiation between Aboriginal and non-Aboriginal persons. And as the trial judge acknowledged, Aboriginal woman (and children) are every bit as entitled to protection of the law as non-Aboriginal woman (and children).

However, a little later he added:

> So while Aboriginality itself must be irrelevant to the sentencing process, the fact that an offender has spent his entire life in a remote community and has a cultural and spiritual connection to the land of that community and has difficulties with the English language, will properly be taken into account at the time of sentence because they bear upon the impact which a sentence of imprisonment will have upon that offender.
>
> (at p. 416)

Decisions of the Queensland Court of Criminal Appeal in the 1980s acknowledged the practice of imposing more lenient sentences on Aboriginal defendants because of the mitigating factors of disadvantage, dispossession and demoralization, but, at the same time, noted that the need to protect victims must not be neglected (Anthony 2010: 2). The importance of taking into account community attitudes was also recognized and encouraged (Mackenzie and Stobbs 2010: 72). More recent decisions have denied that Aboriginality in itself justifies different or special treatment or lighter sentences and have downplayed the mitigating effect of indigenous factors.[5]

The shift in the impact of disadvantage and membership of a dysfunctional community from mitigation to aggravation is demonstrated by *KU and others* (2008), a decision which can also be interpreted as devaluing the role and views of the community. The horrific facts of the case (involving a rape of a 10-year-old Aboriginal girl by six young males from her community of Aurukun on the York Peninsula), and the lenient sentences imposed on the perpetrators attracted headlines around the world (Warner 2008; Eames 2008). In quashing the sentences the Court of Appeal held that the sentencing judge had given excessive weight to the offenders' dysfunctional community and to historical and current factors of social disadvantage. These factors, the Court held, did not absolve the judge from the necessity of imposing a sentence that took into account the seriousness of the offences and the need to protect the community. Moreover, the social disadvantage of living in Aurukun was something of two-edged sword. The need for the criminal law to protect vulnerable and innocent victims was said to be more compelling in a community unequal to this task and the arguments against non-custodial sentences were said to be less compelling in a community where rehabilitation is less likely to be achieved by community sanctions.

The Court of Appeal's decision in *KU* has been criticized on four principal grounds by a former judge of the Victorian Supreme Court (Eames 2008). First, he described the judgment as 'close to a counsel of despair' that allowed too little room for mitigation by reason of historical and current disadvantage (p. 30). Second, the Court's criticism of the sentencing judge for requiring proof that the offenders had suffered from the history of colonization and dispossession and from current social disadvantage was dismissed on the grounds that the sentencing judge had extensive experience with the community and 'that a judge sitting on a one-day circuit was entitled to conclude, unless the contrary was proved, that any young offender of the ages and with the criminal histories of these offenders was bound to have been adversely affected by the social and historical deprivations which the Aurukun community generally experiences' (p. 35).

[5] See, e.g., *Daniel*.

Third, the Court was also criticized for undervaluing the role of the indigenous community in the sentencing process by failing to seek information from the Aurukun Community Justice Group about the sentence and the offenders. Finally, Eames attacked the judgment for focusing on the failures of the judge and the prosecutor and omitting to highlight the broader failures that the case exposed. These included the government's failure to address the underlying causes of offending which had been highlighted almost eighteen years earlier by the Royal Commission into Aboriginal Deaths in Custody and the failure to acknowledge the ineffectiveness of the criminal justice system in dealing with community dysfunction. By imposing harsher sentences in the name of deterrence, the court was implicitly accepting that the courts could provide long-term answers to the dysfunctional features of some remote indigenous communities.

Canada

Section 718(2)(e) of the Canadian Criminal Code, which requires sentencing judges to consider all available sanctions other than imprisonment and to pay particular attention to the circumstances of Aboriginal offenders, has been interpreted by the Supreme Court in *Gladue* (1999) and *Wells* (2000) as directing sentencing judges to undertake the sentencing of Aboriginal offenders (First Nations, Metis and Inuit) differently because of their unique circumstances. In *Gladue*, the Court summarized their approach to the requirements of section 718(2)(e) in twelve propositions, which include the central assertion that the section's purpose is remedial in nature, namely to ameliorate the serious problem of the overrepresentation of Aboriginal people in prisons. Pursuant to this purpose, in sentencing an Aboriginal offender, a judge must consider:

(A) The unique systemic or background factors which may have played a part in bringing the particular Aboriginal offender before the courts; and

(B) The types of sentencing procedures and sanctions which may be appropriate in the circumstances for the offender because of his or her particular Aboriginal heritage or connection (at para. 93).

In doing so the judge is required to take judicial notice of the broad systemic and background factors affecting Aboriginal people and of the priority given in Aboriginal cultures to a restorative approach to sentencing; in addition case-specific information will come from counsel and a pre-sentence report addressing the above matters. In crafting a sentence which is meaningful to Aboriginal persons, the goals of restorative justice may properly be given greater weight. The Court emphasized that the different method of analysis does not mean that Aboriginal offenders must always be sentenced in a way which gives most weight to principles of restorative justice and less weight to goals such as deterrence, denunciation and separation. If there is no alternative to incarceration, the *Gladue* approach does not mandate an automatic reduction in the prison sentence, but acknowledges that the 'jail term for an Aboriginal offender may in some circumstances be less than the term imposed for a non-Aboriginal offender'.

However, the more violent and serious the offence, the more likely it is that terms of imprisonment will be close to or the same as that imposed on non-Aboriginals, even taking into account their different concepts of sentencing (at para. 79). This was the case on the facts of *Gladue*, where the sentencing judge's error in failing to consider the systemic or background factors that may have influenced the offender's conduct in killing her spouse did not make the sentence of three years' imprisonment inappropriate. Applying the *Gladue* methodology in the later decision of *Wells*, a case of sexual assault, the Supreme Court of Canada held that it was open to the trial judge to give primacy to the principles of denunciation and deterrence on the basis that the crime was serious and violent. However, the Court did not foreclose the possibility of giving greatest weight to restorative justice principles in imposing sentence for a serious crime in appropriate cases.

The significantly different circumstances of Aboriginal offenders in Canada tend to be summarized simply as 'systemic or background factors'. In elaborating on this, the Supreme Court in *Gladue* referred to the impact of years of dislocation and economic development on *so many* Aboriginal peoples which has translated into low incomes, high unemployment rates, lack of opportunities and options, lack or irrelevance of education, substance abuse, loneliness and community fragmentation (para. 67). In addition, Aboriginal offenders are more likely to be adversely affected by incarceration and less likely to be rehabilitated because the internment milieu is often culturally inappropriate and discrimination towards them so often rampant (para. 68).

The *Gladue* 'method of analysis' applies to all Aboriginal offenders wherever they reside, to those who live in reserves or rural areas and to those in urban areas (para. 91). In *Gladue*, the Supreme Court took care to emphasize that section 718(2)(e) was neither discriminatory nor unfair to non-Aboriginal people. Rather, its fundamental purpose was to treat Aboriginal offenders fairly by taking into account their different or unique circumstances as part of weighing the multitude of factors which must be taken into account when determining a fit sentence.

Debating the issues

The Supreme Court's claim that the *Gladue* methodology is not unfair to disadvantaged non-Aboriginal offenders and does not infringe the principle of equality before the law has been challenged by scholars. The decision was condemned in the media as a 'race-based discount' (Ives 2004: 131). Academics such as Stenning and Roberts (2001) argued that it offends principles of fairness and parity and that social deprivation or adversity should be taken into account for all offenders regardless of racial or cultural background. They disputed that the systemic or background factors identified by the Supreme Court were unique and different in kind from those of non-Aboriginal offenders or that they were relevant for all Aboriginal offenders. It follows, they argued, that to adopt a different sentencing methodology which can result in different outcomes and shorter sentences compared with a similarly circumstanced non-Aboriginal offender for the same offence is unfair and discriminatory. Moreover, because many offences committed by Aboriginal offenders involve Aboriginal victims, the criminal justice system could come to be perceived as discriminatory against Aboriginal victims, particularly women. Even if the historical treatment and discrimination of Aboriginal Canadians is unique, Stenning and Roberts questioned its unique effects on current circumstances. In any event, they contended, the solution to Aboriginal over-representation in prison populations lies beyond the role of the sentencing judges, who have no brief to redress history or recent discrimination.

These criticisms have been partly answered by a subsequent line of decisions of the Ontario Court of Appeal which have not exactly extended the *Gladue* factors to other disadvantaged minority groups but have indicated that social or economic disadvantage is a mitigating factor open to all if it precipitates crime. In *Borde* (2003), Rosenberg JA, having noted that the *Gladue* methodology only applies to Aboriginal offenders, stated:

> However, the principles that are generally applicable to all offenders, including African Canadians, are sufficiently broad and flexible to enable a sentencing court in appropriate cases to consider both systemic and background factors that may have played a role in the commission of the offence and the values of the community from which the offender comes. (at para. 32)

In *Hamilton* (2004) Doherty JA applied the reasoning in *Borde* and held that if racial and gender bias suffered by an offender explain why an offender committed a crime they can be said to have 'played a role in the commission of the offence' and can be taken into account at sentencing. However, there needs to be a connection between institutional racism and gender inequality and the particular circumstances of the offender. None was established on the facts. Nevertheless, the poor economic circumstances of the two African Canadian single mothers were mitigating factors.

As a result of *Gladue*, *Borde*, and *Hamilton*, it seems that social disadvantage is a relevant mitigating factor irrespective of the offender's membership of a disadvantaged minority group which has suffered systemic discrimination. Questions remain about what weight this factor can have, particularly in 'serious and violent' cases. In the context of Aboriginal over-representation there were questions about the effectiveness of the *Gladue* approach in reducing Aboriginal imprisonment rates despite its promise (Anand 2000: 416; Stenning and Roberts 2001: 166). Subsequent research has shown that neither the statutory sentencing reforms nor the Supreme Court decisions interpreting these reforms have reduced the rate of Aboriginal over-representation in Canada's prison populations (Roberts and Melchers 2003). There are questions, too, about the relevance of the 'unique circumstances' of indigenous Canadians beyond social and economic disadvantage and the particular salience of restorative justice practices to Aboriginal Canadian communities. Developing *Gladue's* reference to the impact of 'the legacy of dislocation' on Aboriginal offenders, Rudin and Roach (2002: 19) argue that unique factors include not only social and economic disadvantage that have helped to bring Aboriginal offenders to court and the relevance of restorative approaches to crime, but also the impact of colonialism, which has made Aboriginal people 'feel that they both personally and as a people ... [are] inferior and unable to accomplish anything of merit'.

Roberts and Stenning's rejoinder to this is that while colonialism has played a significant role in generating the disadvantage experienced by most Aboriginal Canadians today, its relevance to the response to Aboriginal over-representation is open to question. In particular, if it is to be taken into account, the Supreme Court has failed to make it clear how it should influence the determination of an appropriate sentence in the individual case (Roberts and Stenning 2002: 82–3). Supporters of the Aboriginal sentencing provision assert that it can be defended as a means of symbolically showing concern for the problem (Daubney 2002: 41; Carter 2002: 67), whereas its detractors argue that such symbolism is unprincipled and unfair, addressing historical injustices is beyond the appropriate role of a sentencing court and it diverts attention from the real root causes of the disproportionate representation of Aboriginal people (Roberts and Stenning 2002: 89–91). At the heart of the debate is the basis on which Aboriginal status justifies a different response and who should be responsible for ameliorating social disadvantage.

FINDING RELEVANT DIFFERENCES IN ABORIGINALITY

The Australian and Canadian experience of dealing with difference in the context of the sentencing of indigenous Australian and Canadian offenders has provided the opportunity to develop and debate the relevance of socio-economic disadvantage as a mitigating factor as well as other factors associated with Aboriginality. Despite theoretical debates in the literature about the relevance of socio-economic disadvantage, courts in Australia and Canada have had little difficulty in accepting the relevance of social and economic disadvantage provided that it can be linked with the offending for which an offender is now being sentenced. It does not offend the principle of proportionality because if it helps to explain offending behaviour, then it reduces the offender's level of culpability – one of the two branches of a proportional sanction. And because it applies to all offenders and is not restricted in its application to Aboriginal offenders, it does not offend the principle of equality before the law. What of the other claimed unique differences beyond social and economic disadvantage? Is it possible to tease out these differences and take them into account in a way that is acceptable in principle?

Harsher impact

It can be argued that there is a principled justification for taking into account the harsher impact of imprisonment on indigenous offenders, particularly those from remote communities who have a spiritual attachment to the land and for whom the imprisonment regime is culturally inappropriate.[6] It is not only indigenous offenders who benefit from the impact of imprisonment as a mitigating factor. The exceptional impact of imprisonment has also been recognized as mitigating for members of ethnic minorities who would face grave cultural difficulties in the prison

[6] *Daniel*, Fitzgerald P at p. 532(v); *Gladue* (1999) at para. 68; *Richards* (2008) at p. 416; see also Nicholson (1999: 88–9) for an explanation why separation from group, culture and land is a uniquely harsh experience for an Australian Aboriginal prisoner.

system.[7] Similarly, the disproportionately harsh impact of imprisonment for those who have some special mental or medical condition which makes imprisonment more painful has been recognized in many Australian decisions (Edney and Bagaric 2007: 300).

In England there is 'scattered support' for mitigation on the basis of exceptional impact because of illness or old age (Ashworth 2010: 183). *Bernard* (1997) stands for the principle that a reduced sentence is not automatically available to those with a serious medical condition, even when it is difficult to treat within prison, although a court might impose a reduced sentence as an act of mercy rather than a principle of law (Ashworth and Player 1998: 256). In some cases, therefore, life-threatening illnesses have resulted in reduced sentences, but there is no duty on the court to take impact into account or for mitigation to have precedence over factors relating to the seriousness of the offence (Easton and Piper 2008: 214). The problems in leaving the matter as a matter of mercy is that it is entirely discretionary and provides no real guidance to sentencers (Ashworth 2010: 186). A preferable approach is to regard the relevance of exceptional impact of a prison sentence as an application of the principle of equal impact, the principle that 'the system should strive to avoid grossly unequal impacts on offenders with differing resources and sensitivities because that would be unjust' (Ashworth 2010: 99).

One problem with accepting exceptional impact as a mitigating factor is that there are many contexts in which a person may suffer abnormally as a result of the sentence imposed, and this leads to difficulties as to where the line should be drawn. Australian courts have accepted that the fact that a prison sentence will be unduly harsh because the prisoner is at risk of harm from other prisoners is a mitigating factor (*Rostum* (1996), *York* (2005)), although it must not merely be assumed that protective custody will involve harsh conditions, greater deprivations or danger (*Mostyn* 2004). In *York* (2005), where there was persuasive evidence that the appellant was at grave risk of harm in prison, McHugh J stated:

> The common law's equal concern for the physical safety of each citizen makes it appropriate for a sentencing judge to take into account the grave risk that a convicted criminal could be killed while in jail. What weight should be given to the risk of a person being killed or injured will depend on all the circumstances of the case including the likelihood of its occurrence.
>
> (at para. 23)

[7] For a recent English case see *Athwal* (2009).

The approach of the English Court of Appeal is that the offender's treatment by other inmates is not generally a factor to which a court 'can have proper regard' (*Nall-Cain*, at p. 150). Against this it can be argued that the principle of equal impact is an acceptable basis for considering danger to a prisoner where there is clear evidence that the prisoner's safety is a real concern. However, the relevance of other collateral consequences of conviction and sentencing, such as loss of employment, profession and associated benefits has a less secure foundation (Ashworth 2010: 184; Easton and Piper 2008: 219). Taking such matters into account can lead to discrimination rather than equal treatment.

INTOXICATION, SUBSTANCE ABUSE AND EMOTIONAL STRESS

In Australia, Canada and the United Kingdom, intoxication and substance abuse are generally regarded as aggravating rather than mitigating (Ashworth 2010: 164; Edney and Bagaric 2007: 179–85). But, as discussed above, when alcohol and substance abuse by indigenous offenders are linked with social disadvantage, dispossession, loss of culture and demoralization, it can be justified as a relevant difference which helps to explain offending behaviour. Emotional stress, which is linked to strained community relationships, racism and tensions (*Neal* 1982) or to childhood separation caused by displacement or paternalistic colonial policies (*Fuller-Cust* 2002), is also relevant to culpability. In these ways the impact of colonialism on the identity and self-esteem of Aboriginal people is a unique difference which can impact on the current circumstances of many Aboriginal people. In such cases it is the reduced culpability by reason of the relationship of such factors with offending which justifies giving mitigatory weight to such factors. It is not Aboriginality alone. As with social disadvantage and offending, some evidence of a link between emotional stress, demoralization, childhood separation and offending is necessary for it to be a mitigating factor.

REMEDYING PAST INJUSTICES AND CURRENT OVER-REPRESENTATION

Some of the remarks of the Supreme Court in *Gladue* clearly suggest that the *Gladue* methodology is designed to remedy past injustices. Reference to the judges' 'remedial role' and to the 'limited role that sentencing judges will play in remedying injustice' (para. 65), and the statement that the 'direction to consider these unique circumstances flows from the staggering injustice currently experienced by Aboriginal peoples with the criminal justice system' are examples (para. 88). Moreover, the assertion that the central purpose of the Aboriginal sentencing provision in the *Criminal Code* is to address the issue of over-representation is an acknowledgment that its purpose is to remedy present injustices even if over-representation does not stem from discriminatory sentencing. Stenning and Roberts have argued that it is not the role of the courts to redress historical injustices and there are problems with expecting the courts to do so, not the least of which is the way it distracts attention from the need to address the underlying causes of Aboriginal over-representation.

In a similar vein, Australian courts have counselled against an approach to sentencing indigenous offenders which hints at 'paternalism or collective guilt' for the harm caused to the Aboriginal race by white settlement (*Fernando*: 63; *DPP* v. *Terrick* 2009: [46]). Attempting to address the over-representation of indigenous persons in prison by adopting a lenient approach to Aboriginal offenders has also been rejected by Australian courts (*Richards* 2008: 416). However, there is a distinction between remedies for past injustice and over-representation (and appropriate social policy to achieve this) and recognizing the impact of past injustices. Recognizing the differential impact of past injustices on the Aboriginal people is not inconsistent with substantive equality. It is a difference or unique circumstance which can be relevant to an understanding of the offender and his or her offending.

Proof of the link between the systemic or background factors associated with Aboriginality and offending is critical. In Canada this is facilitated by the *Gladue* judicial notice approach, which accepts the universal impact of dispossession and dislocation on the Aboriginal population. In Australia there are advocates of a similar approach (Nicholson 1999: 89; Edney and Bagaric 2007: 265), but the courts have not gone so far. Arguably, recognizing a general principle of mitigation is compatible with substantive equality, if it is not an automatic discount. The benefit could be lost for legitimate reasons, such as the impact of loss of culture having been overcome in the particular case or perhaps overwhelmed or diminished by serious violence (as in *Gladue*). This latter qualification would recognize that victims of domestic violence and abused children also have rights to equality before the law.

CONCLUSION

It has been argued that many Canadian and Australian indigenous offenders have unique differences which can be taken into account in mitigation of penalty in a way which conforms with the principles of fairness such as equality before the law and equal impact. Such differences include:

- social and economic disadvantage;
- alcohol and substance abuse when it is linked to social and economic disadvantage;
- the potentially harsher impact of imprisonment on indigenous offenders;
- emotional stress diminishing culpability when contributed to by strained community relationships and racial tension, or when childhood separation caused by paternalistic colonial policy has created fears of rejection.

All these factors can have sufficient connection with offending to make them relevant to culpability or can be justified on the grounds of equal impact. While the *Gladue* approach, the *Fernando* principles and the approach of Eames J in *Fuller Cust* provide support for taking these unique differences into account, there are a number of obstacles to Aboriginal factors operating effectively as mitigation.

First, there may be difficulty in establishing the necessary causal connection with the particular factor and offending. In Canada, the *Gladue* approach seeks to address this issue by allowing courts to take judicial notice of Aboriginal disadvantage and discrimination and by making provision for '*Gladue* reports'. In Australia, as cases such as *KU* demonstrate, there may real difficulties in ensuring that the circuit courts in particular have the appropriate information prior to sentence. There are also questions about the strength of the causal connection, questions which also arise in relation to the weight that should be given to social disadvantage more generally (Ives 2004:154).

Second, the courts have made it clear that less weight is to be given to indigenous factors in serious and violent offences. In Canada, the *Gladue* approach has limited application in such cases. And in Australia, concerns with the need to protect vulnerable indigenous victims (echoed in Canada) and the inability of dysfunctional communities either to protect victims or to restore or support offenders has led to mitigating factors being trumped by consideration of deterrence and denunciation. There is force in the observation that community dysfunction seems to have become an aggravating rather than a mitigating factor in some cases. As has been argued above, the imposition of harsh sentences in the name of deterrence implicitly suggests that through sentencing the courts can provide an answer to the endemic violence which exists in some indigenous communities. The impact of allowing mitigation for indigenous sentencing factors is limited. It can do little to remedy the underlying causes of over-representation. As the courts have recognized, 'the criminal law is a hopelessly blunt instrument of social policy' and an inadequate substitute for improved health, housing, education and employment opportunities for Aboriginal communities.[8] But it does not follow from such a concession that courts should discount mitigation for historical and current disadvantage in favour of an approach which suggests deterrence and denunciation. This, too, suggests that such an approach provides an answer to the problem of violence rather than attacking the causes of community dysfunction.

Third, there is a problem in determining the weight which should be given to indigenous factors once it is determined that they are relevant. This is a common objection to personal mitigation but should not be a ground for refusing to give a factor any weight at all. Sentencing is not a precise exercise and the weight given to such factors will have to be a matter of judgement. Transparency suggests that, as is common in the case of guilty plea discounts, it would be useful for sentencers to specify the weight which has been given to indigenous factors by first specifying the sentence without indigenous factors and then the adjusted final sentence with reasons why the indigenous factor is mitigating. This has the added advantage of explaining to the victim, the offender and the public why it is that the sentence should be mitigated to produce equality of treatment.

There are obvious limitations in striving for fair and just sentences in societies riven with inequality and injustice (Ashworth 2010: 99). It is unlikely that sentencing can have any impact on addressing the problem of Aboriginal over-representation, and it should not claim to seek to redress past and current injustices. Nevertheless, sentencing should at least strive not to exacerbate inequalities or contribute to the problems of over-representation of disadvantaged groups such as indigenous minorities. Taking into account social and economic disadvantage and other indigenous factors can be done in a way that is consistent with fundamental principles of fairness, proportionality and equality before the law. And equality principles as a justification for mitigation avoid

[8] *Daniel*, 530; *Newman* (2004), 377; *Richards* (2008), 416.

some of the paternalistic overtones of mercy. Notwithstanding endemic problems of violence and dysfunction in some indigenous communities, courts should not encourage the impression that the solution to such difficulties lies in harsh sentencing. Instead, the limitations of the criminal law in protecting the vulnerable should be recognized and the need for governments and communities to deal with the underlying causes emphasized. Acknowledging the limits of the criminal law in addressing these issues creates a space for developing community engagement in criminal justice processes and a search for restorative and community approaches that offer better protection for victims.

REFERENCES

Anand, S. (2000). 'The Sentencing of Aboriginal Offenders, Continued Confusion and Persistent Problems', *Canadian Journal of Criminology and Criminal Justice*, 42: 412–19.

Anthony, T. (2008). 'Late-modern Developments in Sentencing Principles for Indigenous Offenders: Beyond David Garland's Framework', *Proceedings of the 2nd Australian and New Zealand Critical Criminology Conference*, Crime and Justice Research Network, University of New South Wales.

(2010).'Sentencing Indigenous Offenders', *Indigenous Justice Clearing House*, Brief 7.

Ashworth, A. (2010). *Sentencing and Criminal Justice*, 5th edn. Cambridge University Press.

Ashworth, A. and Player, E. (1998). 'Sentencing, Equal Treatment and the Impact of Sanctions', in A. Ashworth and M. Wasik (eds.), *Fundamentals of Sentencing Theory*. Oxford University Press.

Australian Bureau of Statistics (2009). *Prisoners in Australia*, Cat. 4517.0.

Australian Human Rights and Equal Opportunity Commission (1997). *Bringing Them Home: Report of the National Inquiry into Separation of Aboriginal and Torres Strait Islander Children from their Families*. Sydney: Australian Human Rights and Equal Opportunity Commission.

Bentham, J. (1970). *The Collected Works of Jeremy Bentham: An Introduction to the Principles of Morals and Legislation*, ed. J. H. Burns and H. L. A Hart. London: Athlone Press.

Carter, M. (2002). 'Of Fairness and Faulkner', *Saskatchewan Law Review*, 65: 63–74.

Daubney, D. (2002). 'Nine Words: A Response to "Empty Promises: Parliament, the Supreme Court, and the Sentencing of Aboriginal offenders"'. *Saskatchewan Law Review*, 65: 35–43.

Dicey, A. V. (1959). *Introduction to the Study of the Law of the Constitution*. 10th edn. London: Macmillan.

Eames, G. (2008). 'Criminal Law and Sentencing Issues amongst Indigenous Communities: Questions from Aurukun', *Australian Indigenous Law Review*, 12: 22–40.

Easton, S. and Piper, C. (2008). *Sentencing and Punishment: The Quest for Justice*, 2nd edn. Oxford University Press.

Edney, R. and Bagaric, M. (2007). *Australian Sentencing*. Melbourne: Cambridge University Press.

Ives, D. (2004). 'Inequality, Crime and Sentencing: *Borde*, *Hamilton* and the Relevance of Social Disadvantage in Canadian Sentencing Law', *Queen's Law Journal*, 30: 114–55.

Mackenzie, G. and Stobbs, N. (2010). *Principles of Sentencing*. Sydney: Federation Press.

Mauer, M. and King, R. (2007). *Uneven Justice: State Rates of Incarceration by Race and Ethnicity*. Washington, DC: The Sentencing Project.

Nicholson, J. (1999). 'The Sentencing of Aboriginal Offenders', *Criminal Law Journal*, 23: 85–9.

Riley, J., Cassidy, D., and Becker, J. (2009). *Statistics on Race and the Criminal Justice System 2007/8*. London: Ministry of Justice.

Roberts, J. V. and Hough, M. (2005). *Understanding Public Attitudes to Criminal Justice*. Maidenhead: Open University Press.

Roberts, J. V. and Melchers, R. (2003). 'The Incarceration of Aboriginal Offenders: Trends from 1978 to 2001', *Canadian Journal of Criminology and Criminal Justice*, 45: 211–42.

Roberts, J. V. and Stenning, P. (2002). 'Colloquy on "Empty Promises: Parliament, the Supreme Court and the Sentencing of Aboriginal Offenders": The Sentencing of Aboriginal Offenders in Canada: A Rejoinder', *Saskatchewan Law Review*, 65: 75–95.

Royal Commission into Aboriginal Deaths in Custody (Commonwealth of Australia) (1991). *National Reports*.

Rudin, J. and Roach, K. (2002). 'Broken Promises: A Response to Stenning and Roberts' "Empty Promises"'. *Saskatchewan Law Review*, 65: 3–34.

Spigelman, J. (2008). 'Consistency and Sentencing'. *Sentencing 2008 Conference*, National Judicial College of Australia, Canberra, 8 February.

Statistics Canada (2009). Incarceration of Aboriginal People in Adult Correctional Services, *The Daily*, 21 July, available at www.statcan.gc.ca/daily.

Stenning, P. and Roberts, J. (2001). 'Empty Promises: Parliament, the Supreme Court and the Sentencing of Aboriginal Offenders', *Saskatchewan Law Review* 64: 137–68.

von Hirsch, A., Ashworth, A. and Roberts, J. V. (eds.) (2009). *Principled Sentencing: Readings on Theory and Policy*, 3rd edn. Oxford: Hart Publishing.

Warner, K. (2008). 'Sentencing Review 2007–2008', *Criminal Law Journal*, 32: 368–83.

TABLE OF CASES

Athwal [2009] EWCA 789.
B *v*. DPP [2005] TASSC 16.
Bernard [1997] 1 Cr App R (S) 135.
Borde (2003) 8 CR (6th) 203.
Bux *v*. Police [2009] SASC 353.
Chambers (2003) 145 A Crim R 15.
DPP *v*. Terrick [2009] VSCA 220.
Daniel [1998] 1 Qd R 499.
Fernando (1992) 76 A Crim R 58.
Fuller-Cust (2002) 6 VR 496.
Hamilton [2004] OJ No 3252.
Gladue [1999] 1 SCR 688, 171 DLR (4th) 385.
KU, *Ex parte* Attorney-General [2008] QCA 154.
Matadeen *v*. Pointu [1999] 1 AC 98.
Mostyn (2004) 145 A Crim R 304.
Nall-Cain (Lord Brocket) [1998] 2 Cr App R (S) 145.
Neal (1982) 149 CLR 305.
Newman (2004) 145 A Crim R 361.
Peters *v*. Police [2009] SASC 1.
Postiglione (1997) 189 CLR 295.
Richards (2008) 185 A Crim R 413.
Rostum [1996] 2 VR 97.
Scobie (2003) 85 SASR 77.
Waters [2007] NSWCCA 219.
Wells [2000] 1 SCR 207.
Wurramara (1999) 105 A Crim R 512.
York (2005) 79 ALJR 1919.

CHAPTER EIGHT

PERSONAL MITIGATION: AN EMPIRICAL ANALYSIS IN ENGLAND AND WALES

Jessica Jacobson and Mike Hough

Personal mitigation casts into sharp focus some fundamental issues about sentencing principles and judicial discretion. Is justice best served by sentencing the offence or the offender? What balance ought to be struck between the two? Surprisingly, mitigation has been an under-researched topic, despite its evident significance in the sentencing process and the contentious issues it raises (Ashworth 2010: 168–94). Previously, the only detailed empirical study that specifically focused on the role of mitigation in the English criminal courts was that of Shapland (1981), who examined the mitigation deployed in the sentencing of one hundred adult defendants in magistrates' courts and the Crown Court. Other empirical studies of sentencing that have explored mitigation include Flood-Page and Mackie (1998) (on sentencing practice in magistrates' courts and the Crown Court), Hedderman and Gelsthorpe (1997) (on the sentencing of female defendants by magistrates) and Parker et al. (1989) (on the sentencing of young offenders by magistrates).

CHAPTER OVERVIEW

In this chapter we present key findings of an empirical study conducted in England and Wales which addressed the following two questions:

This research was mounted as a joint enterprise between the Institute for Criminal Policy Research and the Prison Reform Trust. We are very grateful to the Esmée Fairbairn Foundation and the Cripps Foundation for funding ICPR's and PRT's work.

- What is the role of personal mitigation in sentencing decisions made in the English criminal courts?
- What are the main components of personal mitigation?

The study

There were two main elements to our study of mitigation: observations of sentencing hearings (a total of 132 cases involving 162 defendants and 52 sentencers) and one-to-one interviews with forty sentencers. The study therefore includes 162 sentencing decisions. Both the observations and interviews were carried out across five Crown Court centres in cities in England and Wales. While the study was limited to sentencing of adult offenders in the Crown Court, the issues addressed have direct relevance also to sentencing in magistrates' courts and sentencing of children and young people. Throughout, we use the term 'mitigation' to refer to *any* aspect of a case that reduces the severity of the sentence passed – in terms of sentence *length* or *type*. 'Aggravation', conversely, refers to factors that increase the severity of a sentence. We use the term 'personal mitigation' to refer to mitigation that relates largely to the background or circumstances of the *offender* rather than the facts of the *offence*.

Types of factor and their impact

Most sentencing decisions taken in the Crown Court are not based on the facts of the offence or offences alone. Rather, sentencing tends to involve close consideration of the *offender* as well as the *offence*. Many of the offender-related factors that play a part in sentencing decisions are mitigating factors (and are referred to as 'personal mitigation' in this report); some, however, have an aggravating effect.

In analysing sentencing decisions, we developed a categorization of relevant factors. While we drew on previous research and Court of Appeal decisions in constructing this typology, it was primarily a 'data driven' classification of factors which were cited as mitigating factors in the course of the study. We proposed six categories:

1. factors relating to the criminal act, including harm caused to any victim;
2. factors relating to the immediate circumstances of the offence;
3. factors relating to the defendant's wider circumstances at the time of the offence;

4. factors relating to the defendant's responses to the offence and prosecution;
5. factors relating to the defendant's past; and
6. factors relating to the defendant's present and future.[1]

These categories are by no means discrete: they overlap with and merge into each other. Drawing boundaries between the different sets of factors is thus a somewhat arbitrary process, but is an attempt to bring analytic clarity to a confused and complicated empirical reality. Table 8.1 sets out potential mitigating factors in each category (this is not intended to be an exhaustive list). The range of factors is very broad indeed. As noted by Ashworth, 'the factors which have been recognized as mitigating sentences in England are a much more heterogeneous collection than the aggravating factors' (2010: 168).

The factors in category 1 can, clearly, be described as *offence-related*; and some of these may be incorporated in the specific charge or charges faced by the defendant. The factors in categories 3 to 6 can be described as *offender-related* (although in the case of 'supportive attitude of victim'; in category 4 the factor relates to the victim more than the offender). Category 2 is a grey area, within which the factors are neither purely offence- nor purely offender-related. The aggravating factors in this category are often seen as contributing to an offender's *culpability*, and hence to the overall seriousness of the offence. By the same token, mitigating factors in this category – and, arguably, some of the factors in categories 3 and 5, such as youth, psychiatric problems and a history of deprivation – can be seen as reducing the offender's culpability.

Observation findings on the role of personal mitigation

On the basis of the sentencing remarks made during the observed hearings, we sought to identify which, if any, of the mitigating factors expressed in the plea in mitigation, and in any reports referred to, had an impact on the sentence. Table 8.2 shows the frequency with which the different kinds of mitigating factors were mentioned by sentencers, across all 162 decisions observed. The factors in category 1 are strictly offence-related, while those in categories 3 to 6, and some in category 2,

[1] Shapland (1981) categorized the mitigating factors cited in mitigation speeches as: reasons for the offence; descriptions of the gravity of the offence; attitudes of the offender to the offence; present personal circumstances of the offender; past personal circumstances of the offender; future personal circumstances of the offender; factors concerned with the probation service; factors concerned with court processes; and 'others'.

TABLE 8.1. Potential mitigating factors

Category 1: the criminal act
Low level of impact
No violence/low level of violence
Poorly executed/unsophisticated
Played minor role in relation to others
Defendant suffered 'rough justice'
Category 2: immediate circumstance of the offence
Spontaneous offence
Low level of recklessness/unintentional
Provocation
Acted under pressure from others
Category 3: wider circumstances at time of the offence
Offended in response to pressing need
Vulnerability to the influence of others
Social/intellectual limitations
Youth/immaturity
Offence linked to (treatable) psychiatric problems
Under severe stress at time of offence
Category 4: response to offence and prosecution
Remorse/acknowledgment of offence
Efforts at reparation
Co-operation with authorities
Court processes have been stressful/long-running
Has spent time in custody (on remand)
Has been addressing problems since arrest
Supportive attitude of victim
Consistency with co-defendants
Category 5: defendant's past
Good character or limited previous offending
Positive responses to previous sentences
Has led a productive/worthwhile life
Disadvantaged/disrupted background
Traumatic life events
General improvement in behaviour
Category 6: defendant's present and future
Unlikely to reoffend/cause harm
Can address/is addressing problems (e.g. drug, alcohol problems)
Psychiatric problems are being/can be treated
Has family responsibilities
Has support from family/partner
Currently in work/training/studying or has prospects of work/training/studies
Physical illness, disability or old age

TABLE 8.2. Mitigating factors cited by sentencers (as affecting sentence)

Category of mitigation	Type of mitigation	Number of times cited
Category 1: the criminal act	Lack of seriousness/impact of offence	19
	Played minor role in relation to others	12
	Total	*31*
Category 2: immediate circumstances of the offence	Acted under pressure from/on behalf of others	4
	Total	*4*
Category 3: wider circumstances at time of the offence	Youth	19
	Pressing personal or family need	10
	Vulnerable/immature/naïve	7
	Psychiatric illness/problems	5
	Total	*41*
Category 4: response to offence and prosecution	Faced up to/understands criminal behaviour	12
	Remorse	9
	Has been addressing problems in custody/ time on remand has been difficult/salutary	9
	Co-operation with authorities	6
	Total	*40*
Category 5: defendant's past	Good character or limited/irrelevant/gap in previous offending	21
	Has led a productive/worthwhile life	7
	Has shown a general improvement in behaviour	7
	Offence uncharacteristic/'let yourself down'	5
	Total	*40*
Category 6: defendant's present and future	Can address/is addressing drug problems	14
	Has family responsibilities	11
	Unlikely to reoffend/cause harm (general point)	6
	Prison will not benefit defendant and/or the public	6
	Supportive family/partner	6
	Currently in work/training or prospects of work/training	5
	Can address/is addressing alcohol problems	5
	Total	*53*

Note: excludes citations by fewer than five participants.

TABLE 8.3. Perceived impact of mitigation on sentence

Impact of mitigation	Percentage of sentences (rounded up)
Custody → non-custodial sentence	28
Custody → suspended custodial sentence	4
Custody → deferred sentence	2
Sentence unknown → conditional discharge	1
Sentence unknown → fine	1
Shorter custodial sentence: factors other than/ additional to a guilty plea	31
Shorter custodial sentence: reflecting guilty plea *only*.	17
Minimal/no impact	16
Hospital order because of mental illness	1
Total	*100*

are offender-related. While it is impossible to make a hard-and-fast distinction between the two sorts of factor, it is clear that a large proportion of mitigating factors cited by sentencers were offender-related and can hence be described as personal mitigation.

While Table 8.2 records mentions of mitigating factors, it does not show what impact these had on the sentencing decision itself. Table 8.3 shows the impact of mitigation of all kinds on the sentences passed. It includes only those cases – amounting to 127 of the 162 offenders we observed being sentenced – in which the sentencing remarks revealed the impact of the mitigation. In 43 of the 127 cases (34%), the judge said that the offence(s) merited custodial sentences, but mitigation had pulled the sentence back from immediate custody.[2] Of these cases, thirty-five (or 28% of the total) resulted in a non-custodial sentence, five in a suspended sentence, and three had sentencing deferred. *Personal* mitigation played a major, and usually *the* major, part in at least thirty-eight of

[2] These forty-three cases covered a wide range of offences – including Class A drugs offences, passport-related offences and offences of possessing or making indecent images of children. In six cases the primary offence committed by the defendant was burglary, and in another six assault occasioning actual bodily harm.

these forty-three non-custodial sentencing decisions. Personal mitigation was also central to the decisions to conditionally discharge one offender and to impose a fine on another. In twenty cases, mitigation appeared to have a minimal or no impact on sentence. In a total of sixty-one cases, mitigation resulted in the passing of a shorter custodial sentence than would otherwise have been imposed. In twenty-one of these cases, the only mitigating factor cited by the judge was a guilty plea. In the remaining forty cases, other mitigating factors – including, in at least thirty-four cases, personal mitigation – played a part.

In short, personal mitigation was evidently a factor in just under half of all 162 cases we observed. Taking into account only those 127 cases in which the impact or non-impact of mitigation was made explicit, in almost a third of cases personal mitigation was a key factor pulling the sentence back from immediate custody; and in just over a quarter personal mitigation contributed to the passing of a shorter custodial sentence.

Interview findings on the role of personal mitigation

All forty sentencers interviewed for this study were asked the following open-ended question: 'What kinds of *personal* mitigation most frequently influence the sentences that you pass?' Their unprompted responses to this question are summarized in Table 8.4. (Categories 1 and 2 do not appear in this table because of the question's explicit emphasis on personal mitigation.)

We found that the range of factors cited by sentencers when discussing personal mitigation in the abstract are broadly consistent with the factors cited by the sentencers in our observed cases. For example, Category 6 factors (relating to the defendant's present/future) appear to have particular significance within both data sets. However, rather to our surprise, many of our respondents were hesitant or reluctant to generalize about the kinds of personal mitigation that influence their sentences. Their answers indicated that they had not previously considered the concept of mitigation in terms of theory or general principle. Several argued that the question was difficult to answer because 'each case is different'. One respondent said that he did not like the question, because he is always influenced by whatever mitigation there is. He was not happy to categorize mitigation: 'We're paid to listen.' Two respondents said that the answer to any such question has to be, 'it depends'. In two cases, respondents initially said that they could not comment on which mitigating factors tend to carry weight, but went on to discuss the issue in some detail. They eventually reached the conclusion that, in the

TABLE 8.4. Sentencer references to personal mitigation factors

Category of personal mitigation	Type of personal mitigation	Number of mentions
Category 3: wider circumstances at time of the offence	Youth	9
	Difficult family/social circumstances	8
	Financial pressures	7
	Social/intellectual limitations	4
	Psychiatric illness/problems	4
	Total	*32*
Category 4: response to offence and prosecution	Remorse (and efforts at reparation)	13
	Has been addressing problems since arrest	5
	Total	*18*
Category 5: defendant's past	Good character or limited/irrelevant previous offending	11
	Difficult or deprived background	4
	Total	*15*
Category 6: Defendant's present and future	Family responsibilities	20
	Can address/is addressing drug problems	15
	Physical illness/disability (including terminal illness)	13
	Currently in work/training or prospects of work/training	9
	Can address/is addressing problems (general)	6
	Supportive family/partner	5
	Total	68

Note: excludes citations by fewer than four participants.

one case, 'the more you think about it, the more factors there are'; and, in the other case, 'Now I think about it, maybe mitigation does play a bigger part than I first indicated.'

Ashworth has made the point that when asked about their calculations, judges and magistrates 'have a tendency to retreat behind the "no two cases are the same" argument' (2010: 190). Similarly, in their report on the sentencing of young offenders by magistrates, Parker et al. write of how sentencers justify their sentencing decisions 'with the magic words, "we judge each case on its merits"' (1989: 173).[3] The question raised, in turn, by the 'no two cases are the same' response is whether justice would better be served by a sentencing framework within which certain over-arching principles – relating to mitigation among other matters – are more clearly articulated. This is a question to which we return in the concluding section of this chapter.

The weighting of sentencing factors

In order to explore the relative weight given to different types of specific mitigating factors, our interviews included a short sentencing exercise. Each respondent was asked to consider three sentencing scenarios, attached to which were various alternative mitigating factors. These scenarios are presented in the appendix. Each mitigating factor had to be 'scored' by the respondent as follows:

A: major impact – e.g., shift from custodial to non-custodial sentence, or halving of sentence length;
B: moderate impact – e.g., some reduction in sentence length;
C: minimal or no impact.

Table 8.5 ranks the mitigating factors in terms of the significance accorded to them by our respondents, from most to least significant. It was clear that respondents were in agreement about some of the mitigating factors. As the table shows, the factor assigned most significance, overall, was severe clinical depression in the case of the assault occasioning ABH (actual bodily harm). The three lowest-scoring factors were all from the burglary scenario: offender had partner and young child; offender was illiterate; offender had been abused as a child. The low scores for these factors reflected a general sense among our respondents that these were unremarkable (if, in the cases of childhood abuse and illiteracy, unfortunate) factors that did not merit special treatment. ('They're all like that', said one judge with respect to the illiteracy factor, and gave it a C.) While there was a broad consensus among the respondents about the significance (or insignificance) of some of the factors,

[3] With reference to the tendency of sentencers to assert that 'each case is different', Hawkins (2003) argues that decision-makers in the criminal justice system 'do not confront for practical purposes a unique world of distinctive events, problems and people. Matters are simplified and made sense of by seeking patterns, by using past experience and aligning the present with the past.' This can be described as a process of 'typification'.

TABLE 8.5. Ranking of mitigating factors, from most to least significant

Rank*	Average importance score*	Factor	Scenario
1	3.4	Severe clinical depression	ABH
=2	2.8	Support from victim's family	Death by dangerous driving
=2	2.8	Motivated to get drug treatment	Burglary
4	2.5	Intense remorse	Death by dangerous driving
=5	2.2	Profound regret	ABH
=5	2.2	'Moment of madness'	ABH
7	2.1	Married with three children	Death by dangerous driving
8	1.9	Steady job	Burglary
9	1.6	Respected individual	ABH
10	1.1	Support from defendant's family	ABH
=11	0.9	Partner and young child	Burglary
=11	0.9	Functionally illiterate	Burglary
13	0.6	Abused and in care as a child	Burglary

* Ranking is produced by assigning the values to the mitigation scores as follows, A=4, A/B=3, B=2, B/C=1, C=0, and calculating the average (mean) for each factor.

there was marked inconsistency in their views on others. For example, the 'moment of madness' mitigation in the case of ABH had a 'major impact' for nine respondents, and 'minimal or no impact' for seven. The 'motivation to get drug treatment' factor in the burglary scenario was scored as 'major impact' by nineteen respondents and 'minimal/no impact' by seven. These findings underline the need for guidance to reduce some of the variability in perceptions of relevance.

MITIGATION AND THE EXERCISE OF DISCRETION

The importance of personal mitigation or, more broadly, offender-related factors in sentencing makes it inevitable that sentencers exercise a considerable degree of discretion, within the parameters set by legislation and sentencing guidelines. Sentencing, in other words, involves responding to the characteristics, circumstances and life history of the individual, which potentially brings into play any number of variables to be weighed up by the court. Moreover, in according significance to certain aggravating or mitigating factors, sentencers are (implicitly) prioritizing certain sentencing rationales over others.

Mitigation and social disadvantage

What is the relationship between mitigation and social disadvantage? Some theorists have argued that disadvantage, particularly in the form of early deprivation, should mitigate. This argument is usually made from a just deserts perspective which assumes that a seriously disadvantaged defendant is less culpable. As Odudu has suggested, for example, 'The moral blameworthiness of the deprived is different because the choices the deprived face and what motivates their action is different' (2003: 418).[4] In contrast, von Hirsch is hesitant about the extension of the principle of proportionality to take account of reduced culpability resulting from deprivation. His view is that 'a sentencing scheme, on any theory, scarcely can compensate for the effects of wider social ills'; nevertheless, proportionality 'permits this issue of social deprivation to be raised'. He concludes:

> If, on the one hand, deprived persons (or some of them) might arguably be entitled to something less than the full measure of the prescribed punishment, but if, on the other, granting such special mitigated treatment is likely to encounter serious theoretical or practical obstacles, one

[4] See also, among others, Hudson (1995).

> possible solution remains: to keep such matters in mind, when setting a [sentencing] scale's anchoring points.
>
> (1993: 108[5])

Whatever the academic arguments for and against disadvantage as a source of mitigation, defence advocates routinely assume that sentencers *are* swayed by accounts of their clients' social deprivation. Many of the pleas in mitigation that we heard in court made much of the misfortunes experienced by the defendants, particularly as children: numerous unhappy stories were told of child neglect and abuse, family breakdown and bereavement. Whether these accounts were claims of reduced culpability, or simply attempts to engage the sympathy of the judge, was rarely made clear by defence counsel.

As has been noted above, for their part sentencers appear to be somewhat deaf to claims of disadvantage – other than when the circumstances are truly exceptional, or the defendant is very young, or the defendant has evidently strived to overcome the adversity he has faced. There is a simple reason for this: the vast majority of defendants are disadvantaged in one way or another (and often in many ways), which effectively rules out special treatment on these grounds. As one respondent dismissively noted, 'There is a sob story in everyone.' A related point is that while a great many defendants are seriously disadvantaged, many are also highly inadequate individuals leading chaotic lives. As one judge commented, defendants are usually 'completely disorganized. There are the real crooks, but the vast majority are just hopeless.' They are people 'who cannot cope with life and manifest that by committing stupid offences.' This kind of inadequacy is very often rooted in early deprivation, as was made clear by another judge, who said, 'Some people simply *can't* – can't cope with past [traumatic] events . . . and it's a component of their approach to life, and therefore their [lack of] ability to cope with pressure and resist temptations and all the other factors that lead to offending.'

While *disadvantage* often fails to mitigate (notwithstanding the apparent belief to the contrary of defence advocates), it appears that *advantage*, in some circumstances, can mitigate. More specifically, a defendant's employment or degree of family support is sometimes treated by sentencers

5 Likewise, von Hirsch and Ashworth conclude that social deprivation should not be treated as reducing culpability, but a case can be made for mitigation on compassionate grounds, taking into account the deprived offender's 'diminished incentives for compliance' and the fact that 'these diminished incentives reflect a *societal* failure' (2005: 66).

as a mitigating factor. When this occurs, the rationale is unrelated to culpability. Rather, the mitigation is often based on the assumption that the relatively advantaged defendant poses little risk of reoffending, or has good prospects for reform. Sentencers may also assume that the advantaged defendant has more to lose than other defendants, and will therefore suffer more – and be disproportionately punished – if a custodial sentence is passed.

When culpability is brought into the equation, the advantages enjoyed by a defendant can, conversely, be treated as aggravating factors. As some of our respondents suggested, for example, an employed defendant 'should know better' and therefore is more culpable when he commits a crime. However, the notion that advantaged defendants should in practice receive more severe punishment than others is unlikely to attract much support – both because it could lead to accusations of discrimination and disproportionate punishment, and because it would undermine rehabilitative concerns. In short, consideration of the impact of advantage/disadvantage on sentencing brings to light various dilemmas that merit further attention by policymakers and practitioners.

One of our respondents, an experienced judge, described a case that provides an appropriate conclusion to this discussion. It involved a 21-year-old who had set up a company to organize charitable events, in relation to which he was convicted for fraudulent trading. The young man was from a 'good family', and had had a public-school education. He had many references asserting that he was a very good boy who had never been in trouble before. In passing sentence, the judge was struck by the fact that this young man was quite unlike the usual people who stood before him: he was someone who had enjoyed all kinds of advantages, but had not used them. With this in mind, the judge passed a sentence of eight months' custody. The custodial sentence was successfully appealed; in its place, the Court of Appeal imposed a community sentence. In describing the case to us, the judge commented that all this had happened a couple of years ago, but the Appeal Court's decision 'still rankles'.

Mitigation, offence seriousness and guilty pleas

We have shown that sentencers may consider a range of offender-related factors, and make an implicit choice between different sentencing rationales. The context for these decisions is set by the level of seriousness of the offence. Many of our respondents stressed the point that personal mitigation is much more of a consideration when the offence is not very serious, and hence the decision to be made is about the kind of sentence to be passed, rather than the length of a custodial sentence. This is not to deny, however, that personal mitigation can and frequently does impact sentence length – as indeed we found to be the case in many of our observed cases.

There are two elements to the apparently common-sense assumption that the more serious the offence, the less personal mitigation matters. First, it is clear that some mitigating considerations – for example, the desire to avoid disrupting the defendant's employment or family life, or his motivation to undertake drug treatment – only apply if the decision is about sentence type, and particularly custody versus non-custody, rather than sentence length. Second, it appears that some offences are viewed as so serious that the associated personal mitigation is deemed irrelevant – or a very minor concern next to the much greater issue of the crime that has been committed. In the words of Henham, writing specifically about the mitigation of good character, 'It is evident that, where serious offences are concerned, the gravity of the offence is merely regarded as an aggravating factor which automatically extinguishes mitigation to the point where the sentence reflects the ceiling for that offence' (1997: 268). One of our respondents made this point. He was a judge who had recently sentenced a group of young boys who had stabbed someone and broken his jaw. They had pleaded not guilty, but had been convicted at trial. The defendants had previous good character, and 'stacks of testimonials'; their parents clearly considered them 'gentle, loving, church-going boys'. However, the judge commented that 'when you see them strutting their stuff on CCTV' and consider what they have done, the fact that they go to church and are nice to their younger brothers and sisters does not count and should not have an impact on sentence.

Looking at the inverse relationship between the significance of personal mitigation and the seriousness of the offence, one might question the fairness of, essentially, 'rewarding' certain forms of mitigation if the offence is of relatively low seriousness, but discounting that same mitigation if the offence is more serious. A related issue is that the significance of some aspects of personal mitigation may diminish as offenders become more persistent. Evidence of remorse, for example, inevitably carries much more weight for a first-time offender than for a recidivist.

The nature of the defendant's plea also shapes the context within which mitigation is considered by the sentencer. Usually – as our respondents pointed out – personal mitigation plays a greater role if the defendant pleads guilty. This is because many of the important mitigating factors, such as remorse, and a willingness to address the problems underlying the criminal behaviour, cannot logically proceed from a plea of not guilty. One judge commented in interview (adding that this was something he had not thought about before), that the defendant who pleads guilty not only can claim remorse, but also 'engages the court's sympathy much more readily'. Given that the discount in sentence for a guilty plea is to be calculated *after* any relevant mitigating factors have been taken into account,[6] this effectively means that the plea permits a double discount on the sentence – the fairness of which can perhaps be questioned. Some theorists, it should be noted, have argued that the guilty plea discount in itself is problematic, given that it 'provides a powerful incentive to innocent persons to plead guilty' and significantly increases the sentence to be served by a defendant who is wrongly convicted after a trial (Tonry 2002: 97).[7]

The plea of guilty may be on a basis of plea, agreed with the prosecution, that differs markedly from the original charge and thereby not only minimizes the seriousness of the offence but also offers further scope for personal mitigation. (Although the basis of plea can be challenged by a judge who subsequently hears the case, leading to a Newton hearing,[8] this is not often done.) For example, we observed a domestic violence case in which mitigation concerning the defendant's reconciliation with his partner – of which the sentencer evidently took account – would have been more difficult to sustain had the defendant been convicted of the original, more serious charges. One of our respondents voiced his frustration with the fact that a dishonest defendant who pleads guilty to the minimum that the prosecution will accept will be sentenced on that basis and thus rewarded for his dishonesty. In contrast, an honest defendant who admits to the court all he has done, in an effort to 'wipe the slate clean', is likely to receive a harsher sentence.

6 See the guideline on reduction in sentence for guilty pleas, paragraph 2.3 (SGC, 2004).

7 Tonry also notes that sentencing disparities affecting Afro-Caribbean defendants can be exacerbated by sentence discounts, since, as research by Hood (1992) has found, Afro-Caribbean defendants are less likely than others to plead guilty (see also Darbyshire (2000) for a vehement critique of guilty plea discounts).

8 A Newton hearing is a procedure used where the defendant offers a guilty plea, but the two sides offer such conflicting evidence about the facts of the case that a judge sitting alone (that is, without a jury) decides which party is telling the truth.

'What one person thinks about another: sentencing as a subjective process'

Issues of mitigation point to the inevitably subjective element in sentencers' decision making. One respondent, a female judge, talked in vivid terms about the process of making a sentencing decision:

> When the offender comes into court, and you have that first long hard look at him, you can see so much in that first split second. That direct relationship between the Bench and the dock – you can see, are you looking at a fool? Are you looking at someone who doesn't give – anything? Are you looking at someone who's just been knocked about from day one? You can tell a lot.

She went on to say that sentencing can be 'terrifying, because it's a very subjective exercise – there are all these objective parameters put in place, but in the end it's down to what one person thinks about another'.

This intuitive, subjective dimension of sentencing was stressed by a number of our respondents – such as one who said that sentencing is about a 'personal and sometimes emotional response to a particular set of circumstances'. In speaking in these terms, the respondents sometimes made the point that sentencing – like advocacy, it seems – is 'an art, not a science'. (Ashworth (2010: 49) notes the general tendency of the judiciary to describe sentencing in this way.)

Indeed, if subjective factors, such as a defendant's remorse and his motivation to address his problems, are potential mitigators, it is inevitable that sentencing becomes partly a matter of what our respondents referred to as 'experience and feeling' or 'gut feeling rather than careful calculation'. One judge told us that 'if you see a fully grown man in the dock crying' this can be seen as a clue that he will not offend again in the future. Another of our respondents commented, 'I know there are actors in the dock as much as on stage . . . but it's easy to under-estimate the importance of the face-to-face contact you have with the offender – particularly if you take the trouble to make eye contact.' Like several of our other respondents, this judge acknowledged the difficulty of making assessments of character and motivation for the purpose of sentencing. He added, however, that while he might be 'conned' by a defendant pretending to be remorseful, 'I'd rather make that mistake than find a [genuinely] repentant, reformed offender and reject his pleas . . .'

Notwithstanding the general emphasis on subjective, intuitive decision-making, a number of our interviewees (particularly, but not only, recorders and less experienced judges) also stressed that they personally favour a structured approach to sentencing, which they distinguished from the more instinctive approach of others. One judge described sentencing as 'a cold, intellectual analysis of the relevant criteria'. She described how she always makes note of the relevant guideline cases before sentencing, and will adjourn a case if necessary to allow her to review all the applicable legal arguments. She said that she sometimes asks counsel to talk through the factors, as reflected in case law, if required – which can be a 'very painful process'.[9] A newly appointed recorder spoke of how she had developed her own 'template' to guide her through each sentencing decision, although more experienced judges (especially those, unlike her, from criminal law backgrounds) had told her that, when it comes to sentencing, 'You just do it.' She thinks that her approach not only reflects her lack of experience, but also the fact that sentencers receive more training today than they did in the past, and this training tends to emphasize structured decision-making.

Another recorder said that she takes longer than most sentencers to make a decision because she always looks up the relevant legal guidelines and provisions, thinks about the issues carefully and drafts her sentencing remarks in advance. She has sometimes felt under pressure from counsel who complain that she is too slow, but she refuses to sentence 'off the cuff' because it is a complex process which demands time. The judge who described sentencing as a matter of 'what one person thinks about another' also spoke about the need to deal in a structured way with the wide range of factors that come into any sentencing decision. Otherwise, she said, 'It all just swims about in my head.' Hence before going into court she always notes the aggravating and mitigating factors of a case, and the potential sentence. Another judge said that if he is passing sentence after a trial, he likes to allow time for the 'dust to settle' so that he can approach the decision afresh, 'remote from the battle as to guilt'. He added that, nevertheless, 'I don't detract from some people who have the ability to sentence as if from a machine gun.' Perhaps the important point to draw from this is that sentencing decisions can still benefit from structure even when they involve subjective judgement and intuition.

[9] Of all our forty respondents, this was the only one who would not score the mitigating factors in the scenario on death by dangerous driving in our sentencing exercise – saying that she did not wish to provide answers without looking up the relevant guidance.

CONCLUSION

The role of mitigating factors in sentencing decisions has been under-researched, and this empirical study is the first of its sort to have been conducted in England and Wales over the last thirty years. The study has shown how sentencers attach significant importance to mitigating factors, and that personal mitigation plays a large part in the sentencing decision. Its findings serve as a corrective to the belief that judges primarily sentence the offence, and only secondarily take offender characteristics into account.

The Sentencing Guidelines Council, now replaced by the Sentencing Council, issued guidance on mitigation, including personal mitigation, in its definitive guideline on overarching principles (Sentencing Guidelines Council 2004). It is fair to say that this largely restated current practice, and listed types of personal mitigation that should be taken into account. It did not attempt to articulate any broader principles against which claims for mitigation could be tested. The advice on mitigation offered by the Sentencing Advisory Panel (2010) did not go much further, although it extended the list of factors that are routinely cited in mitigation – drawing substantially on the research presented in this chapter. The question remains, therefore, whether the Sentencing Council should set out more fully the sorts of principle and consideration that sentencers should apply when considering issues of mitigation.

We think they should do so. There are clear conflicts in existing practice – for example, one judge may regard an offender's privileged background as an aggravating factor, while another might advance arguments about the greater punitive bite of imprisonment on those who have lost their job and their social status following conviction. In resolving such conflicts, there may be no right answer. But in our view it would be better for the Council to state a position on the issue, and provide reasons for it, than to say nothing. Sentencing should be a process that is transparent to all those involved in it.

Some sentencers – and some academic commentators (e.g., Cooper 2008; Lovegrove 2010) – are opposed to attempts to articulate principles in this way, and about the ambition of structuring sentencers' decision-making in an attempt to achieve greater consistency. Their arguments, at heart, are that cases are much more diverse than is recognized by those without experience of sentencing, and that this diversity makes generalization impossible, even within particular categories of crime. Lovegrove (2010) argues that the complexity and interrelatedness of the factors considered by sentencers, especially in relation to mitigation, mean that the traditional judicial approach – that of 'intuitive synthesis' – will yield better justice than structured guidelines. And, as Cooper put it, the guidelines have yielded welcome predictability, but . . .

> Where the guidelines fail to serve the profession is in those cases which do not fit any standard pattern, and some would argue that these form the majority of criminal cases.
>
> (Cooper 2008: 280)

These are, of course, some of the most central of penological issues. We think it important for the judiciary – and in particular for the Sentencing Council – to articulate the principles against which sentencing decisions should be made. We think that it is also possible for statements to be made about the relative weight to be attached to different principles. It should then be possible to draw on these principles in elaborating guidance for particular categories and sub-categories of offence and offender. Such a process should be applicable to issues of personal mitigation as much as to specific types of offence. Whether this position is defensible turns very much on whether the majority, or only a minority, of criminal cases are indeed ones which, in Cooper's words, 'do not fit any standard pattern'.

APPENDIX: SENTENCING EXERCISE SCENARIOS

Scenario 1: Burglary

Offender	Victim
22-year-old man; several previous shoplifting convictions	76-year old woman
Early guilty plea to burglary	Alone in house

Mitigating factors

(i) Physically and emotionally abusive parents. Childhood mainly in care

(ii) Lives with 20-year-old girlfriend and daughter of 18 months. Shown himself to be a devoted father.

(iii) Dependent on heroin for five years. Now highly motivated to get treatment; started on a drug programme following arrest.

(iv) Functionally illiterate (mother discouraged school attendance) and never had a regular job.
(v) Has had same job for eighteen months. Letter of support from employer confirming prospect of promotion.

Scenario 2: Death by dangerous driving

Offender	Victim
45-year-old woman of previous good character Early guilty plea to causing death by dangerous driving Lost control on motorway, distracted by radio	Her passenger A personal friend

Mitigating factors

(i) Letter from victim's family saying that they forgive the offender and don't want her sent to prison. Are in court to offer support to defendant.
(ii) Defendant married with children aged 8, 10 and 13.
(iii) Defendant intensely remorseful; attempted suicide.

Scenario 3: Assault occasioning actual bodily harm (ABH)

Offender	Victim
35-year-old man of previous good character	Bus driver
Early guilty plea to assault occasioning ABH (Offences against the Person Act 1861, s. 47)	Received facial cut requiring stitches & severe bruising
Dispute over change	

Mitigating factors

(i) Psychiatric report indicates severe clinical depression; offender under treatment at time of offence.
(ii) Defendant's family has attended all court hearings and offers practical, financial and emotional help.
(iii) Defendant has expressed profound regret. Has written to the court to stress his remorse, and has written to the victim and victim's family.

(iv) Defendant is a respected individual with responsible job. Stress of prosecution extremely high.
(v) Offence utterly out of character: a 'moment of madness'. Under stress after break-up with girlfriend.

REFERENCES

Ashworth, A. (2010). *Sentencing and Criminal Justice*, 5th edn. Cambridge University Press.

Cooper, J. (2008). 'The Sentencing Guidelines Council – A Practical Perspective'. *Criminal Law Review*: 277–86.

Darbyshire, P. (2000). 'The Mischief of Plea Bargaining and Sentence Rewards', *Criminal Law Review*: 895–910.

Flood-Page, C. and Mackie, A. (1998). *Sentencing Practice: An Examination of Decisions in Magistrates' Courts and the Crown Court in the mid-1990s*, Home Office Research Study 180. London: Home Office.

Hawkins, K. (2003). 'Order, Rationality and Silence: Some Reflections on Criminal Justice Decision-Making', in L. Gelsthorpe and N. Padfield (eds.), *Exercising Discretion: Decision-Making in the Criminal Justice System and Beyond*. Cullompton: Willan.

Hedderman, C. and Gelsthorpe, L. (eds.) (1997). *Understanding the Sentencing of Women*, Home Office Research Study 170. London: Home Office.

Henham, R. (1997). 'Anglo-American Approaches to Cumulative Sentencing and the Implications for UK Sentencing Policy', *Howard Journal*, 36: 263–83.

Hood, R. (1992). *Race and Sentencing*. Oxford: Clarendon Press.

Hudson, B. (1995). 'Beyond Proportionate Punishment: Difficult Cases and the 1991 Criminal Justice Act', *Crime, Law and Social Change*, 22 (1): 59–78.

Lovegrove, A. (2010). 'The Sentencing Council, the Public's Sense of Justice, and Personal Mitigation', *Criminal Law Review*: 906–23.

Odudu, O. (2003). 'Retributivist Justice in an Unjust Society', *Ratio Juris*, 16 (3): 416–431.

Parker, H., Sumner, M. and Jarvis, G. (1989). *Unmasking the Magistrates: The 'Custody or Not' Decision in Sentencing Young Offenders*. Milton Keynes: Open University Press.

Sentencing Advisory Panel (2010). *Overarching Principles of Sentencing: The Sentencing Advisory Panel's Advice to the Sentencing Guidelines Council*. London: Sentencing Council, available at www.sentencingcouncil.org.uk.

Sentencing Guidelines Council (2004). *Overarching Principles: Seriousness*. London: Sentencing Council, available at www.sentencingcouncil.org.uk.

Shapland, J. (1981). *Between Conviction and Sentence*. London: Routledge & Kegan Paul.

Tonry, M. (2002). 'Setting Sentencing Policy through Guidelines', in S. Rex and M. Tonry (eds.), *Reform and Punishment: The Future of Sentencing*. Cullompton: Willan.

von Hirsch, A. (1993). *Censure and Sanctions*. Oxford University Press.

von Hirsch, A. and Ashworth, A. (2005). *Proportionate Sentencing*. Oxford University Press.

CHAPTER NINE

EXPLORING PUBLIC ATTITUDES TO SENTENCING FACTORS IN ENGLAND AND WALES

Julian V. Roberts and Mike Hough

Our volume now moves away from the theory and practice of mitigation and aggravation at sentencing to consider the views of the community. The next chapter, by Austin Lovegrove, reports findings from a project involving members of the public and judges in Australia. In this chapter we draw on a number of large-scale quantitative surveys to explore public attitudes to the factors that aggravate or mitigate sentence. The purpose of this essay is to describe recent research findings which illuminate public attitudes to a number of common sentencing factors. These results challenge the view that the public are inflexible, punitive sentencers with little interest in mitigation, and shed light on the model of sentencing to which many people subscribe.

CHAPTER OVERVIEW

The chapter begins by discussing some recent survey trends with respect to public attitudes to sentencing. We then discuss some reasons why we might want to know about attitudes to mitigation and aggravation. Some methodological caveats are issued; different approaches to measuring public attitudes will yield very different responses. This discussion is followed by a presentation of some specific research findings from a study involving a large, representative sample of the public in England and Wales. Finally, we draw some conclusions for the sentencing process.

This chapter draws on research reported in Hough et al. (2009), which was conducted with Jessica Jacobson and Nick Moon for the Sentencing Advisory Panel.

Public criticism of sentencing and sentencers

Opinion polls around the world routinely document high levels of public dissatisfaction with sentencing and sentencers. Thus in 2008, three-quarters of the polled public in England and Wales expressed the view that sentencing was too lenient (British Crime Survey 2009). A decade earlier a similar percentage of the public held this view (Hough and Roberts 1998). In fact, over 70 per cent of the polled public has expressed this view on every administration of the survey. Similar trends emerge from surveys exploring this issue in many other jurisdictions (see Roberts and Hough 2005, for a review). These trends suggest that the public are punitive sentencers who may be blind to issues such as an offender's level of culpability or potential for rehabilitation. If this is an accurate reading of public opinion it would imply little public interest in claims for mitigation. Another reading of the polls is that people may not distinguish between different mitigating factors in terms of their relative importance at sentencing. One of the goals of this chapter is to call into question these two characterizations of public opinion.

Polls about sentencing also suggest that there may well be a disagreement between courts and the public about the factors considered at sentencing – that is, the gap between the courts and the community may involve more than a disagreement about severity. Newspaper accounts of sentencing often report sentencers' remarks out of context, leaving the reader with the impression that the judge considered an inappropriate sentencing factor or failed to give sufficient weight to a specific factor. The British Crime Survey has repeatedly demonstrated that the public perceive sentencers to be 'out of touch with what the ordinary person thinks' (e.g., Hough and Roberts 1998; British Crime Survey 2009). This perception of being out of touch may arise from or refer to disagreement about relevant sentencing factors.

The relevance of public views

If a guidelines authority such as the Sentencing Council of England and Wales is concerned with ensuring public comprehension of its guidelines (and public support for sentencing practices) it needs to know what the public thinks about sources of aggravation and mitigation. The necessity is twofold. First, it is important to document where the gap between sentencing practices (or guidelines) and the public is greatest – with a view to correcting any public misperceptions. Consider the guilty plea discount, for example. If the public strongly oppose the discount offered to offenders who plead guilty, a guidelines authority needs to defend this practice publicly by drawing attention to its justifications.

Similarly, courts sometimes impose a mitigated punishment – usually a community order instead of custody – where the victim makes an appeal for leniency, to avoid harming third parties such as dependents of both victim and offender (Ashworth 2010: 387). If the offence is relatively serious, this concession to third-party interests may antagonize the public. No research, however, has systematically explored public reaction to factors which may affect crime seriousness. Simply put, promoting a degree of consistency between courts and community requires an understanding of public opinion. If courts apply sentencing factors considered extra-legal by the public, this will exacerbate criticism of the sentencing process.

Another reason for wanting to know more about public attitudes to sentencing factors is more contentious. Some scholars have argued that public views should influence sentencing practices, including the nature and weight ascribed to sentencing factors. Paul Robinson and his colleagues, for example, argue that a sentencing process which was more closely aligned with community views would be perceived as more legitimate (Robinson 2009). This enhanced perception of legitimacy would, so the theory runs, promote compliance with the law. A sentencing system which considered factors opposed by the public, or which ignored factors regarded by the community as important at sentencing would lack legitimacy, and this, as noted, would undermine efforts to achieve compliance with the law.

It is hard to say to what extent 'outcome justice' as measured by sentencing practice shapes perceptions of the legitimacy of the law. There is a growing body of evidence to suggest that it is *procedural* justice that is the more important factor (cf. Tyler and Huo 2002; Tyler 2007). Hough et al. (2010) argue that criminal justice systems may derive their legitimacy from a combination of procedural justice and 'moral alignment' (following Beetham 1991). If this is correct, judicial systems need to keep sentencing practice broadly in step with public opinion to ensure that the public retain a sense that the courts share their moral values.

Another way of stating this argument is that a sentencing system which attempts to convey censure must by definition reflect community beliefs about the factors which enhance or reduce crime seriousness and culpability. Otherwise the sentencing process would involve the imposition of sanctions which lacked censure; offenders would feel punished but not censured by a legitimate authority. The power of the criminal law to effect moral transformation through legal censure would diminish (Roberts 2009).

This perspective on public opinion therefore ascribes some normative value to community views – a sentencing factor assumes relevance or importance because the community regards it as affecting the seriousness of the offence or the degree of the offender's level of blameworthiness. The dangers of this approach are clear; public views may ascribe importance to a variable that has no deontological value at sentencing, or they may ignore a factor which does carry weight. The idea of 'sentencing by plebiscite' is self-evidently undesirable; yet a sentencing system that loses all resonance with public views is equally unthinkable. Resolving the tension between sentencing practices and community views is beyond the scope of this chapter. The question is complex, and recently a number of publications have addressed the subject (for a selection of views see Roberts 2011). For the present purposes it is sufficient to note the utility of understanding public views – if only to correct misperceptions about sentencing.

Prior research

Public attitudes to sentencing have been the subject of much research since the first empirical study in Britain was published forty years ago (Silvey 1961), but until recently the empirical literature on public attitudes to sentencing factors was relatively sparse. Research is available from other jurisdictions, although it is now quite dated. For example, more than a generation ago the Canadian Sentencing Commission asked a sample of respondents to state whether various factors should always, sometimes or never be taken into account at sentencing. The three most important factors (cited by at least four out of five respondents) were premeditation, the extent of harm to the victim and the offender's criminal history (Roberts 1988, Table 21). The only factor in the survey relating to mitigation sheds little light on the nature of public opinion: 28 per cent of the sample believed that 'personal circumstances – for example employment and educational history' should always be taken into account.

In England and Wales, the Home Office Sentencing Review (2001) explored public reactions to sentencing factors using a representative sample of the public. Respondents were required to rate the importance of a number of mitigating and aggravating factors at sentencing. Unfortunately, the Review's report provides little information about public responses, listing only respondents who cited a given factor as one which 'should have a great deal of influence on a sentence' (ibid., Appendix 5, Fig. 4). The two factors that attracted most support were previous convictions and the likelihood of future convictions – suggesting public interest in the past and the future of the offender, a subject to which we return later in this chapter. Finally, prior to the research reported here, the Sentencing Advisory Panel (SAP)[1] commissioned two public opinion research projects into perceptions of specific offences or offence categories, namely domestic burglary and rape. Both studies asked members of the public about mitigating factors (Russell and Morgan 2001; Clarke et al. 2002). One of these (Clarke et al. 2002) used a small sample (of only sixty-two participants), making it hard to draw conclusions about attitudes in the population. Moreover, since in both studies the context was offence-specific it is hard to generalize the findings to the sentencing process as a whole.

A note on methodology

Research on public opinion assumes many forms, qualitative and quantitative in nature. In our view a number of prerequisites must be fulfilled before a study may be considered scientific. First, the sample should be composed in such a way as to permit generalization to the population from which it is drawn.[2] Research that uses volunteers or special populations such as college students participating for academic credit (as is often the case in North American research) suffers from a clear validity issue: the samples are not representative of the general population. Second, if experimental manipulations are used, researchers should employ random assignment to condition. Third, research should have a qualitative component to flesh out the conclusions derived from responses to a fixed-choice question on a survey, but a representative sample is always necessary. One important advantage of survey research is that the exact research question – and information provided to the respondent – is on record for subsequent readers to evaluate. This is not the case with focus groups – where the reader of any subsequent account does not have access to a record of the discussions – or demonstration projects involving practitioners discussing cases with small samples of

[1] The SAP was one of two statutory bodies responsible for sentencing guidelines, the other being the Sentencing Guidelines Council. Both were replaced in 2010 by the Sentencing Council of England and Wales (www.sentencingcouncil.org.uk).

[2] The tables presented here derive from representative quota samples. Each involved 1,023 face-to-face, in-home interviews, of adults aged 18+ in England and Wales (for further information see Hough et al. 2009).

the public. The research project we draw on here fulfilled these criteria. In our research we explored public opinion by asking survey respondents to identify (i) factors which should enhance crime seriousness or mitigate sentence severity; and (ii) circumstances which might justify a community order in place of custody.

AGGRAVATING FACTORS

To explore reactions to aggravating factors, survey respondents were presented with fifteen different circumstances which conceivably increase the seriousness of the offence, and were asked whether each factor 'always, often, only sometimes, or never makes a crime more serious'. Table 9.1 summarizes responses and reveals clear differentiation among the factors: Some were seen as always or often increasing the gravity of the criminal conduct, while others were seen as being far less important to the determination of crime seriousness. The factor generating the highest degree of consensus among respondents was whether the offender had used a weapon to commit the crime: 88 per cent of respondents stated that this circumstance *always* increased the seriousness of the offence. Other factors that many believed always increased crime seriousness included 'the victim is a child', 'crime was committed in the presence of children', 'the victim was elderly', 'premeditation', 'the offender was the ringleader in the commission of the offence', and 'the offender has previous convictions'. All these circumstances were identified as always increasing crime seriousness by at least 65 per cent of respondents (see Table 9.1).

The pattern of findings seen in Table 9.1 reveals a relatively coherent approach to aggravation on the part of the public. The issues of harm, victim vulnerability and offender culpability are clearly uppermost in people's minds. The discrimination among the factors from the least to the most often likely to increase seriousness suggests a considered approach to considering the grounds for aggravation. Moreover, although limitations on space do not permit a factor-by-factor comparison, the circumstances seen to increase crime seriousness are also those which are identified by the guidelines authorities in England and Wales.[3] In this sense there appears to be a reasonable 'fit' between public opinion and practice as reflected in the current guidelines.

[3] See the definitive guideline *Overarching Principles: Seriousness*, available at www.sentencingcouncil.org.uk.

TABLE 9.1. Public perceptions of factors increasing crime seriousness

	Always increases seriousness %	Often increases seriousness	Sometimes increases seriousness	Makes no difference
1. Weapon was used	88	6	2	4
2. Victim was a child	80	9	5	6
3. Crime was committed in the presence of children	69	16	7	8
4. Victim was elderly	68	16	6	9
5. Offender planned crime	67	16	7	10
6. Offender was the ringleader	66	19	5	10
7. Offender has prior convictions	65	17	6	12
8. Victim attacked for religion/race	58	16	7	19
9. Offender abused a position of trust	53	22	15	10
10. Offender part of gang	52	25	9	14
11. More than one victim	47	25	12	16
12. Victim was a relative or spouse of the offender	40	19	19	20
13. Offender has prior, unrelated convictions	38	22	22	18
14. Offender was drunk at time of crime	24	26	20	29
15. Theft was from the state rather than an individual victim	21	18	22	39

Q: 'In general, some circumstances of a case make the crime more serious. I am going to read you a list of circumstances. Does each always, often, sometimes or never makes a crime more serious. Or does it make no difference?' Source: Hough et al. (2009).

The importance of prior compliance and prior offending

Findings from a number of public opinion studies demonstrate that for the public an important source of information is the offender's history of complying with the law. The absence of any prior offending is perceived to justify a significant reduction in sentence – the first-offender discount. On the other hand, prior offending is also perceived by the public to justify harsher sentencing. The evidence for this comes from several surveys. First, two items on the list of potential aggravating factors relate to previous convictions. 'Offender has previous convictions' was seen as always increasing crime seriousness by fully 65 per cent of the sample. Russell and Morgan (2001) reported a similar pattern in their study of attitudes to sentencing burglary: the second most important aggravating factor cited by their respondents was whether the offender had been convicted of burglaries in the past. These findings demonstrate the link between previous convictions and crime seriousness in the public mind.

Second, another item asked about the relevance of prior, *un*related convictions. It is interesting to note that the percentage of the sample that saw this as always increasing crime seriousness was much lower: 38 per cent. Thus whether the previous offending was related to the current offence is clearly of interest to members of the public when considering the aggravating effect of prior convictions. This is also consistent with section 143(2) of the Criminal Justice Act 2003, which identifies the relationship between the current and previous offending as one of the considerations for a court determining whether the prior offending is relevant for current sentencing purposes.

Additional proof of the impact of prior offending on public perceptions comes from earlier research, in which people are asked to sentence offenders, some of whom are first offenders, some of whom are recidivists. Thus Roberts (2008b) divided a representative sample of the public into three groups. Respondents in each third were asked to sentence the same offender (convicted of assault) but under a different criminal history description: no previous convictions, two previous, related convictions, or five prior convictions. People were asked to choose between imposing custody, a community order or a fine, and those who chose to impose a term of custody were further asked to specify the duration of imprisonment. Even a relatively short criminal record (i.e. two prior convictions) had a dramatic impact on public sentencing preferences. The custody rate rose from 11 per cent for the first offender to 65 per cent for the offender with two prior convictions, and then to 83 per cent for the offender with five priors. To summarize, when sentencing, members of the public ascribe a high level of importance to an offender's criminal antecedents. Whether for reasons of desert or dangerousness, offenders with previous convictions are sentenced more harshly by the public.[4] At

[4] Public opinion research in this and other jurisdictions suggests that the public regard repeat offenders as both more culpable and more likely to reoffend (Roberts 2008b).

the same time, the fact that the offender has not previously been convicted is seen as an important justification for leniency.

MITIGATING FACTORS

Offender-related factors that justify a more lenient sentence

In the light of the generally punitive public response to opinion polls about sentencing one might expect an equally hard line towards appeals for mitigation. As will be seen, this was not the case. Strong support for the use of custody would place great emphasis on the nature of the offence – and its associated level of harm – without leaving room for mitigating factors to reduce the severity of sentence. On the other hand, a more nuanced approach to sentencing would be open to the possibility that even a relatively serious crime may attract a community penalty, if certain mitigating circumstances relating to the offence or the offender are present. How, then, do the public react to claims for mitigation?

Respondents were asked to consider a list of potential mitigating circumstances, and to decide which factors justified a more lenient sentence. Response options were 'in all', 'most', 'only some cases', or 'should never result in a more lenient sentence'. The specific factors were selected to represent a range of forms of personal mitigation. Table 9.2 lists the factors according to the degree to which respondents saw them as justifying leniency at sentencing and reveals considerable support for a wide range of common mitigating circumstances. Thus, for twelve of the thirteen factors, over half the sample believed that it should result in a more lenient sentence in all, most or some cases (Table 9.2). Only one factor – the fact that the offender was only 18 years of age – was rejected as a potential mitigating factor by more than half (57%) of the respondents.

Public responses to this question also demonstrate the strong public support for a degree of individualization at sentencing: the most popular response category was 'should result in a more lenient sentence in *most* cases' – respondents were clearly unwilling to accept a categorical position that the factors listed in Table 9.2 should *always* (or *never*) result in a more lenient sentence. Their reluctance categorically to endorse a factor as mitigating in all cases suggests that the public support a sentencing model which permits courts the discretion to make this determination. This interpretation is supported by findings from surveys which have explored public reaction to mandatory sentencing. That research has shown strong support for judicial discretion rather than mandatory sentences (Roberts 2003).

TABLE 9.2. Public reaction to factors which might result in a more lenient sentence

	Should result in more lenient sentence in all or most cases %	Should result in more lenient sentence in some cases %	Should never result in more lenient sentence %
1. Crime was committed in an emergency	25	53	19
2. No prior convictions	24	52	22
3. Offender played a minor role in crime	24	59	15
4. Offender shows remorse	21	56	23
5. Offender has assisted police	20	57	22
6. Offender receiving medical care	18	57	23
7. Offender 'led on' by others	15	51	33
8. Offender treated for depression at time of offence	15	61	23
9. Offender elderly	14	43	41
10. Offender was abused as a child	14	51	33
11. Offender is the main carer for an elderly relative	13	48	37
12. Offender is a single parent with two children	11	47	41
13. Offender is young (18)	10	33	57

Q: 'Now I would like to ask you about the offender. Some characteristics of the offender may justify a more lenient sentence. I am going to read out some statements about the offender. Should this result in a more lenient sentence in all, most, or some cases? Or should it never result in a more lenient sentence?'
Source: Hough et al. (2009).

Most significant sentencing factors

Five factors were endorsed as justifying the imposition of a more lenient sentence in all or most cases by at least one-fifth of the sample: if the crime was committed in an emergency; if the offender had no prior convictions; if the offender played a minor role in the commission of the crime; if the offender showed remorse for the crime; and if the offender had assisted police in the prosecution of other offenders. Less support emerged for a set of factors related to what might be termed the vulnerability of the offender – whether he had been depressed at the time of the offence, was elderly, was currently receiving medical treatment or was a single parent with children. The public may have reasoned that these circumstances did not reduce the culpability of the offender and therefore should play a lesser role.

Offence v. offender-related sources of mitigation

One clear pattern in Table 9.2 is that the public seem to be more concerned about personal mitigation that is related to the offence rather than the offender. Thus the four factors attracting the highest levels of public support were: committing the crime in an emergency; having a clean record; playing a minor role in the crime; and helping the police. In contrast, claims for mitigation associated with social circumstances or personal characteristics – for example, being a single parent with two children or caring for an elderly relative – attracted a less sympathetic response from the public (see Table 9.2).

Why is there less public support for mitigation based on the offender's individual circumstances? One explanation involves public expectations of the offenders in these circumstances. People may reason that such offenders were aware of their vulnerable status before committing the crime, and this awareness may undermine claims for mitigation. The argument is similar to the 'taxi driver' problem in sentencing. People who depend on their driving licence to earn a living sometimes claim excessive hardship when that licence is suspended following a conviction. Defendants who rely on their driving to earn a living generate little sympathy from the public or the courts when their licences are suspended for driving-related offences – the argument being that they should have been aware of the particular consequences before committing the offence.

There may also be a certain degree of public cynicism with respect to claims for personal mitigation arising from, for example, health problems. It is possible that people recognized that sources of personal mitigation associated with the offender's personal circumstances must be taken on faith to a greater degree than mitigating factors relating to the crime. For example, assisting the victim after the commission of the crime, or voluntarily turning oneself in to the police are easy to document. Whether the offender provided information which assists in the prosecution of other offenders is often acknowledged by the Crown. In contrast, the source of information about the severity of health problems is usually the offender himself.

Table 9.2 also sheds light on the model of sentencing to which members of the public subscribe. Previous research conducted has demonstrated that proportionality in sentencing is fundamental to community views of legal punishment (Darley, Carlsmith and Robinson 2000; Roberts and Gebotys 1989). This suggests that the public may be retributively oriented sentencers, since proportionality constitutes the spine of retributivism. However, the current findings make it clear that the public are not strict retributivists who focus exclusively on the seriousness of the offence and the offender's level of culpability. If they were, there would be no support for factors such as remorse or assisting the criminal justice system. These circumstances are unrelated to crime seriousness or the offender's level of culpability and are therefore deemed extra-legal by retributivist sentencing theorists.

As can be seen in Table 9.2, however, significant majorities of the public view these factors as capable of mitigating the severity of sentence. For example, if the offender was remorseful, 21 per cent of the sample believed that this should result in a more lenient sentence in all or most cases, and a further 56 per cent 'in some cases'. This finding is consistent with research that has explored the impact of remorse on public sentencing decisions. Members of the public tend to be more lenient in their sentences when the offender is remorseful (e.g. Robinson, Smith-Lovin, and Tsoudis 1994).

Factors which may justify imposition of a community order

Another way of exploring public opinion regarding mitigating factors is to ask people to identify factors which might justify the imposition of a community order instead of custody. For this issue we moved away from posing a general question and asked about mitigation in the context of two specific crimes. Respondents were asked to consider one of two serious offences, an assault and a fraud. They were asked whether a number of factors definitely or probably justified the imposition of a community order, or definitely or probably did *not* justify a community order (rather than custody). Since previous research has demonstrated that the public has only limited knowledge of community penalties (Roberts and Hough 2005), before being asked to consider factors that would justify the imposition of a community sentence respondents were given simplified definitions of a community order and a term of custody.[5]

Assault

The case of assault was described in the following terms: 'Imagine a court has decided to impose a prison sentence on an offender convicted of assaulting a member of the public. The victim sustained cuts and severe bruising for which medical treatment was required, and was off work for three weeks.' This case would likely result in custody under current sentencing practices (see Sentencing Council 2010). Respondents were asked to consider six factors – listed in Table 9.3 – which might justify imposition of a community order rather than custody. As can be seen, all these factors were seen as definitely or probably justifying a community order by half the sample or more. Indeed, the high level of community support for these sentencing factors is striking.

The absence of previous convictions emerged as the most powerful justification for a community penalty: 69 per cent of respondents agreed that this definitely or probably justified the imposition of a community penalty. This finding sustains the importance of the offender's criminal history to public views to which reference has already been made. It is noteworthy that first-offender status was regarded as an important justification for a community penalty rather than a term of custody, even though the assault was quite serious in nature. An equally noteworthy finding is that 69 per cent of the sample believed that the victim's wish for a community penalty definitely or probably justified the imposition of a community order rather than custody. This reflects the strong appeal of victims' interests to members of the public. The factor that attracted the lowest level of support as a justification for a community order was the circumstance that the offender was only 18 at the time of the offence. However, even for this factor, respondents were more likely to support than oppose it: 56 per cent believed to some degree that it justified a community penalty while 44 per cent responded that it probably or definitely did not justify imposition of a community order.

[5] The definitions can be found in Hough et al. (2009).

TABLE 9.3. Public reaction to factors which may justify a community order, assault

	Definitely or probably justifies a community order	Definitely or probably does not justify a community order
	%	%
1. Offender has no prior convictions	69	31
2. Victim does not want the offender imprisoned	63	36
3. Victim provoked the offender	69	28
4. Offender is caring for small children	65	34
5. Offender is remorseful and has apologized to the victim	64	36
6. Offender is young (18)	56	44

Q: 'I would like to ask you about circumstances which may make the difference between whether a court imposes a prison sentence or a community order. Imagine a court has decided to impose a prison sentence on an offender convicted of assaulting a member of the public. The victim sustained cuts and severe bruising for which medical treatment was required, and was off work for three weeks. In your view, do you think that this definitely, probably, probably does not, or definitely does not justify the court imposing a community order instead of a prison sentence?' Source: Hough et al. (2009).

Serious fraud

The serious fraud case was described in the following terms: an offender was convicted of a serious fraud against his employer involving £20,000. As with the assault case, this profile of offender would likely result in a term of imprisonment under current sentencing arrangements in England and Wales (Sentencing Guidelines Council 2008). Table 9.4 shows clear parallels with public responses to the case of assault: significant proportions of respondents perceived the factors as justifying the imposition of a community penalty rather than custody. Once again when the victim – in this case the offender's employer – expressed opposition to imprisoning the offender, this was seen by many to justify the imposition of a community order. Almost 70 per cent of the sample believed that this consideration definitely or probably justified the

TABLE 9.4. Public reaction to factors which may justify a community order, fraud

	Definitely or probably justifies a community order	Definitely or probably does not justify a community order
	%	%
1. Employer (victim) does not want the offender imprisoned	69	31
2. Offender is caring for small children	66	33
3. Offender has no prior convictions	64	36
4. Offender is remorseful and has apologized to his employer (the victim)	53	46
5. Offender is young (18)	48	51

Q: 'I would like to ask you about circumstances which may make the difference between whether a court imposes a prison sentence or a community order. Imagine a court has decided to impose a prison sentence on an offender convicted of a serious fraud against his employer valued at £20,000. In your view, do you think that this definitely, probably, probably does not, or definitely does not justify the court imposing a community order instead of a prison sentence?' Source: Hough et al. (2009).

imposition of a community order rather than custody. The fact that the offender was caring for small children was as significant to respondents in this group as those who considered the assault: two-thirds believed that this probably or definitely justified a community penalty.

The offender being only 18 at the time of the crime was the only factor across the two groups of subjects which was seen by a slim majority as *not* justifying the imposition of a community penalty. Why did this factor generate little public support as a source of mitigation (see Table 9.2) or as a justification for a community penalty in fraud or assault cases? This lack of sympathy suggests that the public do not regard a 'young adult' as a different category from 'adult'. Although previous research has demonstrated strong public support for youth as a mitigating factor (Hough and Roberts 2004), the public appear to regard youth-based mitigation as ending at age 18.

COMPARISON BETWEEN MITIGATION AND AGGRAVATION

Is it possible to draw any over-arching conclusions about the relative importance of the two categories of sentencing factors? Mitigating and aggravating factors do not represent different sides of the same coin. Aggravation usually arises out of the circumstances surrounding the commission of the crime – the way it was committed, the vulnerability of the victim and so forth. Few aggravating factors relate to the offender, with previous convictions and custody status (whether the offender was on bail or parole at the time of the offence) being the most obvious examples.

Mitigation, on the other hand, is most likely to arise from the personal circumstances of the offender. Previous research has demonstrated the importance of personal mitigation at sentencing (Jacobson and Hough, this volume). This distinction may mean that making comparisons between mitigating and aggravating factors is a case of comparing apples and oranges. Nevertheless, it is significant that there was greater consensus about the power of the aggravating factors to affect seriousness than about the power of the mitigators. Thus over half the sample believed that ten aggravating factors *always* increased crime seriousness (Table 9.1). None of the mitigating circumstances elicited such a high degree of agreement among respondents. No mitigating factor was viewed by even 10 per cent of the respondents as justifying a more lenient sentence in *all* cases. The most powerful mitigators were 'crime was committed in an emergency' and 'absence of prior convictions'. For the first of these, 7 per cent of the sample believed it mitigated in all cases, and 17 per cent in most cases – for the total of 24 per cent seen in Table 9.4. For the absence of prior convictions, 8 per cent believed that this circumstance should result in a more lenient sentence in all cases and 16 per cent responded 'in most cases' – for the total of 24 per cent seen in Table 9.2.

Even allowing for conceptual differences between the factors, this pattern suggests an asymmetry in public attitudes to sentencing factors: people appear to see aggravating factors to be more central than mitigators to the determination of crime seriousness. Why would this be so? There may be more public scepticism surrounding the claims for personal mitigation: was the offender *really* remorseful? Is he exaggerating the impact of his depression at the time of the offence? Did it really affect his ability to comply with the law? Questions like these may occur to a public which previous research has demonstrated to be very cynical with respect to the sentencing process and defence lawyers who make the appeal for mitigation (see Roberts and Hough 2005).

CONCLUSIONS

Several important conclusions may be drawn from the empirical findings described here. First, these results counter the stereotypical view of the public as punitive sentencers concerned almost exclusively with punishment and focused on the offence at the expense of legally relevant offender characteristics which might justify mitigation. Respondents displayed an interest in the particular circumstances of offences, and avoided making categorical judgements based on crime seriousness alone. Second, although people were more interested in the seriousness of the crime than the offender, the survey revealed that culpability considerations were nevertheless also important. Third, the public clearly favour an individualized model of sentencing, rather than models such as those in use across the United States which employ a two-dimensional sentencing guidelines grid. Under a grid-based guideline scheme with relatively narrow ranges of sentence length there is less scope for courts to tailor the sentence to reflect the individual circumstances of the offender.

Fourth, although a systematic comparison of public views and definitive guidelines in England and Wales was not possible, there was a significant degree of consistency between the two. We see clear parallels between public opinion and current sentencing guidelines. For example, the definitive guidelines issued to date in this jurisdiction are much more likely to contain aggravating factors (see discussion in Roberts 2008a). Moreover, statutory sentencing factors in England and Wales as well as other common law jurisdictions are far more frequently aggravating than mitigating. This suggests that for the public as well as guidelines authorities aggravating factors have a clarity which mitigating factors lack; the significance of the latter depends heavily on personal and case characteristics which cannot be specified in advance by legislatures or guidelines authorities.

Another general conclusion is that the public consider a wider range of factors than strict retributive theorists would incorporate at sentencing. Prior convictions and remorse are two obvious examples. Most retributivists ascribe only a very modest role – or none at all – to an offender's prior convictions, while remorse is viewed as irrelevant because it cannot change the seriousness of the offence or the offender's level of culpability at the time the offence was committed (e.g. von Hirsch 2010). Both these circumstances are seen as being highly relevant by the public in the research reported here. In this sense the public may best be described as *neo-retributivist* sentencers who assign a high level of importance to proportionality at sentencing yet also look beyond the crime and the offender's state of mind at the time of the offence.

The conventional retributive perspective involves the expression of censure – a moral appeal to the offender which is blind to his subsequent response. Thus the repetition of offending is not seen as justifying any harsher punishment, and the expression of remorse is overlooked as a source of mitigation. In contrast, the public generally regard the repeat offender as more blameworthy, and are interested in the reaction of offenders who have been censured. As a number of writers (e.g. Tudor 2008) have recently acknowledged, the expression of remorse carries more significance as a moral indicator than most retributivists are willing to acknowledge. For example, Maslen (2011) argues that an interactive approach to sentencing in which a dialogue exists between the court and the offender represents a superior approach to the unidirectional expression of censure.

Finally, let us return to the question of the degree of correspondence between sentencing practices or guidelines and community views. The findings reported here suggest that the correspondence is relatively close. The differences appear with respect to the weighting of factors, rather than as a fundamental mismatch. However, sentencing guidelines authorities still have a dual function in this area: first, to determine the level of public support for different sentencing factors, after which it will be possible to modify sentencing guidelines – where a sound principle is found in the community reaction; second, to explain to the public why certain factors seen as irrelevant by the community are nevertheless incorporated by the courts at sentencing.

REFERENCES

Ashworth, A. (2010). *Sentencing and Criminal Justice*, 5th edn. Cambridge University Press.

Beetham, D. (1991). *The Legitimation of Power*. Basingstoke: Palgrave Macmillan.

British Crime Survey (2009), unpublished analysis available from the authors.

Clarke, A., Moran-Ellis, J. and Sleney, J. (2002). *Attitudes to Date Rape and Relationship Rape: A Qualitative Study*. London: Sentencing Advisory Panel.

Darley, J., Carlsmith, K., and Robinson, P. (2000). 'Incapacitation and Just Deserts as Motives for Punishment', *Law and Human Behavior*, 24: 659–83.

Home Office (2001). *Making Punishments Work*. London: Home Office.

Hough, M. and Roberts, J. V. (1998). *Attitudes to Punishment: Findings from the British Crime Survey*, Home Office Research Study No. 179. London: Home Office.

(2004). *Youth Crime and Youth Justice: Public Opinion in England and Wales*. Bristol: The Policy Press.

Hough, M., Jackson, J., Bradford, B., Myhill, A. and Quinton, P. (2010). 'Procedural Justice, Trust, and Institutional Legitimacy', *Policing*, 4: 203–10.

Hough, M., Roberts, J. V., Jacobson, J., Steele, N. and Moon, N. (2009). *Determining Crime Seriousness and the Custody Threshold: An Analysis of the Public's View*, available at www.sentencingcouncil.org.uk.

Jacobson, J. and Hough, M. (2007). *Mitigation: The Role of Personal Factors at Sentencing*. London: Prison Reform Trust.

Maslen, H. (2011). 'Remorse and Punishment: Justifying Mitigation within Retributive Theory', unpublished ms., Centre of Criminology, University of Oxford.

Roberts, J. V. (1988). *Public Opinion and Sentencing*. Ottawa: Department of Justice Canada.

(2003). 'Public Opinion and Mandatory Sentences of Imprisonment: A Review of International Findings', *Criminal Justice and Behavior*, 20: 1–26.

(2008a). 'Aggravating and Mitigating Factors at Sentencing: Towards Greater Consistency of Application', *Criminal Law Review*: 264–76.

(2008b). 'Punishing Persistence: Explaining the Enduring Appeal of the Recidivist Sentencing Premium', *British Journal of Criminology*, 48: 468–81.

(2009). 'Explaining the Enduring Appeal of the Recidivist Sentencing Premium: The Role of Blameworthiness', in A. von Hirsch, A. Ashworth and J. V. Roberts (eds.), *Principled Sentencing*, 3rd edn. Oxford: Hart Publishing.

(2011). 'Community Views of Sentencing: Intuitive and Principled Responses to Offending', in M. Tonry (ed.), *Punishment Futures*. Oxford University Press.

Roberts, J. V., and Gebotys, R. (1989). 'The Purposes of Sentencing: Public Support for Competing Aims', *Behavioural Sciences and the Law*, 7: 387–402.

Roberts, J. V., and Hough, M. (2005). *Understanding Public Attitudes to Criminal Justice*. Maidenhead: Open University Press.

Robinson, P. (2009). 'Empirical Desert', in P. Robinson, S. Garvey and K. Ferzan (eds.), *Criminal Law Conversations*. Oxford University Press.

Robinson, D. T., Smith-Lovin, L. and Tsoudis, O. (1994). 'Heinous Crime or Unfortunate Accident? The Effects of Remorse on Responses to Mock Criminal Confessions', *Social Forces*, 73: 175–90.

Russell, N. and Morgan, R. (2001). *Sentencing of Domestic Burglary*. London: Sentencing Council, available at www.sentencingcouncil.org.uk.

Sentencing Council (2010). *Assault and Other Offences against the Person: Definitive Guidelines*, available at www.sentencingcouncil.org.uk.

Sentencing Guidelines Council (2008). *Assault and Other Offences against the Person*, available at http://www.sentencingcouncil.org.uk/guidelines/guidelines-to-download.htm

Silvey, J. (1961). 'The Criminal Law and Public Opinion', *Criminal Law Review*: 349–58.

Tudor, S. (2008). 'Why Should Remorse Be a Mitigating Factor in Sentencing?', *Criminal Law and Philosophy*, 2: 241–57.

Tyler, T. R. (2007). *Legitimacy and Criminal Justice*. New York: Russell Sage Foundation.

Tyler, T. R., and Huo, Y. J. (2002). *Trust in the Law: Encouraging Public Cooperation with the Police and Courts*. New York: Russell Sage Foundation.

von Hirsch, A. (2010). 'Proportionality and Progressive Loss of Mitigation: Further Reflections', in J. V. Roberts and A. von Hirsch (eds.), *The Role of Previous Convictions at Sentencing: Theoretical and Applied Perspectives*. Oxford: Hart Publishing.

CHAPTER TEN

THE PERNICIOUS IMPACT OF PERCEIVED PUBLIC OPINION ON SENTENCING: FINDINGS FROM AN EMPIRICAL STUDY OF THE PUBLIC'S APPROACH TO PERSONAL MITIGATION

Austin Lovegrove

Sentencing has become harsher in recent times, particularly in the more serious cases. One cause of this shift has been public opinion. This holds true for countries around the world, including Australia and Britain. This influence has several strands and is both direct and indirect. Judges in Australia and in England and Wales have come to regard the public as being more punitive than the courts, and as wanting sentences to reflect better the seriousness of the offending and less the interests of the offender. As a consequence, in many types of case, the courts are now imposing tougher sentences. In England and Wales public opinion has had a second and indirect influence. There judges must fashion their sentences around sentencing guidelines, which are structured in terms of offence seriousness and which generally make little allowance for offenders by way of personal mitigation. The effect of these guidelines has been to consolidate the now diminished role of personal mitigation. Public opinion has played its part here in two ways. Of particular importance has been the influence on these guidelines of proportionality theory, said by von Hirsch to reflect common-sense justice (i.e. the public's sense of justice). This theory requires commensurability between offence seriousness and sentence severity, a requirement interpreted quite strictly by the framers of the guidelines. Of secondary importance, the framers of the guidelines have commissioned research on public opinion to inform their judgements about factors relevant to sentence.

One aim of this chapter is to offer an overview of these influences of public opinion on sentencing. In respect of this, the question arises, are the readings of public opinion inherent in these influences well founded?

If they are, then we should observe little support from the public for personal mitigation at sentencing. Thus a second aim of this chapter is to test this hypothesis. This is done by way of an empirical study of the public's approach to personal mitigation, conducted by the author in Victoria, Australia. Members of the public imposed sentences in four real cases and gave reasons for their sentences. This analysis carries implications for how research should be conducted in this area. Indeed, it appears that much of the research on which this change was based was not suited to the phenomenon of personal mitigation. If this is true, then the offender has been falsely counted out of sentencing.

CHAPTER OVERVIEW

In the light of this, the present chapter starts with a description of personal mitigation in traditional sentencing and then analyses the move to harsher sentencing, and the direct and indirect influences of public opinion. This sets the scene for a brief description of the Victorian study, an overview of the findings and a discussion of the implications of the research.

TRADITIONAL JUDICIAL SENTENCING

Less than twenty years ago, in Australia and in other common law jurisdictions such as England and Wales, serious consideration was given to the interests of the offender in sentencing decisions. The judicial instinct was to sentence offenders for committing offences, rather than to adopt a more offence-based approach. Thus, in many cases, even though the offence was serious, judges would regard the circumstances of the offender as justifying significant mitigation on what would be a proper sentence considering the facts of the offence alone. In this, numerous matters in mitigation were of potential relevance. The seriousness of the offence was always important – indeed would sometimes largely override the offender's claim to mitigation – but it was far from being all important.

In judicial sentencing, personal mitigation, as the term is used here, includes offender factors mitigating culpability and matters personal to the offender. It is manifest in three ways. Sometimes an offender is regarded as less than fully culpable for the offence; drunkenness and immaturity may be cited in this respect. In some cases the court sees an offender whose rehabilitation is of importance and a real possibility, in the light of his employment status and response to the offence. Then there are the offenders whose personal circumstances – perhaps their ill health – mean that the otherwise proper punishment would fall unusually harshly on them. Recognizing this represents humanity in sentencing. These matters are assessed by way of individual factors, as illustrated, but also globally. Thus the offender might be seen as being more decent than the bald facts of the offence would suggest, or be regarded as deserving rehabilitation (for empirical studies see Shapland 1981; Lovegrove 1989; Jacobson and Hough 2007).

HARSHER SENTENCING AND PUBLIC OPINION

This traditional approach to judicial sentencing changed in the early to mid 1990s (see generally Roberts et al. 2003). Sentencing became noticeably more severe by way of the more frequent use, and longer terms, of imprisonment, particularly for the more serious offences (for Victoria see Freiberg and Ross 1999; for England and Wales, Millie et al. 2003). The facts of the offence are now more important; less weight is given to personal mitigation.

Unequivocal evidence for this lessening of the importance of personal mitigation is not available. Nevertheless, there are three lines of circumstantial evidence. First, as a matter of logic, harsher sentences necessarily involve less personal mitigation, since mitigation is expressed by way of leniency. Second, appellate courts have taken an increasingly harder line on personal mitigation. For example, in the New South Wales Court of Appeal, Spigelman CJ called for higher sentences for robbery. To this end, he determined that drug addiction – when it is a motive for money – was no longer to be, of itself, mitigating (*R* v. *Henry* 1999). Third, in England and Wales, the Sentencing Council's sentencing guidelines reflect a policy in which personal mitigation is far less important than offence seriousness.[1] This is evident in the general guidance (Sentencing Guidelines Council 2004) and in the offence-specific guidance (see for example, Sentencing Guidelines Council 2006; 2008a, for robbery and assault, respectively). In the general guidance, few mitigating offender factors are listed, and these are far outnumbered by the aggravating factors. And although a lesser sentence may be imposed in

[1] Prior to 2010, sentencing guidelines were issued by the Sentencing Guidelines Council in conjunction with the Sentencing Advisory Panel. In 2010 these two bodies were replaced by a single statutory authority, the Sentencing Council for England and Wales (see Ashworth (2010) for further information).

the interests of an offender's treatment, this concession is limited to cases whose seriousness places them near or just above the custody threshold.[2]

Moreover, in the offence-specific guidance, there is little room for personal mitigation to carry much weight. Seriousness is defined by harm and culpability (the latter as it is closely related to the facts of the offence), and frames sanction severity. For each category or sub-category of offence, there are only a few levels of seriousness, and for each level the presumptive sentencing range is comparatively narrow. Moreover, although departures for mitigating offender factors are permitted, the grounds must be exceptional. As Cooper (2008) has observed, the guidelines are not conducive to much weight being given to personal mitigation. The contrast between this and the traditional approach to mitigation, in which numerous factors are of potential relevance and which in individual cases not infrequently combine to considerable effect, could not be starker. Let it be clear, humanity in sentencing remains today, as is evident in the observations of senior judges (for Victoria see Warren 2006; for England and Wales, Sir Igor Judge 2005), but this humanity is not as strong or certain or as widely in evidence.

Public opinion and law and order

Public opinion has surely played a direct and significant role in this change. This was Millie et al.'s (2003) conclusion based on their analysis of the striking increase in the prison population in England and Wales. In Australia, change has come largely by way of the politicization of sentencing. In this, the 'get tough' lobby, with the help of the tabloid media, has largely controlled the law-and-order debate. Thus politicians and the public have pressured the judiciary to impose tougher sentences – ones thought better to reflect the seriousness of offences and to offer better protection – and politicians also have enacted provisions giving effect to this, toughening aspects of sentencing law and curtailing judicial discretion (see, e.g., Hogg and Brown 1998). Similar processes have been at work in England and Wales (Tonry 2003). Indeed, in respect of public opinion, appellate courts in Australia and in England and Wales have acknowledged the need for tougher sentences in the light of what they have perceived to be significant disquiet – perhaps frustration – in the community over aspects of sentencing practice (see Spigelman CJ, in *R* v. *Jurisic* 1998, citing with approval Lord Bingham).

[2] The former Sentencing Advisory Panel's proposed reforms of the general guidance pay more attention to personal mitigation, but the disparity between aggravation and mitigation remains significant (Sentencing Advisory Panel 2010).

These readings of the community's views appear to be based largely on public expressions of opinion, and simplistic public opinion surveys, the latter routinely revealing that around four-fifths of the public in Australia and Britain, and indeed in other countries, believe that sentencing is too lenient (Roberts et al. 2003). There is a problem with this. Public opinion surveys measure opinions. However, sentencing policy should not be driven by the public's opinion about sentencing, but be guided by their sense of justice. Now, if the judiciary's reading of the public's mood is indeed correct, research should reveal a public who are as least as harsh in their sentencing as the judiciary and who generally place little importance on personal mitigation at sentencing. This would be manifest, in the empirical study to be reported here, in two ways. First, the sentences imposed by the public for the cases in this study – recall they are real cases – should be as least as harsh as the actual sentences imposed by the courts. Second, when the public justify their sentences, they should make few appeals to personal mitigation. This, of course, raises the question how best to research the public's approach to personal mitigation. To this matter we shall return shortly.

Public opinion and sentencing guidelines

In England and Wales, public opinion has influenced sentencing by way of a second, indirect path. It is through the Sentencing Council and its sentencing guidelines. This guidance, as has been explained, is largely structured around the facts of the offence, and affords little room for personal mitigation.[3] What is relevant for present purposes are the sources of the structure and content of the guidance: namely von Hirsch's theory of proportionality and research on public opinion commissioned by the former Sentencing Advisory Panel (Wasik 2008). The relevance of public opinion to the former is real but not patent. It arises thus. Proportionality theory represents a sophisticated intellectual framework developed from what von Hirsch believes is common-sense justice (von Hirsch and Ashworth 2005). Surely this means the public's sense of justice; this is how it is seen to be relevant here.

Roberts[4] has observed that there is no evidence that the guidelines, and hence public opinion by way of the guidelines, have led directly to harsher sentencing. This notwithstanding, I suggest that the guidelines

[3] The guidelines almost certainly do more than just not facilitate individualization – they will tend to inhibit the practice.

[4] Personal communication.

have had a subtle but nonetheless important effect on sentencing. With respect to personal mitigation, they have made explicit and confirmed policies and practices which had already arisen from the judiciary's (and the legislature's) response to perceived public opinion. What is important is that the guidelines' theoretical and empirical underpinnings lend these policies and practices intellectual and academic respectability. Thus it is necessary to examine how proportionality theory understands personal mitigation, and what research on public opinion has concluded about the public's approach to personal mitigation. For only then it is possible to test whether this understanding and these findings, and the guidelines' consequent representation of them, do in fact reflect the public's sense of personal mitigation. Each is considered in turn.

Proportionality and the guidelines

In von Hirsch's theory of proportionality, the severity of the punishment must be commensurate with the seriousness of the offence, the latter comprising harm and culpability (von Hirsch and Ashworth 2005). In this view of just punishment, proportionality is primordial. As a consequence, the scope for personal mitigation is necessarily limited, for the following reasons.

1. Personal mitigation in the theory is restricted to offender factors directly and closely related to culpability for the offending, the censuring function of punishment, and what would amount to inhumane consequences of the sanction for the offender. Relevant matters are considered individually and largely independently of all the circumstances of the case.
2. Human weakness as an excuse for not being deterred by the threat of censure is generally not open to offenders as a source of mitigation.
3. In most cases, the sum of an offender's mitigation will not justify a sanction below or much below the proportionate range of sentence.
4. In the light of this, it makes no sense for there to be more than a handful of factors relevant in any individual case. Thus, factor relevance must be interpreted parsimoniously. It will be confined largely to factors which are not common features of cases, represent exceptional or patent circumstances, and (on this ground, too) directly and closely related to culpability and the offender's experience of the sanction.

The Sentencing Council's guidelines are intended broadly to represent the operationalization of proportionality (see Wasik 2008). Nevertheless, there are differences between the two, these representing a relaxation of strict proportionality theory. Instances are to be found in the general guidance (e.g. general remorse as relevant) (see Sentencing Guidelines Council 2004) and, particularly, in the former Sentencing Advisory Panel's proposed reforms (e.g. extreme disadvantage as mitigating culpability) (see Sentencing Advisory Panel 2010). Moreover, as discussed in the text above, rehabilitation – not part of proportionality theory – is treated as potentially relevant in restricted circumstances under the guidelines (Sentencing Guidelines Council 2004; Sentencing Advisory Panel 2010). Nonetheless, the influence of proportionality theory in the guidelines is patent and strong. The question remains: do the sentencing guidelines, influenced as they are by proportionality theory, represent the public's sense of justice? If they do, then, first, in the sentences imposed by the public and in their justifications for them, the expression of personal mitigation should appear as restricted as it is in proportionality theory; second, the factors which would be deemed relevant for the six offenders under the guidelines should correspond to those cited in the public's justifications for their sentences.

Research and the guidelines

There needs to be careful thought about how to research the public's understanding of personal mitigation. For this purpose, consider the conditions under which judges sentence offenders. Case information comes by way of a detailed account of the circumstances of the offence, together with the past and present behaviour and circumstances of the offender. It is of sufficient detail to paint a vivid picture of the offender as a whole person. Moreover, the offender appears as someone whose future lies in their own hands. And all this is done with a well-thought-out sense of justice – the principles and matters potentially relevant to just punishment, together with experience in applying these in individual cases. Is not the implication clear? Research on the public's understanding of personal mitigation should, as far as is practicable, capture the reality of the sentencing hearing.

In fact, the present study attempted this. Thus real cases were used. The circumstances of each offence and offender were presented as a detailed narrative and biography, and the offender was given a name. Also included were the effects of the crime on the victim/s. As well, in order to encourage the participants to feel that their responses mattered, each case was presented by the sentencing judge, and the exercise was introduced as trialling a process of consultation. Prior to the actual sentencing exercise, the author led a session in which the participants were given an opportunity to think about what matters might be, and how together they might be, of potential relevance to just sentencing. The purpose of this was to help the participants develop their own senses of justice. They were also given information about the sanctions available to the courts. In the light of this, consider the following research studies.

Of particular significance is the study by Hough, Roberts and Jacobson (2009) of matters regarded by the public in England and Wales as relevant to sentence. It was commissioned by the former Sentencing Advisory Panel. Roberts et al. (2009), drawing on the results of this study, concluded that there is no 'fundamental mismatch' between the guidelines and the public's sense of justice; what differences there are, they claim, are 'at the margin' (p.781). In this largely quantitative study, the participants imposed sentences for cases and made judgements about factors by considering their relevance, alone and in the context of cases. The core case descriptions were quite brief, but were elaborated by the addition of single, or combinations of several, factors taken from a list. The offending involved violence and dishonesty, around and just above the custody cusp. The sample was large and cross-sectional. Data collection was primarily by way of 'in-home' interviews. There was also a focus groups component. The seriousness of the offence was found to be important, and generally more important than personal mitigation, but the effects of personal mitigation on sentence were sometimes quite significant. The range of factors was limited, but did relate to culpability, rehabilitation and mercy. In the multivariate analysis, there was no evidence of interaction among factors. However, in the limited qualitative analysis, some of the judgements were individualized and in this sense contextual and interactive. Nevertheless, the focus of this study was the relevance of individual factors.

The study by Hough et al. is sophisticated, but does not satisfy the criteria set out above as being necessary to the proper study of the public's approach to personal mitigation. Indeed, because of this, their picture of personal mitigation – its scope, character and importance – may be incomplete and inadequate for the purpose of answering the questions posed here. There have been other studies, but they have adopted less than adequate methodological approaches. For example, in both Clarke, Moran-Ellis and Sleney's (2002) study on rape and Jacoby and Cullen's (1999) National Punishment Survey in the United States, the offender was found to play little part in the sentencing decision. This is hardly surprising, as the offender played little part in these studies. In the former study, for example, the case vignettes used to facilitate the participants' thinking were brief and had no offender factors; moreover, prompting appeared to be used for offence factors, but not for personal mitigation, age aside. In the latter study, for example, offender factors were few and presented with virtually no context.

THE VICTORIAN STUDY

The purpose of this study, conducted between 2004 and 2006, was to investigate whether what is assumed about the public's approach to personal mitigation by the judiciary and in the sentencing guidelines (including their theoretical underpinning) is in fact well founded (for a full account of the various aspects of this research, see Lovegrove 2007; 2010a; 2010b; 2011).

There were four real cases involving six offenders. In each of the cases the offender/s had strong traditional claims to personal mitigation. The offence facts were, in summary,

- An armed robbery of A$1,100, at a small gambling venue, at night. The offender, 31, had a very extensive record of dishonesty, but not of violence.
- Multiple rapes at knifepoint of a young woman, at night, by a neighbour who broke into her home. This 24-year-old male had priors for car theft, but was not regarded as antisocial.
- Multiple serious stabbings of two young men by a young adult male carrying a knife, and the violent punching of a young woman by his 18-year-old girlfriend, who was also involved in one of the stabbings. The male, who was 21 years old, had served a term in a youth training centre, as a result of a previous stabbing; the female had priors, but not for violence.
- The theft of about A$1,000,000 worth of goods (cigarettes) from a company by two senior employees, over an extended period of time. The male organized the operation; the woman, although a key player, acted under his direction and did not benefit greatly from the crime. Both offenders were otherwise of good character.

The study was conducted at thirty-two different workplaces across Melbourne and around Victoria during working hours. People participated in small groups, each dealing with a single case. In total the sample comprised 471 participants, there being at least 115 for each case.

Participants represented a balanced cross section in respect of factors such as the nature of the work (white-collar/manual) and gender. Each case took about fifty minutes to present; this was undertaken by the sentencing judge. As part of the presentation the four judges considered in general terms the relevance of sentencing principles in the context of each case, and information was given on current sentencing practice. Once each of the participants had written down his or her sentence(s) for the case, the judge announced the actual sentence(s). Then participants, led by the author, were invited to comment on and discuss in their group the judge's sentence. Some participants offered no comments.

Potential threats to validity

There is in this method the possibility of two biases: first, that of privileging the interests of the offender over the seriousness of the offence and the harm to the victim; and, second, of favouring the judge's view of the case over what might be the contrary views of the participants. Thus measures were taken to guard against these potential biases; the following examples illustrate this. In the author's account of sentencing policy, a similar emphasis was placed on matters pointing to severity and to leniency. Moreover, the judges' presentations of the facts of the cases were very detailed, including matters not obviously relevant, thus permitting participants to draw their own conclusions. In any case, the judges did not argue for their approach to the case, but set out the matters thought by them to be potentially aggravating or mitigating or to be not relevant, with no indication of where the balance was struck or how this related to the sentence. In fact, transcripts of the judges' sentences show that much was made of the seriousness of the offending and the need for deterrence. Additionally, participants were told that, since the exercise represented consultation, what was wanted were their own well-thought-out views.

Findings of the Victorian study

Law and order

The question here is whether, having regard to the participants' sentencing data, the judges' reading of public opinion and their consequent toughening of sentencing policy actually reflects the public's sense of justice. Recall that there are two aspects of this: the sentences actually imposed by the participants on the six offenders in the study; and the reasons offered by the participants in support of their sentences.

The sentences

The participants' median sentences (non-parole periods) for the four males in the rape, assault, armed robbery and the theft were, respectively, 4.9, 3.2, 1.9 and 2.0 years. By way of comparison, the corresponding sentences of the judges for these offenders were 6.0, 3.0, 4.5 and 3.5 years. Thus, for three of these offenders, the judges were considerably harsher than the participants; for the fourth (assault), the judge was more lenient, but only marginally. For the two female offenders, the participants' median sentences were: for the theft, a suspended sentence of imprisonment, together with six months' community work (or a modest fine); for the assault, two years' custody in youth training. The judges' sentences for the females were similar to those of the participants: a suspended sentence together with an A$5,000 fine for one (theft), and twenty months' youth training in custody for the other (assault). These conclusions, being based on medians, represent the balance of the participants' sentencing practices.

The expectation was that, if the courts' reading of public opinion was correct, the public's sentencing practices would be found to be at least as harsh as those of the judges. In fact, the finding here is to the contrary. For the four male offenders, there was a strong tendency for the participants' median sentences to be significantly less harsh than the sentences of the judges. And for the two female offenders, although the participants were no less harsh than the judges, the sentences of both were, in view of the seriousness of the offending, very lenient and patently reflected mitigation.

Sentencing justifications

What sorts of reasons were advanced by the participants in support of leniency? Across the six offenders numerous factors were cited, and all could be placed in one of the judicial categories of culpability, rehabilitation or mercy. Consider the following examples of factors relating to culpability. The female in the assault was seen as less than fully culpable, in part because she suffered from a personality disorder arising from her troubled background. Drug addiction contributed to this young woman's maladjustment, but this was not treated as her fault; it was said that in view of her background, her poor education and her youth, she would not have appreciated the potential dangers of drug abuse. And the drunkenness of the male in the assault was seen as mitigating. This is because he was, as people can be, thoughtless about the effects of alcohol on his behaviour. Rehabilitation, too, was a matter exercising participants' minds. They looked for and found evidence of favourable rehabilitation prospects in the offenders' circumstances. Four of these offenders – the rapist, the armed robber and the two in the assault – were vulnerable to serious reoffending as a result of personality problems. Participants discerned this and wanted treatment for them. Imprisonment was seen as deleterious to this – indeed, to an offender's rehabilitation independent of the need for treatment. In regard to the latter, more general considerations, such as the disruption of the socializing influences of family, were important to them. On this basis, despite the seriousness of the offending, there was a preference for shorter rather than longer terms of imprisonment for these offenders.

Then there is mercy. This was for the participants a component of mitigation. It took the form of compassion for the offender and the offender's family. For example, for the female in the theft there was the extreme dependence of her two chronically sick children on her as their sole carer. For the armed robber, there was his having to spend his time in prison under the harshness of protective custody.[5]

The expectation was that, if the courts' reading of public opinion was correct, the participants in justifying their sentences would make few appeals to personal mitigation. In fact, to the contrary, many of the participants were prepared to make allowance, in respect of culpability, for human weakness and challenging personal circumstances. As well, the community was regarded as having a responsibility to provide treatment for those with personal problems relating to their offending, and lesser sentences were seen as warranted to facilitate these measures. Indeed, the rehabilitation of offenders in general was seen as important. Finally, for the participants, penal pain was not something to be dismissed lightly. The difference between this approach and the law-and-order perspective lies in a preparedness to see offenders as fellow human beings, rather than as, in effect, different and less (i.e., as 'other'; see Garland 2001).

The question arises whether these conclusions are an artefact of the method. The weight of argument as well as the empirical evidence is against this. Thus, for example, the participants' discussions were often lively, and their comments were anything but a reflection of the judges' views about the potential relevance of the various case factors. Moreover,

[5] Some participants found much aggravation in the circumstances of the offenders and their offending. But harshness was not predominant in the participants' opinions, as is shown by their median sentences in comparison with the judges' sentences.

the participants' sentencing practices compared with those of the judges' are indicative of the former's justifications for leniency actually carrying significant weight. This issue aside, there is the matter of the generalizability of these findings. Clearly, this study needs to be replicated with other types of offence and offender.

Sentencing guidelines and proportionality theory

The question here is whether the Sentencing Council's guidelines, influenced largely as they are by proportionality theory, represent the public's sense of justice. This is analysed in two ways. First, there is the matter of whether, having regard to the participants' sentences and reasons for their sentences, proportionality theory represents commonsense justice. Second, there is the matter of whether, for the six offenders in the study, the factors which would be identified as mitigating under the guidelines correspond to those cited by the participants. In regard to the first of these two matters, proportionality theory – recall – was found as a matter of principle to restrict personal mitigation in four ways. The approach of proportionality is now compared with the participants' take on personal mitigation, in respect of each of these.

1. For the participants, personal mitigation was not limited, as it is in proportionality theory, to matters closely related to culpability, the censuring function and the inhumane consequences of the sanction for the offender. For them, it did include the first and last of these, but went further. Consider first the concept of culpability. For the participants, culpability included factors related to the offender's commission of the offence as well as those underlying the offending (related to the offender's circumstances). However, it also included the offender's response to the offence and the offender's character. Thus, in the rape, the offender should be treated as less than fully culpable because, for example, he used the knife as a threat, not to inflict actual harm, was of low intellectual capacity, expressed remorse to the victim immediately after the offence, and had no history of violence. Similarly, the armed robber had no intention of being violent (his gun was not loaded), he knew no other life (he lacked life skills), he was remorseful, and previously had given assistance to the police at great risk to himself. The last two factors for each offender, significantly, are no more than indirectly related to the offending, yet they were still seen by the participants as relevant to culpability.

The relevance of these indirect factors arises because the participants not only assessed culpability by way of these individual factors, but more globally. Thus the rapist was seen as a 'poor silly man'. These assessments patently rely not only on the factors more or less directly related to the offending, but also on those no more than indirectly related. Indeed, for the rapist, this assessment appeared to rely in addition on a factor apparently unrelated to the offending (namely, low self-esteem). Similarly, the armed robber was a 'loser'. In this way, factors remote from the offending are integral to the assessment of lesser culpability: the offender being seen as not as bad as would appear on the basis of the facts of the offence considered alone. This is part of what is meant by the expression 'determining a sentence in all the circumstances of the case'. This analysis contrasts with proportionality theory, which is structured around individual factors directly and closely related to culpability.

Next, consider rehabilitation. An offender's need for treatment and, indeed, general rehabilitation prospects were important to the participants, and less severe sentences were seen as being warranted on these grounds, even though the offending was serious. In contrast, rehabilitation is not part of proportionality. Treatment is allowed under the theory, as long as it is part of a proportionate sentence. There is a second difference between the participants and proportionality. The participants, in considering matters relevant to rehabilitation, relied on factors, such as family support and the reduced chances of gaining employment after custody, which are not consistent with proportionality. Finally, in regard to personal mitigation, there is mercy. For the participants this was a matter of concern. It was thought about broadly, and included not only the offender but also the offender's family. Consistent with this, the participants cited the offender's ruined life (male in the theft) and the fate of a new business (the family of the male in the theft). These would not count under proportionality theory; the former would be seen as remote from, and the latter as unrelated to, the impact of the sanction.

2. Proportionality theory does not accept excuses reflecting human weakness. It does permit consideration of factors patently related to an offender's capacity to respond to the threat of censure, such as immaturity. In comparison, the participants went much further in their mitigation of culpability, as has been illustrated above (see also below).

3. When the participants cited factors as mitigating, these were no mere words. For five of the six offenders, these factors had in their totality a substantial mitigating impact on what would be regarded as the proportionate sentence. This can be discerned from an analysis of the

participants' median sentences (see above). No more than several observations for illustrative purposes (compared with a detailed analysis) will be made about this here. Consider the male in the theft case. This theft, although serious, is the least serious of these categories of offence. Moreover, this offender was seen as having few claims to mitigation. Thus his sentence of two years can be assumed to be within the participants' proportionate range. In comparison, the sentence for the armed robber (1.9 years), especially in the light of his appalling record, seems substantially disproportionate and attributable to his considerable personal mitigation. A difference like this would not be expected if proportionality were largely controlling. And the sentence for the female in the theft (effectively, just community service) demonstrates how personal mitigation, when compelling, may overwhelm proportionality, even when the offending is serious. Let it be clear: this is not to say that for the participants proportionality was not important. It was, as the substantial sentences they imposed on the four male offenders attest. But it was far from all important.

4. Personal mitigation must be interpreted parsimoniously when proportionality is controlling. But parsimonious the participants were not. This manifested itself in a number of ways. One was that the participants' threshold for invoking mitigation was low. They demonstrated a high degree of understanding and sensibility. Thus a factor was not required to be exceptional to be deemed relevant; its relatedness could be somewhat remote and its appearance subtle. In respect of culpability, there were many examples of this. For the female in the theft, extricating herself from the tightly knit criminal group would have been difficult, it was said. For the armed robber, his culpability was seen as less because his lack of life skills left him vulnerable to offending. And in regard to mercy, for the male in the theft, there was his mature age (50) and the trauma to his upright family. Moreover, a factor being a common characteristic among the offender population or one of a substantial number found to be relevant in a case, apparently did not deter participants from relying on it as mitigating. Instances of the former are drunkenness and a troubled background (both were present for three of the offenders); evidence for the latter is the large number of factors found by the participants to be mitigating (see below). The expectation was that, if the sentencing guidelines represent the public's sense of justice, the participants' reliance on personal mitigation would appear restricted, as it is in proportionality theory. In fact, to the contrary, for the participants the scope of personal mitigation was wider and its character richer, and it carried much more weight.

Sentencing guidelines

The relevant Sentencing Council guidelines were applied to the six offenders in the study; these were the general guidance (Sentencing Guidelines Council 2004) and the guidelines for robbery, rape, assault and theft (Sentencing Guidelines Council 2006, 2007, 2008a, 2008b, respectively). In fact, only four factors were found to be relevant across the six offenders. These were youth (assault, female), low intellectual capacity (rapist), first act of violence (robber) and lesser role (assault, female; theft, female), although only the first and third were patently significant. Moreover, there were no factors to which the offenders could appeal on the grounds of mercy. In regard to the former Sentencing Advisory Panel's recommendations (Sentencing Advisory Panel 2010), only one of their proposed offender factors would apply here, namely mercy on the grounds of extremely dependent children (theft, female).

By way of contrast, the participants not only found these factors to be relevant, but cited many more. With respect to culpability, the participants together cited as mitigating thirty-three factors more or less directly related, and twelve indirectly related, to the offending. Moreover, four of the six offenders were thought to have claims to mercy, and the participants between themselves relied on a total of ten factors for this. Also, rehabilitation, not generally carrying weight under the guidelines when the offending is serious, was treated as important by the participants in these serious cases. In regard to this, the expectation was that, if the guidelines represent the public's sense of justice, then as the guidelines treat personal mitigation so the participants would see it. In fact, to the contrary, personal mitigation appeared to be much more important to the participants than it did under the guidelines.

Implications for research

To ensure that the guidelines give proper weight to the public's sentiments about punishment, the Sentencing Council draws on research. The major study relevant to the present findings is that of Hough, Roberts and Jacobson (2009), as will be apparent from the review above. The conclusion of Roberts et al. (2009), on the basis of this research, is that the guidelines adequately reflect the public's sense of justice. The present findings point to something very different, namely that the guidelines do not do this. Actually, on the ground which is common, the findings of these two studies are not dissimilar. Thus, seriousness generally trumps personal mitigation, and so on. However – and this is what is important here – the present study found that many factors exercised the minds of the public, demonstrating the narrow scope of the guidelines. Also, in this study, the guidelines were shown to be incompatible with the character of the public's approach to personal mitigation (e.g. it is strongly global); this is a matter which Hough et al. failed to consider. Finally, this study found that personal mitigation often carries substantial weight, even when the offending is serious.

The disparity between the conclusions of these two studies may well be due to differences in method. The case detail and the presentation of the offender as real, in association with the qualitative analysis, appeared to be necessary to finding personal mitigation as multifactorial, global, contextual and interactive, and, indeed, as important. As well, it was probably important in finding the participants as understanding of and sensible to the circumstances of the offenders, as fine-readers of case circumstances and as not shunning a factor simply because it was common. Second, the measurement of the total effect of personal mitigation in all the circumstances of a case required a global index, namely the sentence for a case (cf. sentences in respect of individual factors). Finally, serious offending was required to demonstrate the importance of personal mitigation at a level well above the custody threshold; it also gave personal mitigation a context in which it had a chance to shine. Clearly, there must be some doubt, on the basis of the present findings and the apparent limitations of the past research, whether the guidelines can be said properly to represent the public's – at least the Victorian public's – understanding of personal mitigation.

CONCLUSIONS

The question remains: what are the implications for sentencing of the present analysis of the public's approach to personal mitigation; and what needs to be done in the light of this? In Victoria, sentencing has become harsher over the last fifteen or more years (Freiberg and Ross 1999). This has been achieved in part by way of the offender carrying less weight in the sentencing decision. Behind this has been a perception by the judiciary (and the legislature) of a public largely dissatisfied with judicial leniency and wanting sentences which they believe will better protect them and better mark the seriousness of the offending (*R* v. *Jurisic* 1998; *R* v. *Henry* 1999). There can be no doubt that public opinion as measured by opinion polls overwhelmingly favours harshness. But the public's sense of justice is very different, as is shown in the present study. And this sentiment is what should be the yardstick for sentencing practice. On this basis, the change to tougher sentencing and a narrower and more parsimonious interpretation of personal mitigation seems seriously misplaced. Patently, though, this is not the perception of the general public, whose dissatisfaction remains (Square Holes Pty Ltd 2006; Mirrlees-Black 2001). The problem is, judges will not restore offenders to their traditional place in the sentencing judgment until the public call for it. And this will not happen until the public have in their collective consciousness the true nature of their sense of justice. This will require research appropriate to personal mitigation. This means research, so the present study suggests, taking the offender more seriously than has hitherto been the case. A device not suited to a phenomenon will not detect that phenomenon.

There is a second matter of importance for Victoria. English-style guidelines as a means of controlling judicial sentencing disparity and offering an express statement of sentencing policy appear not to be suited to Victoria. This is because, as the present study shows, they do not represent the balance of the public's sense of justice in respect of personal mitigation – its scope, character and importance. This problem arises largely because of the guidelines' reliance on proportionality; this theory, contrary to its claim, does not represent common-sense justice. Let it be clear; sentencing policy does not have to match exactly the public's sense of justice, but, as Robinson (2008) argues, it should be taken into account.

In England and Wales also, public opinion has driven the move to harsher sentencing (Millie, Jacobson and Hough 2003). In this regard, its effect was direct. But, there, the effect of public opinion on sentencing has also been indirect, by way of the sentencing guidelines. One outcome of these guidelines has been the consolidation of the diminished role of personal mitigation. In regard to the former, the results of the present study cast doubt on the soundness of this on the grounds of an instinctively harsher public. In regard to the latter, the problem, as noted, lies largely with proportionality theory. Perhaps the Sentencing Council should re-examine its approach to guidelines. With this, proportionality would be interpreted less strictly and there would be a guideline structure better able to accommodate the breadth, complexity and importance of personal mitigation. These two conclusions assume that the present results would hold if the method used here were to be applied in England and Wales, and to cases towards the upper end of the seriousness scale. The two jurisdictions do have much in common.

Nevertheless, this remains an empirical question, one deserving thoughtful attention.

Judicial sentencing is harsher than it was once. However, the understanding of public opinion behind this change is not well founded, and its effects have been pernicious. Perhaps personal mitigation needs to be restored to the place it once had in traditional sentencing.[6]

REFERENCES

Ashworth, A. (2010). 'Sentencing Guidelines and the Sentencing Council', *Criminal Law Review*: 389–401.

Clarke, A., Moran-Ellis, J. and Sleney, J. (2002). *Attitudes to Date Rape and Relationship Rape*. London: Sentencing Advisory Panel.

Cooper, J. (2008). 'The Sentencing Guidelines Council – A Practical Perspective', *Criminal Law Review*: 277–86.

Freiberg, A. and Ross, S. (1999). *Sentencing Reform and Penal Change*. Sydney: Federation Press.

Garland, D. (2001). *The Culture of Control*. University of Chicago Press.

Hogg, R. and Brown, D. (1998). *Rethinking Law and Order*. Sydney: Pluto Press.

Hough, M., Roberts, J. and Jacobson, J. (2009). *Public Attitudes to the Principles of Sentencing*. London: Sentencing Advisory Panel.

Jacobson, J. and Hough, M. (2007). *Mitigation*. London: Prison Reform Trust.

Jacoby, J. and Cullen, F. (1999). 'The Structure of Punishment Norms: Applying the Rossi-Berk Model', *Journal of Criminal Law and Criminology*, 89: 245–312.

Judge, I. (2005). 'The Sentencing Decision', Atkin Lecture, available at www.judiciary.gov.uk/media/speeches/2005/the-atkin-lecture-the-sentencing-decision.

Lovegrove, A. (1989). *Judicial Decision Making, Sentencing Policy, and Numerical Guidance*. New York: Springer.

(2007). 'Public Opinion, Sentencing and Lenience: An Empirical Study Involving Judges Consulting the Community', *Criminal Law Review*: 769–81.

(2010a). 'Proportionality Theory, Personal Mitigation, and the People's Sense of Justice', *Cambridge Law Journal*, 69 (2): 321–52.

(2010b). 'The Sentencing Council, the Public's Sense of Justice, and Personal Mitigation', *Criminal Law Review*: 906–23.

(2011). 'Putting the Offender Back into Sentencing: An Empirical Study of the Public's Understanding of Personal Mitigation', *Criminology and Criminal Justice*, 11: 37–57.

[6] For recent judicial thinking in regard to this in Victoria, see the judgment of Warren CJ and Redlich JA in *WCB* v. *The Queen* (2010).

Millie, A., Jacobson, J. and Hough, M. (2003). 'Understanding the Growth in the Prison Population in England and Wales', *Criminal Justice*, 3 (4): 369–87.

Mirrlees-Black, C. (2001). *Confidence in the Criminal Justice System*. London: Home Office.

Roberts, J., Hough, M., Jacobson, J. and Moon, N. (2009). 'Public Attitudes to Sentencing Purposes and Sentencing Factors: An Empirical Analysis', *Criminal Law Review*: 771–82.

Roberts, J., Stalans, L., Indermaur, D. and Hough, D. (2003). *Penal Populism and Public Opinion*. Oxford University Press.

Robinson, P. (2008). 'Competing Conceptions of Modern Desert: Vengeful, Deontological, and Empirical', *Cambridge Law Journal*, 67: 145–75.

Sentencing Advisory Panel (2010). *Overarching Principles of Sentencing*, available at www.sentencingcouncil.org.uk/.

Sentencing Guidelines Council (2004). *Overarching Principles*, available at www.sentencingcouncil.org.uk/.

(2006). *Robbery*, available at www.sentencingcouncil.org.uk/.

(2007). *Sexual Offences Act*, available at www.sentencingcouncil.org.uk/.

(2008a). *Assault and Other Offences against the Person*, available at www.sentencingcouncil.org.uk/.

(2008b). *Theft and Burglary in a Building Other than a Dwelling*, available at www.sentencingcouncil.org.uk/.

Shapland, J. (1981). *Between Conviction and Sentence*. London: Routledge & Kegan Paul.

Square Holes Pty Ltd. (2006). *Courts Consulting the Community*. Adelaide: Square Holes.

Tonry, M. (2003). 'Evidence, Elections and Ideology in the making of Criminal Justice Policy', in M. Tonry (ed.), *Confronting Crime*. Cullompton, Devon: Willan.

von Hirsch, A. and Ashworth, A. (2005). *Proportionate Sentencing*. Oxford University Press.

Warren, M. (2006). 'Sentencing Considerations', statement by the Chief Justice of Victoria, available at www.supremecourt.vic.gov.au/wps/wcm/connect/0e2a60004056e12aa76fbfe505682c73/Speech06_SentencingConsiderations.pdf?MOD=AJPERES

Wasik, M. (2008). 'Sentencing Guidelines in England and Wales – State of the Art?', *Criminal Law Review*: 253–63.

TABLE OF CASES

R *v.* Henry (1999) 106 A Crim R 149.

R *v.* Jurisic (1998) 101 A Crim R 259.

WCB *v.* The Queen (2010) VSCA 230.

CHAPTER ELEVEN

ADDRESSING PROBLEMATIC SENTENCING FACTORS IN THE DEVELOPMENT OF GUIDELINES

Warren Young and Andrea King

This chapter explores the more practical challenges confronting sentencing guidelines authorities. Drawing on the recent experience creating sentencing guidelines in New Zealand, this chapter addresses the benefits of providing guidance to sentencers with respect to mitigation and aggravation. Particular emphasis is placed on factors which are problematic in some respect.

CHAPTER OVERVIEW

In this essay we discuss the approach taken in New Zealand to developing guidance on aggravating and mitigating factors. After summarizing recent developments in this country, including the creation of a Sentencing Council, we outline the traditional approach taken to aggravation and mitigation in New Zealand before going on to discuss the ways in which the guidelines addressed some of the problems with this traditional approach and the difficulties faced in doing so.

Background to sentencing reform in New Zealand

In 2006, New Zealand's government accepted a recommendation from the Law Commission to establish a New Zealand Sentencing Council to draft sentencing (and parole) guidelines. The Commission made this recommendation in response to what it saw as significant problems with the country's current sentencing and parole structure. These problems were manifest in a rising prison population, an inability of successive governments to manage the increasing pressure on the prison estate and developing concern about what New Zealand's penal policy was costing the country in social and financial terms (for a full discussion of the background to the Council and its establishment see Young and King 2010).

In the Commission's view, the establishment of a Sentencing Council was necessary to ensure greater consistency in sentencing, particularly for lower-level offences, where existing guidance in New Zealand is patchy or non-existent. A Council would enable a greater range of perspectives to be brought to bear on sentencing policy, not only through the Council's membership (which was to include a mix of judicial and non-judicial members) but also through statutory requirements on the Council to consult on draft guidelines and to present the guidelines to Parliament for its scrutiny. These latter two aspects would also encourage a more informed political and public debate about appropriate sentencing levels and the relative cost of punishment compared with other priorities.[1] Because the guidelines would enable the impact of sentencing levels in the future to be more accurately predicted, the guidelines would also lead to a better ability to manage penal resources and, in particular, to plan prison capacity. At the Commission's recommendation, the legislation to establish the Council, the Sentencing Council Act 2007, required that an inaugural set of guidelines come into force at one time. To ensure that the guidelines could be implemented as soon as possible, the government asked the Law Commission to develop a comprehensive set of draft guidelines that the new Council could consider. A Sentencing Establishment Unit (SEU) was established in the Commission, staffed by members of the Commission and four judges who were seconded part-time for this purpose.[2]

THE TRADITIONAL APPROACH TO MITIGATION AND AGGRAVATION IN NEW ZEALAND

New Zealand's sentencing system, as with such comparable jurisdictions as Australia, Canada and the United Kingdom, traditionally exhibited many features of the common law approach. The legislature tended to provide little guidance to sentencing judges about appropriate sentencing levels. Instead, in reaching an appropriate sentence, judges were limited only by an offence's maximum penalty (which was intended to

[1] When consulting on draft guidelines, the Council was required to provide an accompanying statement regarding their cost-effectiveness and impact on the prison population.

[2] The draft guidelines are available from the Law Commission on request, but, due to their uncertain official status, they have not been made widely available.

provide guidance only as to the upper limit in the worst class of case) and the types of sentence that the legislature made available (e.g. imprisonment, a community-based sentence or a monetary penalty). No statutory guidance was provided about the purposes and principles of sentencing or about relevant aggravating or mitigating factors.

In lieu of any statutory guidance, New Zealand sentencing judges have relied on other sources of guidance. These have included recommendations about the appropriate sentence in pre-sentence reports prepared by probation officers, and prosecution and defence submissions on sentence. However, by far the most important source of guidance has been appellate guidance arising from an appeal against sentence by either the defence or the prosecution. This has included guideline judgments issued by the Court of Appeal, which, while developed in the context of an individual appeal against sentence, provide more general guidance about sentencing for the relevant offence or offence type.[3]

The Sentencing Act 2002

As a result of increasing public scrutiny and criticism of the entire sentencing and parole system (Brown and Young 2000), a citizen-initiated referendum, which included a call for 'minimum sentences and hard labour for all serious violent offences', was held in conjunction with the 1999 general election and received a resounding 92 per cent vote in favour. This led to the Sentencing Act 2002, which included a number of measures designed to take a tougher approach to sentencing, particularly with respect to more serious offences. For example, a seventeen-year minimum term of imprisonment was introduced for offenders receiving a life sentence for a murder accompanied by one or more specified aggravating factors (such as a murder committed with a high degree of brutality, cruelty, depravity or callousness).[4] This replaced the previous minimum term of ten years' imprisonment. The indeterminate sentence of preventive detention was also expanded to cover a greater range of offences and offenders.[5]

However, the Act was also notable for other reasons. In particular, it represents the New Zealand legislature's first real incursion into the common law of sentencing. The Act specifies, for the first time, the purposes of sentencing,[6] the principles that the court must take into

[3] See, e.g., *R v. Terewi* (cannabis cultivation and supply); *R v. Taueki* (serious violence); *R v. Fatu* (dealing in Class A drugs).

[4] Sentencing Act 2002, s. 104. [5] Ibid., s. 87. [6] Ibid., s. 7.

account when sentencing an offender[7] and the purposes of particular offence types.[8] The Act also includes a non-exhaustive list of aggravating and mitigating factors that judges must take into account to the extent they are applicable in a case. Section 9 of the Act identifies the following aggravating factors:[9]

(a) actual or threatened violence or actual or threatened use of a weapon;
(b) unlawful entry into, or unlawful presence in, a dwelling place;
(c) an offender on bail or still subject to a sentence;
(d) the extent of any loss, damage or harm resulting from the offence;
(e) particular cruelty in the commission of the offence;
(f) an abuse of a position of trust or authority in relation to the victim;
(g) a particularly vulnerable victim due to his or her age or health or any other factor known to the offender;
(h) an offence committed in the context of a 'hate crime';
(i) an offence committed as part of, or involving, a terrorist act;
(j) the nature and extent of any connection between the offending and the offender's participation in an organized criminal group or involvement in any other form of organized criminal association;
(k) the existence and extent of premeditation;
(l) the number, seriousness, date, relevance and nature of any previous convictions of the offender and of any convictions for which the offender is being sentenced or otherwise dealt with at the same time.

A smaller number of mitigating factors are also identified:[10]

(a) the age of the offender;
(b) whether and when the offender pleaded guilty;
(c) the conduct of the victim;
(d) that the offender had limited involvement in the offence;
(e) that the offender has, or had at the time the offence was committed, diminished intellectual capacity or understanding;
(f) any remorse shown by the offender, or any offer, agreement, response or measure to make amends;
(g) any evidence of the offender's good character.

[7] Ibid., s. 8.
[8] See, e.g., s. 46 of the Sentencing Act 2002, which provides guidance on the purpose of a supervision sentence, and s. 56 of the Act, which provides guidance on the purpose of a sentence of community work.
[9] Ibid., s. 9(1). [10] Ibid., s. 9(2).

The Sentencing Act's purposes, principles, and aggravating and mitigating factors mostly codified the current approach to sentencing. In particular, the identified sentencing factors did not represent Parliament's view about any new sentencing policy, but instead were, broadly, those most commonly relied on by the courts when imposing sentence. However, this codification was still an important development in a constitutional sense because it demonstrated Parliament's view that identification of these matters should be a legislative, rather than judicial, responsibility.

In terms of providing practical statutory guidance to sentencers, section 9 has a number of limitations. First, it does not specify the relative weight that must be given to each factor. In fact, section 9 specifically provides that nothing about a factor's weight is to be taken from the inclusion of a factor in section 9.[11] Although it might be expected that the inclusion of these factors in legislation would be designed to promote uniformity in how they are applied (Roberts 2003), it is hard to see how it would do so in the absence of any attempt at prioritization or weighting. Judges must inevitably continue to make their own decisions about the weight of each statutory factor in the light of the culpability of the offender and the seriousness of the offence in front of them.

Second, despite the fact that some factors are clearly more relevant to some offences than others, no guidance is provided about how each factor applies to a particular offence. The factors are instead generic across all offences and offence types. Nor is the list complete. There are many offences for which the statutory factors have only limited relevance to the appropriate sentence.

Finally, the Act provides no guidance as to why a factor aggravates or mitigates – that is, the precise relationship between the factor and the offender's culpability or blameworthiness. Instead, the reliance of judges on these factors in the past is essentially taken as sufficient justification for their continued use in the sentencing process in the future.

The development of a comprehensive set of sentencing guidelines required that these issues regarding section 9 be resolved. While providing a useful beginning, section 9 needed to be supplemented with guidance on relevant aggravating and mitigating factors for each offence or offence type linked to appropriate sentencing ranges. The guidelines needed to specify what factors aggravate or mitigate each offence, why, when and to what extent.

[11] Ibid., s. 9(4).

THE APPROACH TO AGGRAVATION AND MITIGATION IN THE DRAFT GUIDELINES

The draft set of guidelines prepared for the Council comprises fifty-nine guidelines. Forty-two are offence-based guidelines that provide guidance on sentencing for particular offences or offence types. These guidelines are confined to offences that come before the courts in high volumes (e.g. drink-driving or driving while disqualified), that result in a high proportion of sentences of imprisonment (e.g. attempted murder) or that are otherwise core criminal offences (e.g. offences relating to chid neglect). A further seventeen guidelines provide guidance on matters that apply across offence types. These include, for example, the recognition that should be given to a guilty plea, sentencing for multiple offences and how the guidelines apply to inchoate offences such as conspiracies and attempts.

The structure of the guidelines

The offence-based guidelines, unlike those promulgated by the Sentencing Council in England and Wales, generally aggregate offences into generic categories or offence types. For example, the assaults guideline covers all assault offences from common assault through to attempted murder and manslaughter. The robbery guideline covers robbery and aggravated robbery, as well as other, related, offences such as assault with intent to rob. This approach enables coherent guidance to be provided for the behaviour covered by the category or type, and makes irrelevant the anomalies and inconsistencies that can be apparent in police charging practice and in the offences themselves.

The offence-based guidelines are organized into bands of seriousness, accompanied by ranges of sentence length for each band. An offence is placed within a particular band on the basis of a small number of factors ('band choice factors') that were identified in the SEU as the primary determinants of seriousness. After the offence is placed within the appropriate band, a number of second-order factors ('band placement factors') then determine where within the band the offence falls. That dictates the appropriate sentence before the application of discounts for a guilty plea and any assistance the offender provides to the authorities to resolve offending by others.[12]

[12] Separate guidelines were prepared covering both matters. Both guidelines largely codify existing practice. The draft guideline on guilty pleas was incorporated by the Court of Appeal into its guideline judgment on guilty pleas – see *Hessell v. R* (C.A.), although that decision has now been overturned by the Supreme Court in *Hessell v. R* (S.C.).

TABLE 11.1. Robbery and associated offences: bands and sentence ranges in New Zealand guidelines

Band 1	Offending accompanied by some or all of the following factors: • minimal actual violence or a threat of violence in the absence of a weapon • target of minimal potential value • minimal victim impact	Sentence range: from community work and/or supervision up to 9 months' imprisonment
Band 2	Offending accompanied by some or all of the following factors: • a single act of low-level violence or the threatened use of a weapon without an immediate ability to inflict serious harm • target of low to moderate potential value • moderate victim impact	Sentence range: from home detention up to 3 years' imprisonment
Band 3	Offending accompanied by some or all of the following factors: • moderate actual violence, or the threatened use of a weapon with an immediate ability to inflict serious harm • target of significant potential value • high victim impact	Sentence range: from 3 years' imprisonment up to 6 years' imprisonment
Band 4	Offending accompanied by some or all of the following factors: • serious actual violence • target of high potential value • very high victim impact	From 6 years' imprisonment up to 10 years' imprisonment

In relation to the draft guideline for robbery and associated offences, for example, the band choice factors are the use of threatened and actual violence, potential value of the target and victim impact. The band placement factors are targeting a vulnerable victim, co-offenders and the use of planning, skill and preparation. This is reflected in bands and sentence ranges as in Table 11.1.

The sentence ranges within the bands are not definitive. While guidelines ought to cater for the vast majority of offences, it was always recognized in the development of the guidelines that some flexibility was required to enable judges to cater for the exceptional case. This is recognized by section 21A of the Sentencing Act, which provides that, when sentencing an offender, the court must impose a sentence that is consistent with any sentencing guidelines that are relevant to an offender's case, *unless the court is satisfied that this sentence would be contrary to the interests of justice*. A generic guideline was also developed that identifies when departure from the guidelines may be justified.[13]

The approach to band choice

The first task in the development of offence-based guidelines within a framework of this sort is to determine the band choice factors for each offence or offence type. In essence, this required the SEU to do what the legislature in enacting the Sentencing Act refrained from doing: prioritizing the purposes of sentencing set out in section 7 of the Act and determining the weight that should be given to particular aggravating and mitigating factors.

In relation to the purposes of sentencing, the structure of the guidelines and the approach taken to their application emphasizes the seriousness of the offence and the culpability of the offender. This places the guidelines firmly within a desert-based framework. The initial reference points in determining the appropriate sentence, and the purposes that are integral to the guidelines, are those set out in section 7(a), (b) and (e) of the Sentencing Act: the need to hold the offender accountable for the harm done; to promote in him or her a sense of responsibility for the offence; and to denounce the conduct. As we shall discuss shortly, in relation to some offences other purposes, such as deterrence and the protection of the community, sometimes intruded into SEU discussions on the appropriate content of a guideline. In particular, criminal history often emerged as a significant driver of what members of the SEU regarded as the appropriate sentence range, even though its inclusion led to a considerable degree of conceptual untidiness. But in general terms the band choice factors are those relevant to seriousness and culpability, while factors relevant to other section 7 purposes – such as

[13] Identified grounds for departure included, for example, if the offender's criminal history or concurrent convictions for other offences demonstrate a particularly high risk of further offending from which the public requires protection, if the applicable band of seriousness does not enable the commission of multiple offences adequately to be taken into account, if the sentence indicated by the guidelines would have a disproportionately severe impact on the offender or his or her family, if appropriate regard cannot otherwise be had to a restorative justice process, if there are strong rehabilitative prospects, or if the offender has already been substantially rehabilitated.

the need to provide for the interests of victims, to provide reparation for the harm done by the offending and to assist in the offender's rehabilitation and reintegration – are relegated to band placement factors.

However, while the prioritization of purposes in section 7 was an important first step in developing the guidelines, it was still only of limited utility in identifying appropriate band choice factors. That is because there are obviously a large number of aggravating and mitigating factors that potentially affect assessments of seriousness and culpability. The SEU took the view that, if the guidelines were to provide meaningful assistance to judges and produce a significant measure of consistency, the band choice factors needed to be confined to the small number that regularly influence the choice of sentence. This approach recognizes the reality that for any particular offence or offence type, some factors are more relevant than others to determining the appropriate sentence. It is appropriate that these factors primarily determine the sentencing policy for that offence or offence type.

The approach the SEU took to band choice departs from that often taken by the New Zealand Court of Appeal in promulgating guideline judgments. These judgments identify a large number of 'band choice factors' and provide that the presence of any of these factors in a particular number determines the appropriate band (and sentence range). For example, in its guideline judgment for sentencing serious violent offences, the Court has identified thirteen aggravating factors, all of which may be relevant to determining the appropriate band.[14] The Court's approach avoids the problems (discussed below) that can arise in determining where the boundary between band choice and band placement should lie. Nevertheless, we think it is limited in the amount of guidance it can provide, and for the following reasons.

First, the approach appears to assume that the primary drivers of seriousness for a particular offence will vary markedly from case to case; that is, because no two cases are the same, judges must be free to select the relevant factors according to the particular circumstances of the offence and the offender. We think this assumption is questionable. A review of hundreds of sentencing notes over the course of the exercise of the guidelines reinforced our view that, for any particular offence or offence type, there is a remarkable similarity in the circumstances in which an offence is committed as well as in the circumstances of offenders.

[14] *R v. Taueki*, at para. 31.

In addition, providing guidance via a large number of aggravating and mitigating factors – any one of which may be relevant to band choice – risks undermining the purpose of providing guidance. Consistency is undermined due to the number of factors and available combinations of those factors which are available to sentencing judges. Transparency is undermined due to the risk that judges will not apply the guidance as intended. In particular, it is likely that judges will not treat all the listed factors as being of equal weight, but will instead routinely treat particular factors as relevant to band choice and the remaining factors as being of secondary importance.

For example, on its face, the Court's sexual violation guideline judgment requires that the extent of violence that the offender inflicted on the victim or the scale of the offending should be given weight equal to consensual sexual activity immediately before the offence.[15] In our view, while all three factors are relevant, the first two factors, which go to the very essence of the offence, are much more determinative of the offender's culpability than the latter. We expect that most sentencing judges will be of the same view and will adjust their sentencing practice accordingly.

Finally, the approach does not enable a clear sentencing policy to be set. In relation to violent offending, for example, the relevant draft guideline identifies the level of violence that the offender intended to inflict on the victim as the primary determinant of seriousness (combined, in some cases, with the scale of the offending, a victim targeted due to his or her public role or particular vulnerability, or premeditation). In contrast, the relevant guideline judgment requires that these factors be given the same weight as the actual injury caused to the victim, the offender's motive, whether or not the offence involved a 'home invasion', the presence of multiple attackers, or an offence committed in the context of gang warfare.[16] No coherent sentencing policy to sentencing serious violence seems discernible from this approach.

In fact, in relation to most offences, we found that the process of identifying the relevant band choice factors was a relatively easy one. The starting point was an analysis of current sentencing practice, including relevant guideline judgments, to identify the factors that were generally relied on by judges when sentencing a particular offence. This was followed by further analysis and discussion within the SEU

[15] *R v. AM*, at paras. 37–62. [16] *R v. Taueki*, at para. 31.

about what factors *ought* to aggravate and mitigate the offence (whether the same or different from current practice) and how those factors should be articulated. There was a wide measure of agreement, among both those drafting the guidelines and those who were consulted on draft guidelines, about the primary drivers of seriousness and culpability in relation to most offences.

Some band choice factors in the draft guidelines are generic factors that appear in section 9 or that have their basis in those factors. For example, the band choice factors in the burglary guideline (victim impact, the scale of the offending, the level of planning and skill and the offender's criminal history for dishonesty offending) can all be found in section 9 of the Sentencing Act. Most of the band choice factors in the arson and intentional damage guidelines (knowledge of risk to life or safety, value of property targeted and/or damaged, the offender's motive and the scale of offending) also have their basis in section 9.

For other guidelines, the relevant aggravating and mitigating factors are almost entirely offence-specific and bear only limited resemblance to factors identified in section 9. For example, the band choice factors in the draft guidelines covering various aspects of drug dealing are the quantity of the drug dealt and whether or not the offending was motivated by profit. The band choice factors in the draft guideline for offences against the administration of justice (e.g. perjury or fabricating evidence) are the seriousness of the investigation or proceedings, the offender's actual and intended impact on the administration of justice and the level of the offender's persistence and sophistication. Equally, in relation to most offences, there was a large measure of agreement about the second-order aggravating and mitigating factors that, while not primary drivers of seriousness, ought to be recognized as band placement factors because they are relevant to the eventual choice of sentence.

None of this is surprising. The factors that determine how seriously a crime is viewed by the public are generally recognized and non-contentious. It is at the margins that controversy arises and that public concern (and sometimes outrage) is generated (see the chapter by Roberts and Hough in this volume). And it was at the margins that the SEU encountered the most problems in framing the guidelines.

Problematic sentencing factors

The problems that the SEU encountered fell into four categories: disagreement about whether a factor is aggravating or mitigating at all; disagreement about the weight that should be attached to an agreed aggravating or mitigating factor; difficulties in articulating a factor in a way that indicates how it should be applied; and disagreement as to the rationale for regarding a factor as aggravating or mitigating.

Disagreement about whether a factor is aggravating or mistigating at all
There was fairly fundamental disagreement, both within the SEU and among those we consulted, whether some factors aggravate or mitigate at all or the circumstances in which they should do so. Two examples will suffice to demonstrate the point.

Prevalence of the offence. First, many New Zealand judges would take the view that the prevalence of a particular offence in their local community should aggravate an offence, resulting in a harsher sentence. Their primary reason for this view is their belief that doing so 'sends a message' to other potential offenders that such offending will not be tolerated and deters further offending of that kind. When questioned about the evidence to support their view, judges are likely to point to individual instances where a stern sentencing approach has had a demonstrable effect on the local prevalence of an offence. It is beyond the scope of this article to review the considerable amount of research that has been undertaken on the effects of exemplary sentencing on general deterrence. For our purposes, it is sufficient to say that the evidence for such an effect is minimal (see, e.g., von Hirsch et al. 1999; Bottoms and von Hirsch 2011). Consultation with relevant groups and individuals during the development of draft guidelines indicated some support for being able to take into account the local or national prevalence of an offence. In addition to believing in the deterrent effects of doing so, those consulted argued that it was important for the public's confidence in the courts and judicial system that the courts were seen to respond appropriately to matters of local or national concern.

Ultimately, the SEU decided that the local or national prevalence of an offence was an aggravating factor that may justifiably be taken into account in sentencing. However, the relevant draft guideline requires that cogent evidence of the prevalence of the particular offence (such as statistics from an objective source) must be placed before the judge before any alteration of sentence may occur on this basis.[17] It is perhaps debatable whether this latter requirement would have led to prevalence impacting on sentences in a more restrictive way than currently occurs.

[17] In this respect, the approach is similar to that adopted by the English Sentencing Council (see its *Overarching Principles: Seriousness* guideline, available at www.sentencingcouncil.org.uk, and discussion in Ashworth (2010), 102–3).

Provocation by the victim. The circumstances in which the victim's conduct should mitigate an offence is another difficult issue. It is relatively uncontroversial that a victim's conduct can mitigate an offence in some circumstances. Most members of the community would accept the view, for example, that provocation by the victim should mitigate an assault where the offender has been subjected to sustained abuse by the victim over a number of years and has finally 'snapped' and caused the victim harm. In New Zealand, this is recognized by the inclusion of the conduct of the victim as a mitigating factor in section 9. However, the application of this factor to particular offences creates difficult questions of sentencing policy. For example, what of the situation where an offender is convicted of breaching a domestic violence protection order when the breach arose out of contact initiated by the victim? It is arguable that an offender in this situation is, all else being equal, less culpable than an offender who sought the victim out.

The counter-argument is that treating this factor as mitigating is inconsistent with the efforts in New Zealand and elsewhere to prevent and reduce domestic violence, which has included placing responsibility for violence squarely on the offender. A domestic protection order is in place because the offender has previously caused harm to the victim. Consistent with the aims of the order (to protect the victim from the offender), a 'zero tolerance' approach to any breach of the order by the offender should arguably be taken. Doing otherwise also brings with it a connotation of 'victim blaming'. This, of course, ignores the fact that one breach can be more or less serious than another. Much will depend on the circumstances. For example, no regard should be had to this factor if the protected person made contact with the offender for a legitimate purpose such as organizing access arrangements to children. However, it is difficult to see why the offender's culpability should not be mitigated if the situation was deliberately orchestrated by the victim to give rise to a breach. Those consulted on a draft guideline generally supported this view.

The relevant draft guideline, therefore, identifies this factor as mitigating but requires that it be considered in a broader context. In particular, the guideline notes that the victim's actions need to be considered in the context of the history of the relationship, the victim's motivation for the contact and the nature of the contact resulting in the offence. Victim-initiated contact will not always be mitigating in its own right. If, for example, the breach was in the form of serious violence, then the fact that the contact arose at the victim's instigation should matter very little.

It will also be of little relevance if the victim initiated contact for a legitimate purpose.

Disagreement about the weight that should be placed on an agreed factor. For some factors there was general agreement that they aggravated or mitigated, but much less agreement about the weight they should be given. In the guidelines context, this becomes most apparent at the boundary between band choice and band placement. Whether a factor is relevant to band choice or band placement is a matter of judgment that can be contentious. In relation to the draft guideline for sexual violation, for example, there was significant debate within the SEU about the weight to be given to factors such as the impact of the offence on the victim or a breach of trust. Both factors were eventually identified in the guideline as relevant to band placement but not to band choice. This was on the basis that other factors (in particular, the level of aggression and intimidation, length of detention, scale of offending, targeting a vulnerable victim, acting with co-offenders and premeditation) had, all else being equal, a greater impact on offence seriousness.

Even if agreement can be reached about a factor's weight, the stakes arguably become higher when these judgments are made explicit and established as a transparent sentencing policy. For example, the nature of the offence of sexual violation makes it difficult to apply an approach which requires a policy to be expressed about what makes one instance of the offence more or less serious than another. There is an understandable level of discomfort in establishing, as the draft guideline did, that the impact on the victim of the offence or the fact that the offence involved a parent offending against his or her child are of secondary importance to other factors.

This discomfort was clearly shared by New Zealand's Court of Appeal when it developed its guideline judgment for sexual violation drawing on the SEU's draft guideline. In particular, there was significant discussion at the appeal hearing about the approach to be taken to breach of trust and some uneasiness with the prospect of this factor being identified as a band placement factor as in the draft guideline. This may be one reason why the Court opted for an approach that listed a large number of factors, rather than making distinctions between band choice and band placement.[18] However, by doing so it simply avoided making the hard decisions and failed in its task of providing guidance for courts of first

[18] *R v. AM.*

instance. As noted above, if a guideline does not adequately distinguish between the more significant and the less significant factors, individual judges will do so (inconsistently) on a case-by-case basis.

Difficulties in articulating a factor in a way that indicates how it should be applied. Sometimes an aggravating or mitigating factor that is commonly agreed to be a significant driver of the choice of sentence is difficult to articulate in a way that provides any real guidance to or constraint on judicial sentencing practice. In our process of developing sentencing guidelines, this was demonstrated by the inclusion of 'planning and premeditation' as a band choice factor.

In the burglary guideline, for example, all the judges involved in the process agreed that the four band choice factors should be potential and actual victim impact, scale of offending, planning and skill, and a history of dishonesty offending. The 'planning and skill' factor was described in the lowest level band as 'offending that was opportunistic in nature, showing little planning or skill', in the middle band as 'offending showing some planning or skill' and in the upper band as 'offending showing significant planning or skill'. However, when we tested the utility of the band choice factors as a guide to actual sentencing practice by giving a sample of actual cases to some SEU judges and asking them to sentence according to the guideline, we discovered a problem. In essence, because all burglaries involve some element of planning, the boundaries between each of the bands in terms of this factor were expressed so vaguely that they gave judges the opportunity to place offenders in any band they chose, in order to arrive at the sentence they intuitively thought appropriate in the circumstances. As a result, the guideline proved to be of relatively little assistance in ensuring a consistent sentencing outcome. Yet we found it difficult to find any more precise language that would adequately capture the varying degrees of planning and premeditation that were likely to arise. We have therefore been left with a draft guideline that appears conceptually sound (with the possible exception of the inclusion of criminal history, which is discussed further below), but is unlikely to work well in practice.

Disagreement whether a factor is aggravating or mitigating

Finally, there were sometimes divergent views as to the rationale for the inclusion of a particular factor as aggravating or mitigating. Criminal history in particular proved problematic from the outset.

In three draft guidelines – possession of Class A drugs, possession of instruments for burglary or car conversion, and driving while disqualified – criminal history is the sole band choice factor. That is because the offence itself does not vary significantly from one offence to another. For example, cases involving the possession of Class A drugs, where the quantity of drugs falls below the threshold at which the presumption of possession for supply applies, cannot readily be differentiated on the basis of the characteristics of the offending; the only discriminator between cases is the characteristics of the offender, among which previous criminal history looms large. In all three guidelines, the criminal history relevant to band choice is confined to cognate offending: a history of drug offending, dishonesty offending and driving while disqualified respectively.

In the other ten draft guidelines where criminal history features as a band choice factor, it is only one of a number of relevant factors (generally three or four). For example, the band choice factors in the draft guideline on forgery are the value of the benefit obtained or intended to be obtained, victim impact, the scale of the offending and a history of dishonesty offending. The band choice factors in the draft guideline on indecent behaviour are the degree of offensiveness, victim impact, the targeting of a vulnerable victim, the scale of offending and a history of indecencies or other sexual offending. Criminal history features as a band choice factor in these guidelines primarily because it was recognized by the SEU as a primary driver of current sentencing practice in relation to the offences covered by these guidelines. For example, while the number of current burglary offences and the value of the property taken are major determinants of current sentencing practice in relation to burglary, it is clear that criminal history is equally as important, if not more so. Again, however, criminal history as a band choice factor in the draft guideline is confined to offending that is similar to the current conviction: for example, previous dishonesty offending in relation to the guidelines on theft, receiving, obtaining by deception, forgery and car conversion; previous drink-driving in relation to the guideline on drink-driving offences; and previous imprisonable traffic offending in relation to the guideline on driving causing injury or death.

However, the rationale for the inclusion of criminal history as a band choice factor in a small number of guidelines, but only as a secondary band placement factor in the rest, is not well articulated. Nor is the use of only cognate criminal history as a band choice factor, while other unrelated previous offending is relegated to band placement.

Criminal history may be regarded as a major driver of sentencing on the basis that it is indicative of a risk of future offending and therefore requires a more severe sentence for incapacitative or individual deterrent purposes. In either case, it is difficult to see why a distinction should generally be drawn between similar and dissimilar previous offending. It may well be that a burglar with a substantial history of previous burglary offending is at substantially greater risk of committing further burglaries in the future than the burglar with one or two previous burglary convictions but a substantial and versatile history of other offending. But there is no evidence that the former presents a greater risk of serious reoffending of any sort than the latter. Why, then, should the public deserve greater protection from one than from the other?

Criminal history may alternatively be regarded as relevant to the calculation of retributive punishment, on the basis either that the absence of previous convictions demonstrates previous good character and is therefore a mitigating factor that progressively carries less weight as previous convictions accumulate (the 'progressive loss of mitigation' theory (von Hirsch 2010)), or that the number and seriousness of previous convictions enhances the offender's culpability and is therefore an aggravating factor (the 'enhanced culpability' theory (Roberts 2008) that seemed to appeal implicitly or explicitly to most of those with whom we consulted in the course of preparing the draft guidelines). However, while it is easy to understand why the *seriousness* of a person's previous history might affect the extent to which it lessens the mitigating effect of any claim of good character or enhances his or her culpability for the instant offence, it is less easy to understand why the *type* of previous history should matter. If previous history enhances culpability, for example, the burglar with a long history of violent offending, sexual offending and drug offending (interspersed with a few property offences) is surely just as culpable as the burglar who has simply specialized in property offending. To suggest otherwise would be to imply that offenders have several lifelines in respect of each type of offending on which they embark.

Our experience in attempting to incorporate criminal history into guidelines in a clear and coherent fashion therefore ultimately failed. The draft guidelines do not take a consistent and conceptually sound approach and are not based on solid empirical evidence as to the nature of criminal careers. However, in this respect the treatment of criminal history in the draft guidelines simply mirrors the confused and often contradictory way in which it has been approached in sentencing policy and in the sentencing literature.

CONCLUSION

Even before a Sentencing Council was proposed, New Zealand was some way along the path of providing guidance to sentencing judges on the approach to be taken to aggravation and mitigation. Since at least the late 1970s, the Court of Appeal has accepted that it is part of its supervisory function to provide sentencing guidance in order to ensure 'the even-handed administration of justice throughout the country'.[19] In 2002, Parliament's role in providing sentencing guidance was reaffirmed by the inclusion of sentencing purposes and principles and aggravating and mitigating factors in the Sentencing Act 2002. Nonetheless, these existing mechanisms can only go so far. Unless techniques like mandatory minimum sentences are used, statutory guidance can only ever be provided at a high level and usually must apply to all offences and offence types. Appellate sentencing guidance can take an offence-by-offence approach. However, as New Zealand's Court of Appeal has itself acknowledged, the process an appeal court must follow to develop this guidance is necessarily flawed.[20] In particular, it is restricted by the sentence appeal at hand and cannot follow a consultative process like that usually employed by sentencing guidance bodies.

As demonstrated by the approach taken to New Zealand's draft guidelines, the development of sentencing guidelines provides an opportunity to establish a coherent approach to aggravation and mitigation across all offences, while also enabling offence-by-offence guidance to be provided. It forces drafters into the discipline of clearly articulating each aggravating and mitigating factor and explaining how and why it is relevant to an offence. It requires, to the extent possible, that the justification for each factor is developed in a clear and transparent way.

These are all difficult tasks. There has historically been little focus, either in sentencing practice, appellate guidance or academic research, on articulating clear rationales for why particular factors aggravate or mitigate. The approach taken by sentencing judges to aggravation and mitigation tends to be second-nature and instinctual. When questioned, they can find it difficult to explain why they treat a factor as aggravating or mitigating. Often, views about the relevance of particular factors will differ from judge to judge, depending on their respective background and experience. A clear articulation of relevant aggravating and mitigating factors also requires some explicit and sometimes uncomfortable

[19] *R v. Pawa* [1978]. [20] *R v.* AM, at para. 7.

judgments to be made about what makes one instance of an offence more serious than another. These were all difficulties which confronted those drafting sentencing guidelines in New Zealand. Sometimes they were overcome, so that a clear statement of aggravation or mitigation emerged. Sometimes, as with criminal history, they were not. However, even when they were not, the sentencing guidelines process was an improvement on the status quo, because it provided a systematic process for a debate about and resolution of differences in perspectives and views, many of which remain unspoken and often unrecognized in traditional court-driven sentencing policy.

Notwithstanding this, the government elected at the end of 2008 announced that it did not intend to establish the Sentencing Council, on the rather contradictory basis that sentencing policy was a legislative responsibility and that the discretion of judges should not be constrained by guidelines. New Zealand's proposed Sentencing Council is therefore in abeyance. While the Sentencing Council Act 2007 remains in force, no members to the Council have been appointed.

The future for sentencing guidelines in New Zealand is therefore uncertain. In *Hessell* v. *R*, the Court of Appeal indicated its intention to resume its practice of issuing guideline judgments. However, the Supreme Court's decision to overturn the Court of Appeal's *Hessell* judgment calls that into question.[21] Even if the practice does remain, the use made of the guidelines by the Court of Appeal to develop a sexual violation guideline judgment demonstrates that this is doomed to be an inferior and inadequate process.

REFERENCES

Ashworth, A. (2010). *Sentencing and Criminal Justice*, 5th edn. Cambridge University Press.

Bottoms, A. and von Hirsch, A. (2011). 'The Crime Preventive Impact of Penal Sanctions', in P. Cane and H. Kritzer (eds.), *The Oxford Handbook of Empirical Legal Research*. Oxford University Press.

Brown, M. and Young, W. (2000). 'Recent Trends in Sentencing and Penal Policy in New Zealand', *International Criminal Justice Review*, 10 (1): 1–31.

[21] The Supreme Court stated that the principle of consistency in s. 8 of the Sentencing Act 2002 carries a greater weight than any of the other principles in that section, and that the sentencing judge must decide on a case-by-case basis how the principles should be balanced. Since the purpose of guideline judgments is to promote consistency, it is difficult to see, on this approach, what utility they would have, since judges would be more or less free to depart from them as they pleased.

Roberts, J. V. (2003). 'Sentencing Reform in New Zealand: An Analysis of the Sentencing Act 2002', *Australian and New Zealand Journal of Criminology*, 36 (3): 249–71.

(2008). *Punishing Persistent Offenders*. Oxford University Press.

von Hirsch, A. (2010). 'Proportionality and the Progressive Loss of Mitigation: Some Further Reflections', in J. V. Roberts and A. von Hirsch (eds.), *The Role of Previous Convictions at Sentencing: Theoretical and Applied Perspectives*. Oxford: Hart Publishing.

von Hirsch, A., Bottoms, A. E., Burney, E. and Wikstrom, P.-O. (1999). *Criminal Deterrence and Sentence Severity: An Analysis of Recent Research*. Oxford: Hart Publishing.

Young, W. and King, A. (2010). 'Sentencing Practice and Guidance in New Zealand', *Federal Sentencing Reporter*, 22 (4): 254–61.

TABLE OF CASES

CHAPTER TWELVE

PROOF OF AGGRAVATING AND MITIGATING FACTS AT SENTENCING

Kevin R. Reitz

Beyond questions of substantive law, aggravation and mitigation at sentencing raise important issues of equitable process. Fact-finding at sentencing is often more textured and intensive than at trial, can have an enormous effect on the penalty selected and yet is carried out in an environment of relaxed procedures. The literature has given too little attention to the imperatives of process that stand alongside substantive sentencing goals.

The first aim of this chapter is to give an overview of different processes in common law legal systems for the establishment of aggravating and mitigating facts at sentencing. The inquiry encompasses all fifty-one US jurisdictions (with which the author is generally familiar), supplemented by research into the law and practice of England and Wales, Canada and Australia. Contrasting procedural values can be seen at work across these jurisdictions. In general, the Commonwealth systems are substantially more protective of defendants' rights during the sentencing process than US systems, although there is some heterogeneity in approach in the United States.[1]

After a general survey, the chapter focuses on the specific problem of real-offence sentencing, sometimes referred to as the consideration at sentencing of 'unadjudicated' offences. On many aspects of sentencing procedure, the United States and the Commonwealth take opposing

[1] US capital punishment procedures are not included in the discussion. The death penalty, in the thirty-four states that authorize it, is used in only a tiny fraction of all criminal cases, yet the applicable procedures and constitutional limitations are Byzantine (Zimring 2003).

views; with respect to real-offence sentencing, the disagreement is especially stark. Practices regarded as fundamentally unjust in the Commonwealth raise few eyebrows, and are even celebrated, in the United States. These irreconcilabilities have rarely been noted and never examined closely.

This chapter is a preliminary foray into the subject of comparative sentencing processes. While primarily descriptive, the chapter's observations suggest the need for a procedural theory of sentencing that, for now, does not exist.

TAXONOMY

For the purposes of this chapter, *trial facts* may be defined as facts determined at the guilt stage of the criminal process. They of course include the factual elements proven or admitted in order to establish the defendant's guilt of the charges in the instant case. They may also include defences accepted by the fact-finder at trial or stipulated by the parties. Further, they could arise from allegations rejected by the fact-finder, as when a jury acquits of murder and convicts of manslaughter. An acquittal, in most circumstances, represents a determination that the more serious charge was not proven to the criminal standard of proof.[2]

Sentencing facts may be defined as those beyond the trial facts that a court – or other sentencing authority – is allowed or required to consider when deciding what penalty the offender will receive. There are many different procedural routes to becoming a sentencing fact. Some must be proven during sentencing proceedings through the presentation of evidence. Others, like prior convictions in some systems, may be deemed adequately established by an external legal process. Much of the time, some or all of the sentencing facts are agreed on by the parties. In some settings, sentencing facts are deemed established unless *disproven* by the prosecutor.

In considering the full panoply of sentencing facts, and the procedural treatment they receive, it is important to recognize that there are often multiple sentencing authorities at work in a single case. In cases of indeterminate sentencing, for example, the severity of prison sentences is set (primarily) by the court and a parole-release agency. To the extent

[2] In the United States an acquittal can stem from the jury's nullification power rather than their assessment of the strength of the evidence (*Duncan*).

that the parole board rests its decisions on its own factual conclusions or fact–opinion constructs, it has adjudicated new sentencing facts.

It is generally true – across the systems examined in this chapter, and allowing for jurisdictional variations – that the range of sentencing facts is much broader, and more fine-grained and qualitative, than the relatively stolid and technical category of trial facts. There are isolated exceptions, as when an offence carries a mandatory penalty and no prospect of early release, so that eligible sentencing facts are set at zero.[3]

PROCEDURAL ARCHITECTURE

As opposed to many Continental systems, the US and Commonwealth jurisdictions examined in this chapter bifurcate the guilt and penalty phases of serious criminal cases (Frase 1990: 680; Pizzi 1999: 95–6, 99, 103; Weigend 2001: 188). In some settings, there are distinct decision makers for the two stages, which raises the possibility that the sentencer will view the trial facts differently – and possibly as less definitive in nature – compared with how they were treated when given legal effect at the guilt phase. This raises an interesting question of whether factual continuity within the same case is an important procedural value.

Even if fidelity to prior fact-finding were an agreed-upon goal, it is not always possible. In some cases, the sentencing authority cannot reconstruct the factual reasoning that came before. Matters become especially difficult when more than one mind has been at work to establish the trial facts. Some convictions rest on conflicting views of events, as when a 'unanimous' jury verdict conceals two or more theories among the jurors, or when a guilty plea is entered yet the state and the defence dispute what actually happened (e.g. *R* v. *Tempelaar* 1995; *R* v. *Tolera* 1999).

The phenomenon of different heads at work is well worth pondering. In some systems decisions about the actual length of prison terms are made by parole boards – and their jurisdiction over this subject often dwarfs that of the courts (American Law Institute 2011; Cole and Manson 1990: 193, 196, 351–2; Edney and Bagaric 2007: 314–21). This is essentially a trifurcated sentencing structure, each successive decision point constituting an opportunity for new attitudes towards the facts of the case to emerge. A parole board may not know, or feel

[3] There is a strong argument in such cases that the prosecutor is the de facto sentencing authority. The prosecutor's charging discretion, however, does not operate within the kind of procedural framework discussed in this chapter.

bound by, the premises of a guilty plea, a jury verdict or a judge's sentence. At least in some US states the parole board's mission is to reassess every aspect of the prisoner's case, including the seriousness of the offence and the prisoner's background and character (e.g. Iowa Admin. Code § 205–8.10(906); Rev. Code Neb. § 83–192(1)(f)(v); Tenn. Rules and Regulations § 1100–01–01-.07).

The immediate post-conviction sentencing authority in common law jurisdictions is almost always a trial judge, in some systems subordinate to the potential authority of the appellate courts. Judicial sentence proceedings occur after a conviction is entered – often weeks or months later – and the parties are generally invited to make new submissions to the court, including the presentation of evidence. Depending on the context, other viewpoints and information may also be put forward, including pre-sentence reports, expert opinions and victim input (Ashworth 2010; Edney and Bagaric 2007; Ruby 2004; Campbell 2004). Because of resource limitations, however, the available process is seldom fully exploited. In Canada, for example, sentences are commonly based solely on the submissions of counsel (Manson 2001). In the United States, a typical sentencing was once reported to consume less than thirty minutes, including the judge's preparation time (Frankel 1973) – an estimate that should probably be reduced for the busier court systems of the twenty-first century.

Among all the systems considered in this chapter, judicial sentencing proceedings are less formalized than the trial process for adjudications of guilt in contested cases, and defendants enjoy lesser protections (Ashworth 2010: 375–6; Manson 2001: 163–5; Edney and Bagaric 2007: 32). In the United States the rules of evidence do not apply at sentencing, nor do the exclusionary rule for unconstitutionally obtained evidence, the double jeopardy clause and the confrontation clause. Except for very narrow classes of case, there is no right to a jury at sentencing, and the criminal standard of proof is not required (Lynch 1997; Reitz 1993; Michaels 2003). This step-down in formality might be called the *procedural differential*. While the differential appears to be ubiquitous in common law systems, it is, as we shall see, markedly greater in some jurisdictions than others.

With indeterminate prison sentences there is an additional procedural drop-off that should be noted. However informal the judicial sentencing process may be when measured against a hypothetical trial, the procedural values attending prison-release decisions are much lower still (Frankel 1973; Rhine 2011; Reitz 2011).

Practical reasons exist for the procedural differential between trial and sentencing. Sentencing proceedings occur in a much larger number of cases than full-blown trials – approaching 100 per cent of all convictions. The trial process would be unsustainable if used for so many guilt determinations, as would trial-like process at sentencing. Also, as noted earlier, sentencing facts tend to be more numerous and subjective than trial facts. Cumbersome rules of process are more expensive, and less workable, in an adjudicative milieu of complexities and shades of grey.

VARIABLE BURDENS OF PROOF

The procedural differential between guilt and penalty stages need not include a lower burden of proof for sentencing facts, although common law systems differ on this point. The general rule in the Commonwealth is that aggravating facts must be proven beyond a reasonable doubt, mirroring the trial standard. In Canada aggravating facts must be established beyond a reasonable doubt by statute (Revised Statutes of Canada 1985, c. C-46, s. 724(e)). A similar rule exists in judicial precedent in Australia and England (*Isaacs* (1997); *R* v. *Davies* 2009). With respect to mitigating factors, the burden is the preponderance or 'balance of probabilities' standard (*Guppy* (1995); *R* v. *Olbrich* (1999); Revised Statutes of Canada 1985, c. C-46, s. 724(d) (Can.)).

The Commonwealth approach to aggravating circumstances is based in a strong sense of functional equivalence between fact-finding done at the trial and sentencing stages (*McGrath* (1983); *R* v. *Olbrich* (1999); *R* v. *Gardiner* (1982)). As Andrew Ashworth has put it, '[B]earing in mind the great effect on sentence which such issues may have, they ought properly to be resolved according to rules of evidence no less fair than those applicable at trial' (2010: 375–6).

While there is reasonable uniformity in the Commonwealth, this is not true in the United States. Across fifty-one systems there is wide variety in the prescribed evidentiary standards at sentencing, although none regularly imposes the criminal standard of proof for aggravating facts. Measured against the Commonwealth, the United States is less concerned to prevent erroneous factual findings adverse to the defendant.

The majority US approach has been described by the Supreme Court as follows: 'Sentencing courts have traditionally heard evidence and found facts without any prescribed burden of proof at all' (*Blakely* (2004): 332–3; *McMillan* (1986): 91). For example, an appellate court in Connecticut recently stated that '[w]e have neither found nor been referred to binding federal authority requiring facts at sentencing to be proven by a preponderance of the evidence' (*State* v. *Altajir* (2010): 1032). In Texas, the Court of Criminal Appeals observed that, 'in the absence of statutory direction, there is no burden of proof for sentencing issues' (*Bradley* 2006). According to the Michigan Supreme Court, a sentencing fact will not be disturbed on appeal if 'any evidence' supports the finding (*People* v. *Green* (1986)).

Instead of evidentiary standards, minimum reliability controls have devolved to constitutional law in traditional US sentencing systems. This means that the safeguards reach only the most egregious cases, and are articulated in guarded terms by appellate courts. The due process clause requires only that facts relied on by the sentencing court be 'reliable' or 'materially accurate' (*State* v. *Spears* (1999); *State* v. *Cook* (1998); *U.S.* v. *Santiago* (1993)). A sentence will be overturned if found to have rested on 'materially untrue' information relied on 'by carelessness or design' (*Townsend* (1948): 741), or legally invalid prior convictions, which amount to 'misinformation of constitutional magnitude' (*U.S.* v. *Tucker* (1972): 447). To claim the benefit of these accuracy protections on appeal, the burden rests with the defendant to show that the factual basis for his sentence was 'clearly erroneous' or 'lacking a minimal indicium of reliability' (*U.S.* v. *Chavez* (1997): 349; *U.S.* v. *DuPont* (1994): 8; *Mayes* (1992): 843). The defendant must also demonstrate 'prejudice' – that is, that the inaccurate information had an actual impact on the sentence (*State* v. *Parker* (2010): 1114); *Bauer* (1999: 959)). Adding to the defendants' plight, in most US states, courts are not obliged to give reasons at sentencing. Typically, the factual substratum of their decisions is unknown or cannot be documented.

Beginning in the 1980s, a minority of US jurisdictions shifted to a sentencing guidelines model in which sentencing facts – both aggravating and mitigating – must be proven under the preponderance standard (e.g., N.C. Gen. Stat. § 15A-1340.16(a); Rev. Code. Wash. § 9.94A.530(2)). Also, the court must explain the effect given to aggravating and mitigating factors on the record (e.g., Kan. Stat. § 21–4718 (a)(2); Minn. Stat. § 244.10 subd. 1; 204 Pa. Code § 303.1(d)). Viewed as enlightened reforms, these innovations won the endorsements of the American Bar Association (1994: Standard 18–5.18) and the American Law Institute (2007: § 7.07A). The preponderance standard has thus become the most prominent alternative in the United States to the no-prescribed-burden approach. It has taken root in a number of non-guidelines states as well (e.g., Alaska Stat. § 12.55.025(i); Ariz. Rev. Stat. § 13–702(D)(5)). Notably, however, in public policy debate there has been no important movement towards requiring the criminal burden of proof for aggravating sentencing facts. This is not because it is viewed as an impossibility; the reasonable doubt standard has long been applied to aggravating factors in death penalty proceedings (*Gregg* (1976); *Ring* (2002)). Rather, there is little visceral sense among Americans that parallel burdens at trial and sentencing are needed for fairness purposes.[4]

A surprising lurch in the direction of trial-sentencing equivalency came from the US Supreme Court in 2004, although relatively few cases fall subject to the new rules. In *Blakely* v. *Washington*, the Court held that, under the Sixth Amendment jury trial guarantee and the due process clause, certain kinds of sentencing facts must be tried before a jury and proven beyond a reasonable doubt. The engraftment of jury-trial procedure on to sentencing hearings was a shock to American sensibilities. In its immediate aftermath, *Blakely* was described as an 'earthquake', a 'tsunami', and a 'forty-car pileup' (Parent and Frase 2005; Pfaff 2006). As an erasure of the procedural differential, the holding goes farther than the law of any Commonwealth state, none of which requires juries at sentencing. However, *Blakely*'s mandates attach only to a narrowly defined category of aggravating facts: those that increase the penalty above an otherwise prescribed 'statutory maximum', which the Court held to include the upper limit of an enforceable sentencing guideline (ibid.: 303–4).

A handful of US systems are structured in such a way that they regularly collide with this constitutional requirement, and they have created new sentencing fact-finding procedures to comply (American Law Institute 2007: § 7.07B). Most jurisdictions, however, have been ruled exempt from *Blakely*'s holding, including those that do not structure judicial sentencing discretion in any way, those that employ 'advisory' rather than presumptively enforceable sentencing guidelines and indeterminate systems in which the true severity decisions in prison cases are made by parole boards (*U.S.* v. *Booker* (2005)). While some hoped that the *Blakely* rule would be expanded to cover more cases and system types (Reitz 2005: 1119–22), this has not occurred. In its more recent decisions the Court has held (or reaffirmed earlier holdings) that the

[4] In a much-criticized opinion, one federal Court of Appeals panel suggested that the applicable burden at sentencing should sometimes be raised to the clear and convincing evidence standard (when the alleged aggravating facts would have a great impact on the penalty), but the proposal did not prove influential (*U.S. v. Kikumura*, overruled in *U.S. v. Fisher*).

Blakely rule does not apply to sentencing facts that trigger a mandatory minimum penalty, or to factual findings legally required for the imposition of consecutive prison terms (*U.S.* v. *O'Brien* (2010); *Oregon* v. *Ice* (2009)). Thus, while *Blakely* has drawn some admiration from the Commonwealth (Ashworth 2010: 376), on its home territory it is a quirky constitutional doctrine that does not betoken a fundamental shift in US attitudes towards sentencing process.

NON-CONVICTION OFFENCES

There are many incongruities in sentencing process across the jurisdictions surveyed in this article, but none is more salient than the conflicting treatment of alleged unadjudicated offences (or 'non-conviction offences'). In the United States, sentencing based on non-conviction crimes, and not limited by the offence of conviction, is known as 'real-offence' or 'real-facts' sentencing (Tonry 1981; Breyer 1988; *U.S.* v. *Booker* (2005)). Given a sufficiently distant maximum authorized penalty for the conviction offence, or multiple counts of conviction to raise the punishment ceiling, a judge can often approximate or replicate the penalty that would have followed actual convictions for the unadjudicated crimes (e.g. *U.S.* v. *Juarez-Ortega* (1989)). A contrary rule, which would allow punishment based only on offences for which there has been a conviction, has been called the 'conviction-offence' approach (Reitz 1993).

Real-offence sentencing can take many permutations. These include allegations at sentencing that the defendant was convicted of a crime too low on the grading scale – for example, when the jury verdict or guilty plea has designated a homicide as manslaughter, but there is a factual basis for thinking that the crime was actually an intentional murder. Alternatively, there may be evidence of offences apart from the crime of conviction, such as a famous US homicide case in which the sentencing judge was permitted to credit assertions that the defendant had committed more than thirty non-conviction felonies that had never been charged or proven (*Williams* (1949)). There are important differences in procedural posture among non-conviction offences. For instance, some have never been charged, some have been charged, but were later dismissed – often as part of a plea bargain – and some have been charged and tried, but resulted in acquittal ('acquittal offences').

Legal rules sometimes distinguish between different real-offence categories. For example, in a handful of US states acquittal offences may not be used as sentencing considerations, while all other real-offence variants are allowed (*State* v. *Cote* (1987, at 783–5)); *State* v. *Marley* (1988, at 38–9)). In the US federal system, real-facts sentencing does not extend to wholly unrelated non-conviction conduct, although the sentencing guidelines take the breathtaking step of holding defendants responsible for 'reasonably foreseeable' non-conviction offences committed by accomplices or co-conspirators – a novel form of vicarious real-offence liability (US Sentencing Guidelines, § 1B1.3).

REAL-OFFENCE SENTENCING IN THE COMMONWEALTH

The Commonwealth's general approach to such questions is easy to summarize: unless the defendant admits to non-conviction criminal conduct, real-offence sentencing is proscribed. There is no route by which the prosecution may allege and prove non-conviction crimes as aggravating factors, no matter how high a standard of proof is employed (Ashworth 2010; Freiberg 2001). The prohibition is seen not as a matter of policy or preference, but as a bedrock principle of justice. In the words of the Australian High Court,

> It is fundamental that the respondent only be sentenced in respect of the particular offence to which he had pleaded guilty and of which he had been convicted. Where there are multiple offences of possible relevance to the facts but the accused has been charged and convicted of one or some only, it is a fundamental error to punish the accused on a basis dependent upon particular circumstances of aggravation which would constitute a different offence of which the accused has not been charged or convicted . . . This is a rule of law derived from the basic requirements of fair procedure. (*Weininger*, at 652)

Similarly, the English Court of Appeal has written that a defendant 'may be sentenced only for an offence proved against him [by admission or verdict] . . . these are basic principles underlying the administration of the criminal law' (*R* v. *Canavan* (1998, at 245–6)). While Canadian law has been wavering (see below), the general rule is still that 'offenders are punished in Canada only in respect of crimes for which they have been specifically charged and of which they have been validly convicted' (*R* v. *Larche* (2006)).

Real-offence sentencing is not entirely unknown in the Commonwealth. It is permitted, in a benign form, when a defendant *admits* to non-conviction conduct and *requests* that it become part of the factual basis for punishment. This practice is called 'taking into consideration' (TIC) or 'taking into account' 'other offences' (*R* v. *Sinfield* (2005) (England); Revised Statutes of Canada 1985, c. C-46, § 725(1)(b) and (b.1); Crimes (Sentencing Procedure) Act 1999 (New South Wales), §§ 31–35).The government gains from the TIC arrangement because it clears up crimes that would otherwise remain on the books as unsolved. It benefits defendants because, either by law or longstanding convention, TIC offences cannot be separately charged at a later date (Sentencing Advisory Panel 2010: 4; Revised Statutes of Canada 1985, c. C-46, § 725(2); Crimes (Sentencing Procedure) Act 1999 (New South Wales), § 35(1)(b)). In the right circumstances, the bar on future prosecutions can be a substantial windfall for defendants, because total penalties meted out across separate proceedings are much heavier than when multiple offences are consolidated for a single sentencing – an effect known as the 'bulk discount' (Jareborg 1998; Reitz 2010). There may also be psychological and practical benefits to the defendant in 'cleaning the slate' (Sentencing Advisory Panel 2010: 1). Non-conviction crimes, in short, may play a role at sentencing only if the defendant calculates a personal advantage in allowing it to happen.[5]

REAL-OFFENCE SENTENCING IN THE UNITED STATES

Turning the camera on the United States, there is no universal practice, but the vast majority of US jurisdictions follow an approach that is more or less the opposite of the Commonwealth view. In the name of real-offence or 'real facts' sentencing, judges are permitted (and, in federal law, required) to include non-conviction offences among the factual predicates of sentencing. Throughout most of the United States, all types of non-conviction facts may be considered, including acquittal conduct – a practice specifically upheld by the Supreme Court in 1997 in *U.S.* v. *Watts*. Far from grappling with mighty principles of fundamental justice, the Court announced its decision in a *per curiam* opinion, signalling that it did not find the acquittal-conduct issue sufficiently difficult or

[5] Gestures towards the TIC approach have been made in a small handful of US jurisdictions, but functionally these are far different from their Commonwealth counterparts. For one thing, they do not function as the sole vehicle for real-offence sentencing, which remains freely permitted when the TIC provisions are not invoked. In addition, with the exception of Texas, the use of TIC at sentencing does not bar later prosecution for the offences considered (Ill. Stat. § 5/5–4–2; Texas Penal Code s. 12.45; *State v. Straszkowski*).

controversial to warrant full argument or a signed opinion (Ray 2000: 519–20).

As a general matter in US jurisprudence, no heightened process is required for the proof of real-offence allegations. It is enough that the conduct be shown to whatever standard, and in accordance with whatever informal procedures, ordinarily employed for fact-finding at sentencing. Indeed, the procedural differential between trial and sentencing supplies one of the doctrinal rationales for the most aggressive forms of real-offence sentencing:

> We have explained that 'acquittal on criminal charges does not prove that the defendant is innocent; it merely proves the existence of a reasonable doubt as to his guilt' . . . For these reasons, 'an acquittal in a criminal case does not preclude the Government from relitigating an issue when it is presented in a subsequent action governed by a lower standard of proof.' (*U.S.* v. *Watts*, at 155–6)

Also in startling divergence from Commonwealth sensibilities, the Supreme Court has held that consideration of real-offence conduct at sentencing does not bar later prosecution for those offences. In a 1995 ruling, the defendant had been sentenced in an earlier case based in part on the trial court's conclusion that he was guilty of a number of non-conviction drug crimes. He was given the same penalty that he would have received had he been convicted of the real-offence charges in addition to the conviction counts (knowable because of the mathematical precision of the federal sentencing guidelines). Later, the government initiated a new prosecution for the same offences, and the defendant brought a constitutional challenge under the double jeopardy clause that the government was seeking to punish him twice for the same crimes. The Supreme Court rejected the claim on the reasoning that the earlier sentence had been 'for' the conviction offences, which were made more serious by the real-offence conduct; there had been no earlier punishment 'for' the real-offence crimes themselves (*Witte* 1995).

US courts defend their practices by positing a sharp divide between the guilt and penalty stages of a criminal case, with the proper individualization of sentence in each case turning on consideration of the 'real' facts (*Williams*, at 248). While the trial is structured to bend over backwards to protect defendants' rights, the sentencing is designed to get at the 'best estimate' of the truth, with the presumption of innocence no longer in force (Michaels 2003). It has also been argued that real-offence sentencing serves the 'basic aim of ensuring similar sentences for those who have committed similar crimes in similar ways' by not allowing punishment to differ with the vagaries of the charges of conviction (*U.S.* v. *Booker* (2005, at 252)).

The peculiarly US sense that trial facts are not binding on sentencing facts is almost certainly related to the heavy reliance on plea bargaining in the United States compared with other countries (Wright, in press). US judges often view the version of offence attached to a guilty plea as only a fractional statement of the defendant's true guilt, at the absolute minimum of what the prosecutor was willing to accept, or else a made-up story to accommodate a plea agreement to a reduced charge (Schulhofer 1984: 757). The factual recitation in a guilty plea is, in essence, no more than a technical necessity to move beyond the guilt stage. Widespread under-punishment would result if judges were to take the formal boundaries of conviction too seriously. There is little anxiety that it is more important to avoid over-punishment errors than under-punishment errors. Quite the contrary, the endurance of real-offence sentencing across most of the United States surely owes something to the cultural shift towards high punitiveness in the late twentieth century, when Americans gave themselves permission to hate, fear and dehumanize criminals (Garland 2002: 6–20; Ruth and Reitz 2003: 68–9).

There are some accounts, however, that actually posit *advantages* to defendants in the real-offence framework. Historically, throughout much of the twentieth century, the need for wide-open factual inquiry at sentencing, including non-conviction offences, was rooted in the optimistic commitment of Americans to the rehabilitative treatment model of sentencing and the belief that therapeutic sanctions would founder if not based on the fullest available information concerning the offender's background and character (*Williams*, at 248). Weak procedural protections are more easily tolerated when the system is portrayed as working for the offender's own well-being (Rothman 1980).

Pursuing a different defendant-friendly tack, some have argued that prosecutors acquire undue power in a conviction-offence framework because they control which conviction facts will be charged and which bargained away. Real-offence sentencing is promoted as a check on this authority, on the fanciful notion that judges will base their sentence on the true facts, even when the parties have agreed to a less than full accounting of the seriousness of the defendant's conduct (Schulhofer 1984: 757–60; *Booker*, at 256–7).This is not terribly realistic given the parties' much greater knowledge of the particulars of the case than judges are able to acquire independently (Scott and Stuntz

1992). Most studies have concluded that real-offence sentencing adds to, rather than subtracts from, the prosecutor's arsenal (Tonry and Coffee 1987; Lear 1993; Reitz 1993; Yellen 2005).

REFORM IN THE UNITED STATES

Although the US and Commonwealth perspectives on real-offence sentencing are reasonably well defined, there are pockets of dissent on both sides of the divide. In the United States, jurisdictions with aberrant approaches have moved towards the Commonwealth systems, and vice versa in the Commonwealth.

A handful of US states that have adopted sentencing guidelines have instituted the conviction-offence programme, including the long-running and well-regarded systems in Minnesota and Washington State (Minnesota Sentencing Guidelines and Commentary § II.A.02; Revised Code of Washington §§ 9.94A.520, 9.94A.530(2); Reitz 1993: 535–42). National law reform organizations in the United States have likewise rejected the real-offence model (American Bar Association 1994: Standard 18–3.6; American Law Institute 2007: § 6B.06). Still, there has not been much action in the US courts or legislatures to curtail the practice of real-offence sentencing in the overwhelming majority of jurisdictions. Indeed, a much-praised decision by the Supreme Court in 2005 was a paean to the 'real conduct' doctrine (*Booker*, at 250–7 (majority opinion of Breyer J)).

BACKSLIDING IN CANADA

Meanwhile, there are signs that commitment to the conviction–offence paradigm is weakening in Canada – at least, there is discord on the question between Parliament and the courts. As part of a major overhaul of sentencing legislation in 1995, the Canadian Criminal Code was amended to state that sentencing judges 'may consider any facts forming part of the circumstances of the offence that could constitute the basis for a separate charge' (Revised Statutes of Canada 1985, c. C-46, s. 725 (1)(c)). The provision would appear to allow sentencing courts to consider additional ('separate') non-conviction offences when imposing sentence, but would not permit the court to substitute its judgment as to the proper grading of a conviction offence. The requirement that non-conviction counts must form 'part of the circumstances of the offence' is also a limit, albeit of uncertain elasticity.

The Supreme Court of Canada's first ruling under the new law came in 2006. In a prosecution of a participant in an alleged drug distribution enterprise across the Canadian–US border, there were two counts of conviction for drug offences in Canada. Under s. 725(1)(c), the trial court based sentence on the conviction crimes plus real-offence allegations that included several drug- and money-laundering crimes in Canada and the United States. The penalty was doubled from three to six years, based on the non-conviction conduct. On first appeal, the Quebec Court of Appeal attempted to nullify s. 725(1)(c) by engrafting a requirement that the provision could not be used without the defendant's consent. In frank disbelief, the Court of Appeal said that '*it cannot be*' (emphasis added), in the light of the presumption of innocence, that the provision was meant to allow non-conviction offences to be considered at sentencing (see also *R* v. *Pearson* (2001)).

The Supreme Court, however, was unwilling to defy Parliament's clear statement of intent to authorize some forms of real-offence sentencing. The Court upheld the trial court's consideration of the non-conviction offences that had taken place in Canada, with the incidental ruling that s. 725(1)(c) was not intended to reach crimes outside Canada's territorial jurisdiction (*R* v. *Larche*). The Court made it clear, however, that it shared the 'legitimate' and 'important concerns' of the Quebec Court of Appeal. It cited ameliorating features of Canadian sentencing procedure: that non-conviction offences must be proven at sentencing to the criminal standard of proof, and that later prosecution for those offences would be statutorily barred. Further, the *Larche* Court sent signals to trial courts that they should do what they can to interpret s. 725(1)(c) narrowly. It took pains to establish that the real-offence sentencing power was permissive, not mandatory, and expressed confidence that 'judges can be relied on, in the exercise of their discretion under s. 725(1)(c), to decline to consider uncharged offences if this would result in unfairness to the accused'. The Court admonished that '[c]are must also be taken, in applying s. 725 over the accused's objection, to ensure that the sentencing hearing is not transformed into a "trial within a trial" '. In short, the Canadian judiciary has shown little enthusiasm for Parliament's real-offence innovation, but the law is in flux.

CONCLUSION

While whole library wings are filled with the literatures of utilitarianism and desert as the substantive meat of sentencing policy, there has been far less debate over what core *process values* are at stake, and their deontological or instrumental origins. Procedural theory in general, and criminal procedure theory in particular, have not made deep incursions into the arena of criminal sentencing (Duff, Farmer and Marshall 2006; Vogler 2005; Damaska 1975; Packer 1968; Bone 2008). On the whole, the variegations in sentencing procedure we see in the Commonwealth vis-à-vis the United States are not debated or explained in sophisticated terms. When argument occurs, much of it is on the level of moral platitudes: that *fairness demands x* or *fundamental justice demands y*. Perorations over the presumption of innocence are not much better.

What is needed is greater elaboration of the moral intuitions that lie behind claims of fairness and legitimacy in sentencing process. Several specific questions arise from this short chapter alone. First, there should be closer examination of arguments that fact-finding at sentencing is essentially similar – or dissimilar – to fact-finding at trial. If an entirely different adjudicative model applies to sentencing, as most Americans believe, why should that be? Second, the principle of consistency in fact-finding across successive procedural stages demands greater thought. While often given voice in the Commonwealth, it is sometimes an impossible goal in bifurcated (or trifurcated) systems. Most US jurisdictions put no stock in it whatsoever, desiring judges to ignore the crudities of conviction facts, and parole boards to second-guess judges. Third, there is great tension between different accuracy models. Do we want a sentencing process that maximizes correct findings overall, or one biased to avoid certain kinds of error? Fourth, the relationship between substantive and procedural values in criminal sentencing must be confronted. A high enough sense of procedural regularity may make some substantive goals, such as rehabilitation and selective incapacitation, less obtainable. On the other hand, one of the most cogent defences of the just deserts programme (to my mind) is that it strictly limits the factual issues in play at sentencing, bringing assiduous process more easily within grasp.

A more powerful analytic might make some difference in the world. The Canadian slippage into real-offence sentencing shows the perils of an under-theorized and under-defended conception of conviction-offence sentencing. The US experience, in failing to make greater headway against the travesties of real-offence sentencing, may owe something to a stunted understanding of the procedural values at stake. The absence of full conversation is in a way a good thing; one never knows how people will respond to new arguments in previously barren territory. Lawmakers' minds are not always closed. One thing that is interesting about the US *Blakely* line of decisions is that even a conservative Supreme Court could find itself confounded by the borderline between trial facts and sentencing facts, and could suddenly perceive as unconvincing the argument that the two procedural contexts are entirely different.

REFERENCES

American Bar Association (1994). *Standards for Criminal Justice: Sentencing, Third Edition*. Washington, DC: American Bar Association.

American Law Institute (2007). *Model Penal Code: Sentencing, Tentative Draft No. 1* (approved May 16, 2007). Philadelphia: American Law Institute.

(2011). *Model Penal Code: Sentencing, Tentative Draft No. 2*. Philadelphia: American Law Institute.

Ashworth, A. (2010). *Sentencing and Criminal Justice*, 5th edn. Cambridge University Press.

Bone, R. (2008). 'Making Effective Rules: The Need for Procedure Theory', *Oklahoma Law Review*, 61: 319–40.

Breyer, S. (1988). 'The Federal Sentencing Guidelines and the Key Compromises upon which they Rest', *Hofstra Law Review*, 17: 1–50.

Campbell, A. (2004). *Law of Sentencing: Third Edition*. Eagan, MN: Thompson West.

Cole, D. and Manson, A. (1990). *Release from Imprisonment*. Scarborough, ON: Carswell.

Damaska, M. (1975). 'Structures of Authority and Comparative Criminal Procedure', *Yale Law Journal*, 84: 480–544.

Duff, A., Farmer, L. and Marshall, S. (eds.), (2006). *The Trial on Trial, Volume 2: Judgement and Calling to Account*. Oxford: Hart Publishing.

Edney, R. and Bagaric, M. (2007). *Australian Sentencing: Principles and Practice*. Cambridge University Press.

Frankel, M. (1973). *Criminal Sentences: Law Without Order*. New York: Hill & Wang.

Frase, R. (1990). 'Comparative Criminal Justice as a Guide to American Law Reform: How Do the French Do It, How Can We Find Out, and Why Should We Care?', *California Law Review* 78: 539–683.

Freiberg, A. (2001). 'Three Strikes and You're Out – It's Not Cricket: Colonization and Resistance in Australian Sentencing', in M. Tonry and R. Frase (eds.), *Sentencing and Sanctions in Western Countries*. New York: Oxford University Press, 29–61.

Garland, D. (2002). *The Culture of Control: Crime and Social Order in Contemporary Society*. University of Chicago Press.

Jareborg, N. (1998). 'Why Bulk Discounts in Multiple Sentencing?', in A. Ashworth and M. Wasik (eds.), *Fundamentals of Sentencing Theory*. Oxford University Press.

Lear, E. (1993). 'Is Conviction Irrelevant?', *UCLA Law Review*, 40: 1179–239.

Lynch, G. (1997). 'The Sentencing Guidelines as a Not-So-Model-Penal-Code', *Federal Sentencing Reporter*, 10: 25–8.

Manson, A. (2001). *The Law of Sentencing*. Toronto: Irwin Law.

Michaels, A. (2003). 'Trial Rights at Sentencing', *North Carolina Law Review*, 81: 1771–863.

Packer, H. (1968). *The Limits of the Criminal Sanction*. Stanford University Press.

Parent, Dale G. and Frase, Richard S. (2005). 'Why Minnesota Will Weather Blakely's Blast', *Federal Sentencing Reporter*, 18: 12–18.

Pfaff, J. (2006). 'The Continued Vitality of Structured Sentencing Following *Blakely*: The Effectiveness of Voluntary Guidelines', *UCLA Law Review*, 54: 235–307.

Pizzi, W. (1999). *Trials without Truth: Why Our System of Criminal Trials Has Become an Expensive Failure and What We Need to Do to Rebuild It*. New York University Press.

Ray, L. (2000). 'The Road to Bush v. Gore: The History of the Supreme Court's Use of the Per Curiam Opinion', *Nebraska Law Review*, 79: 517–76.

Reitz, K. (1993). 'Sentencing Facts: Travesties of Real-Offense Sentencing', *Stanford Law Review*, 45: 523–73.

(2005). 'The New Sentencing Conundrum: Policy and Constitutional Law at Cross-Purposes', *Columbia Law Review*, 105: 1082–123.

(2010). 'The Illusion of Proportionality: Desert and Repeat Offenders', in J. Roberts and A. von Hirsch (eds.), *Previous Convictions at Sentencing: Theoretical and Applied Perspectives*. Oxford: Hart Publishing.

(in press). 'Indeterminate Sentencing', in J. Petersilia and K. Reitz (eds.), *The Oxford Handbook of Sentencing and Corrections*. Oxford University Press.

Rhine, E. (in press). 'The Present Status and Future Prospects of Parole Boards and Parole Supervision', in J. Petersilia and K. Reitz (eds.), *The Oxford Handbook of Sentencing and Corrections*. Oxford University Press

Rothman, David J. (1980). *Conscience and Convenience: The Asylum and Its Alternatives in Progressive America*. Boston: Little, Brown & Co.

Ruby, C. (2004). *Sentencing, Sixth Edition*. Markham, ON: LexisNexis Canada.

Ruth, H. and Reitz, K. (2003). *The Challenge of Crime: Rethinking Our Response*. Harvard University Press.

Schulhofer, S. (1984). 'Due Process of Sentencing', *University of Pennsylvania Law Review*, 128: 733–828.

Scott, R. and Stuntz, W. (1992). 'Plea Bargaining as Contract', *Yale Law Journal*, 101: 1909–68.

Sentencing Advisory Panel (2010). *Advice to the Sentencing Guidelines Council, Offences Taken Into Consideration*. London: Sentencing Advisory Panel.
Tonry, M. (1981). 'Real Offense Sentencing: The Model Sentencing and Corrections Act', *Journal of Criminal Law and Criminology*, 72: 1550–96.
Tonry, M. and Coffee, J., Jr (1987). 'Enforcing Sentencing Guidelines: Plea Bargaining and Review Mechanisms', in A. von Hirsch, K. Knapp and M. Tonry (eds.), *The Sentencing Commission and its Guidelines*. Boston: Northeastern University Press, 142–76.
Vogler, R. (2005). *A World View of Criminal Justice*. Aldershot: Ashgate Publishing.
Weigend, T. (2001). 'Sentencing and Punishment in Germany', in Tonry and Frase (eds.) in M. Tonry and R. Frase (eds.), *Sentencing and Sanctions in Western Countries*. New York: Oxford University Press, 188–221.
Wright, R. (in press). 'Charging and Plea Bargaining as Forms of Sentencing Discretion', in J. Petersilia and K. Reitz (eds.), *The Oxford Handbook of Sentencing and Corrections*. Oxford University Press.
Yellen, D. (2005). 'Reforming the Federal Sentencing Guidelines' Misguided Approach to Real-Offense Sentencing', *Stanford Law Review*, 58: 267–75.
Zimring, F. (2003). *The Contradictions of American Capital Punishment*. Oxford University Press.

TABLE OF CASES

Bauer *v*. State, 983 P.2d 955 (Mont. 1999).
Blakely *v*. Washington, 542 U.S. 296 (2004).
Bradley *v*. State, 2006 WL 1420399 (Tex. Crim. App. 2006).
Duncan *v*. Louisiana, 391 U.S. 145 (1968).
Gregg *v*. Georgia, 428 U.S 153 (1976).
Guppy and Marsh [1995] 16 Cr. App. R. (S) 25 (Eng.).
Isaacs *v*. the Queen [1997] 90 A. Crim. R. 587 (NSW)
Mayes *v*. State, 604 A.2d 839 (Del. 1992).
McMillan *v*. Pennsylvania, 477 US 79 (1986).
Oregon *v*. Ice, 129 S. Ct. 711 (2009) (U.S.).
People *v*. Green, 391 N.W.2d 507 (Mich. 1986).
R v Canavan [1998] 1 Cr. App. R. 243 (Eng.).
R *v*. Davies [2009] 1 Cr. App. R. (S) 79 (Eng.).
R *v*. Gardiner [1982] 2 S.C.R. 368 (Can.).
R *v*. Larche, [2006] 2 S.C.R. 762 (Can.).
R *v*. McGrath and Casey [1983] 5 Cr App R (S) 460 (Eng.).
R *v*. Olbrich [1999] 166 A.L.R. 330 (Austl.).
R *v*. Pearson [2001] R.J.Q. 69 (QU).
R *v*. Sinfield, [2005] E.W.C.A. Crim. 3638 (Eng.).
R *v*. Tempelaar [1995] 1 S.C.R. 760 (Can.).

R *v*. Tolera, [1999] 1 Cr. App. R. (S) 25 (Eng.).
Ring *v*. Arizona, 536 U.S. 584 (2002).
State *v*. Altajir, 2 A.3d 1024 (Conn. App. 2010).
State *v*. Cook, 706 A.2d 603 (Me. 1998).
State *v*. Cote, 530 A.2d 775 (N.H. 1987).
State *v*. Marley, 364 S.E.2d 133 (N.C. 1988).
State *v*. Parker, 992 A.2d 1103 (Conn. 2010).
State *v*. Spears, 596 N.W.2d 375 (Wis. 1999).
State *v*. Straszkowski, 750 N.W.2d 835 (Wis. 2008).
Townsend *v*. Burke, 334 U.S. 736 (1948).
U.S. *v*. Booker, 543 U.S. 220 (2005).
U.S. *v*. Chavez, 119 F.3d 342 (5th Cir. 1997) (U.S.).
U.S. *v*. DuPont, 15 F.3d 5 (1st Cir. 1994) (U.S.).
U.S. *v*. Fisher, 502 F.3d 293 (3d Cir. 2007) (U.S.).
U.S. *v*. Juarez-Ortega, 866 F.2d 747 (5th Cir. 1989) (U.S.).
U.S. *v*. Kikumura, 918 F.2d 1084 (3d Cir. 1990) (U.S.).
U.S. *v*. O'Brien, 130 S. Ct. 2169 (2010) (U.S.).
U.S. *v*. Santiago, 993 F.2d 504 (5th Cir. 1993) (U.S.).
U.S. *v*. Tucker, 404 U.S. 443 (1972).
U.S. *v*. Watts, 519 U.S. 148 (1997) (per curiam).
Weininger *v*. The Queen [2003] 212 C.L.R. 629 (Austl.)
Williams *v*. New York, 337 U.S. 241 (1949).
Witte *v*. United States, 515 U.S. 389 (1995).

CHAPTER THIRTEEN

MITIGATION IN FEDERAL SENTENCING IN THE UNITED STATES

William W. Berry III

Other chapters in the present volume explore sentencing factors in jurisdictions such as South Africa, Canada or New Zealand, where courts impose sentence in the absence of formal guidelines. Across the United States, however, many jurisdictions employ formal sentencing guidelines, often in the form of a two-dimensional sentencing grid. These guidelines establish a 'presumptive' range of sentence for all offences. One of the most well-known and often studied systems is found at the federal level and applies to all offenders sentenced in the federal courts. The US Sentencing Commission issues these guidelines.[1] The federal guidelines employ a two-dimensional grid (offence seriousness; criminal history) with 256 cells that delineates six-month sentencing ranges.

Since their adoption in 1987, the US federal sentencing guidelines have required the use of narrow mandatory sentencing ranges in almost every case, thereby contributing to the creation of one of the largest prison populations in the world (Luna 2005; Stuntz 2001). In determining ranges the mandatory sentencing guidelines identified which aggravating factors must be considered while severely restricting the consideration of mitigating factors at sentencing, disfavouring most potential mitigating factors (Tonry 1996).

In 2005, however, the United States Supreme Court in *United States* v. *Booker* held that the mandatory guidelines were unconstitutional. As a result, the guidelines are now only advisory in nature. With advisory

[1] See www.ussc.gov for further information.

guidelines, consideration of previously disfavoured or forbidden mitigating factors became permissible and widely expanded the ability of federal judges to use such evidence to mitigate the length of sentences.

CHAPTER OVERVIEW

This chapter describes the transformation in the mitigating factors available for consideration in sentencing in the United States federal courts after the *Booker* decision. In addition, the chapter conceptualizes this shift in terms of the theoretical judicial application of competing retributive and utilitarian goals now required under the advisory scheme (Berry 2007). Finally, the chapter examines recent practices in the US federal courts to ascertain the practical effect on sentencing outcomes over the past five years of the reshuffling of aggravating and mitigating factors.

FEDERAL SENTENCING IN THE UNITED STATES, PRE-*BOOKER*

The adoption of the sentencing guidelines

Prior to the adoption of the guidelines in 1987, US federal judges were afforded virtually unfettered discretion in making sentencing decisions (Tonry 1996). This fact, combined with the broad statutory sentencing ranges, resulted in the imposition of inconsistent and disparate sentences for the same or similar crimes (see discussion in Morris 1977; Nagel 1990). Congress sought to address this problem in federal sentencing by passing the Sentencing Reform Act of 1984 (Anello and Peikin 2006). To encourage uniformity and certainty at sentencing, the Sentencing Reform Act established the United States Sentencing Commission as an independent agency in the judicial branch, and charged it with the promulgation of sentencing guidelines to limit the scope of discretion of federal judges. In 1987 the Commission promulgated mandatory sentencing guidelines for federal sentences. The guidelines are comprehensive and attempt to consider almost every potential situation within their framework. As a result, the adoption of the guidelines largely eviscerated the previously expansive discretion of federal judges in sentencing (Tonry 1996).

Calculation of a sentence under the guidelines

Under the guidelines, calculation of an offender's sentencing guideline range depends on the determination of two principal components: the seriousness of the criminal conduct (offence level) and the offender's past criminal conduct (criminal history). The guideline calculation of the offence level includes a number of factors, including the circumstances of the crime, the nature of the victim and the offender's role in the offence. These factors predominantly relate to the culpability of the offender and the degree of harm caused by the criminal conduct. Calculation of the offender's criminal history category quantifies the prior sentences based on their seriousness (offence level) and temporal proximity to the present offence in order to establish the recidivist premium (Roberts 1994). After the offence level of the conduct and the offender's criminal history category have been calculated, the sentencing guideline range is determined in accordance with the Sentencing Table; this contains sentencing ranges, each range being measured in increments of six months of imprisonment. For example, an offender convicted of an offence of seriousness level 36 and who falls into criminal history category III is subject to a sentence within the range of 235 to 293 months. After the final sentencing guideline range has been calculated, the mandatory guidelines (before *Booker*) permit departures from that range only in rare cases.

Mitigation under the guidelines

Grounds for mitigation within the calculation of the guideline range

The guidelines limit mitigation in the calculation of the guideline range to (i) considerations of the offender's role in the offence, and (ii) the offender's acceptance of responsibility for the crime. Where the offender was a 'minimal participant' or 'minor participant', the guidelines provide for lowering the level of the offence between two and four levels (§3B1.2). If the offender 'clearly demonstrates acceptance of responsibility', the guidelines provide for lowering the level of offence seriousness by two seriousness levels (§3E1.1).

Grounds for mitigation from guideline range (downward departures)

Once the calculation of the sentence has been made under the guidelines, a federal judge may choose, in rare situations, to depart downward from the sentencing guideline range based on specified mitigating circumstances (§5K2.0(a)(2)(A)). The grounds for downward departure predominately fall into three categories: the offender's actions during the commission of the crime, the offender's post-offence conduct and, in rare situations, the specific characteristics of the offender.

The reasons for downward departure based on the offender's actions during the commission of the crime are limited to four categories that indicate diminished culpability:

(1) the crime involved a 'lesser harm' (§5K2.11);
(2) the victim's conduct significantly contributed to the offender's conduct (§5K2.10);
(3) the offender acted in response to some degree of coercion (§5K2.12); and
(4) the offender committed a single, brief, unplanned and less serious 'out-of-character' crime (§5K2.20).

The grounds for departure based on post-offence conduct are even more limited; they include providing substantial assistance to authorities and making a voluntary disclosure of the offence (§5K1.1, 2.16). Finally, the guidelines likewise severely restrict the consideration of the specific characteristics, limiting departures to offenders with diminished capacity or a criminal history category that substantially over-represents the seriousness of offender's criminal history or likelihood that the offender will commit other crimes (§5K2.13, 4A1.3).

Disfavoured or impermissible grounds for mitigation

The guidelines create a hierarchy of other possible reasons for mitigation, categorizing them as either 'disfavoured' or 'prohibited'. The disfavoured categories include:

- the age of the offender;
- the offender's educational and vocational skills;
- the offender's mental or emotional condition, physical condition and physique;
- the employment record of an offender;
- the offender's family ties and responsibilities; and, finally,
- any prior good works of the offender (§5H1 et seq.).

The prohibited categories for downward departure include:

- an offender's drug or alcohol dependence, gambling addiction;
- the offender's aggravating or mitigating role in the offence;
- the offender's race, sex, national origin, creed, religion and socio-economic status;
- any evidence of a offender's lack of guidance as a youth or other factors demonstrating a disadvantaged upbringing;

- acceptance of responsibility for the crime, a guilty plea or entry into a plea agreement; and mere fulfilment of restitution obligations without exceptional effort to remedy any harm caused by the crime (§5H1.4, 1.7, 1.10).

Also prohibited as a downward departure during re-sentencing an offender for an offence are the post-sentencing rehabilitative efforts of that offender which were undertaken after imprisonment for that offence (§5K2.19).

THE *BOOKER* JUDGMENT AND ITS EFFECT ON THE GUIDELINES

The *Booker* decision

At his federal trial, Booker was found guilty of possession with the intent to distribute at least 50 grams of cocaine base (crack), based on evidence that he had 92.5 grams in his duffle bag. The applicable statute (21 USC § 841(b)(1)(A)(iii)) prescribed a minimum sentence of ten years in prison and a maximum sentence of life imprisonment for that offence. Based on Booker's criminal history and the quantity of drugs in his possession, the guidelines required the judge to impose a sentence of not less than 210 months (seventeen years, six months) and not more than 262 months (twenty-one years, ten months) in prison. After holding a post-trial sentencing proceeding, the judge, using a preponderance of the evidence standard, concluded that 'Booker had possessed an additional 566 grams of crack and that he was guilty of obstructing justice' (at 227). These findings mandated a new sentencing range of thirty years to life imprisonment, and the judge sentenced Booker to thirty years' imprisonment.

The question before the court in *Booker* was whether the sentence enhancement called for by the guidelines – and resulting in a sentence of thirty years – violated Booker's Sixth Amendment right to a jury trial. Booker claimed that because the enhancement exceeded the original guideline maximum and was based on facts not determined by the jury, his right to a jury trial, pursuant to the Court's prior decision in *US* v. *Apprendi*, had been violated. In other words, it was argued by Booker that the prosecution had to prove these facts to a jury beyond a reasonable doubt, instead of to a judge by a preponderance of the evidence.

In a 5–4 decision, the Supreme Court held that Booker's sentence violated the Sixth Amendment and, as a result, the application of the guidelines in this manner was unconstitutional. Importantly, the Court explained that the mandatory nature of the guidelines, requiring that the judge impose a sentence in excess of the initial statutory range based on facts not proven to a jury, caused the Sixth Amendment violation. The Court also emphasized, however, that the Sixth Amendment requirement that facts be proven to a jury does not limit 'the authority of a judge to exercise broad discretion in imposing a sentence within a statutory range' (*Booker*, at 233–4).

The *Booker* remedy

Curiously, the Court had a different 5–4 split in the second part of the opinion, in which it determined the remedy for the unconstitutional application mandated by the guidelines. The Court chose not to abandon the guidelines, or, in the alternative, to require jury fact-finding in situations where the guidelines procedures would violate the Sixth Amendment; instead, the Court held that 'the provision of the federal sentencing statute that makes the guidelines mandatory, 18 USC § 3553 (b)(1) . . . must be severed and excised' because it was incompatible with the Sixth Amendment (*Booker*, at 245). As a result, the Court's decision in *Booker* made the guidelines effectively advisory. After *Booker*, the federal sentencing scheme still requires a sentencing court to consider guideline ranges as part of the court's inquiry under § 3553(a)(4), but it permits the court to tailor the sentence in the light of 'other statutory concerns as well', specifically the other factors under § 3553(a).

The Court also severed one other statutory section, § 3742(e), because it depended on the guidelines' mandatory nature. The Court replaced the § 3742(e) standard of review for departures from the guidelines with an appellate standard of reasonableness. This significantly expanded the discretion of the federal courts of appeal in reviewing sentencing decisions, allowing a reversal of a sentence based on the view that a district court's sentencing decision was unreasonable.

Current sentencing under the advisory guidelines

After *Booker*, federal courts have adopted a three-step process in making sentencing determinations. First, the sentencing judge must properly calculate the appropriate sentencing guideline range, carefully considering potential grounds for departure. Second, the judge must determine whether a guidelines sentence would adequately serve the factors enumerated by Congress in 18 USC § 3553(a) and, if not, select a sentence that does. Third, the district court must articulate the reasons for the sentence imposed, particularly explaining any departure or variance from the guideline range and its application of § 3553(a).

The requirements of 18 USC §3553

Section 3553(a) articulates a parsimony principle that requires consideration of the four traditional objectives of sentencing (desert, deterrence, incapacitation and rehabilitation). Under this principle, the Court is required to adopt a sentence sufficient, but not greater than necessary, to achieve these purposes.

The statute provides in full:

(a) **Factors To Be Considered in Imposing a Sentence** – The court shall impose a sentence sufficient, but not greater than necessary, to comply with the purposes set forth in paragraph (2) of this subsection. The court, in determining the particular sentence to be imposed, shall consider –
  (1) the nature and circumstances of the offence and the history and characteristics of the defendant;
  (2) the need for the sentence imposed –
    (A) to reflect the seriousness of the offence, to promote respect for the law, and to provide just punishment for the offence;
    (B) to afford adequate deterrence to criminal conduct;
    (C) to protect the public from further crimes of the defendant; and
    (D) to provide the defendant with needed educational or vocational training, medical care, or other correctional treatment in the most effective manner . . . (18 USC §3553(a))

Thus the Court must decide whether the guideline range resulting from the advisory guidelines is consistent with, or contradicts, the parsimony principle. In addition to the above language, the statute also contemplates that, in imposing a sentence, the court must also consider several other factors: the nature and circumstances of the offence and the history and characteristics of the offender, the kinds of sentence available, the kinds of sentence and sentencing range established under the sentencing guidelines, any pertinent policy statement issued by the Sentencing Commission, the need to avoid unwarranted sentence disparities, and the need to provide restitution to any victims.

SENTENCE MITIGATION AFTER *BOOKER*

In his concurrence in *Rita* v. *United States*, Stevens J astutely noted that not only did *Booker* make previously disfavoured or prohibited categories of mitigation available, but now made consideration of such categories *mandatory*. He observed,

> The Commission has not developed any standards or recommendations that affect sentencing ranges for many individual characteristics. Matters such as age, education, mental or emotional condition, medical condition (including drug or alcohol addiction), employment history, lack of guidance as a youth, family ties, or military, civic, charitable, or public service are not ordinarily considered under the guidelines. These are, however, matters that §3553(a) authorizes the sentencing judge to consider. As such, they are factors that an appellate court must consider under *Booker*'s abuse-of-discretion standard [internal citations omitted]. (*Rita* v. *United States*, Stevens J concurring)

In order to determine which of the disfavoured and prohibited guideline categories of mitigation are now permitted and even mandatory, one must examine the degree to which such categories inform the application of §3553 to the calculated guideline sentence. In other words, the Court must consider which of the above-described categories of mitigation inform the question whether a given sentence meets the parsimony sentencing requirement of 'sufficient, but not greater than necessary' to achieve the four articulated purposes of punishment: just deserts, deterrence, incapacitation and rehabilitation. This inquiry does not address the inherent problems in attempting to meet four, often contradictory, purposes (Berry 2007), but instead simply examines which mitigation evidence is now relevant in sentencing determinations.

Applying §3553 to the advisory guidelines

Mitigation and just deserts

Section 3553(a) codifies the principle of proportionality, derived from desert theory, requiring the court to examine whether the advisory guideline sentence calculation is sufficient to reflect the seriousness of the offence, to promote respect for the law, and to provide just punishment for the offence. In determining the appropriate punishment, the theory of just deserts looks principally to the culpability of the offender and the harm caused by the offender's conduct (von Hirsch and Ashworth 2005). This concept of just deserts demands that an offender receive exactly the amount of punishment he deserves for the crime committed – no more or no less (Robinson 2009; Ashworth 2010).

In terms of mitigation, some of the disfavoured categories under the guidelines relate to the culpability of the offender or the harm caused. One possible category of mitigation that could reduce culpability would be the age of the offender. The youth of the offender in certain cases can mitigate a retributive sentence based on a determination that a juvenile possesses a decreased level of culpability (Zimring 1982). Similarly, evidence of a disadvantaged upbringing might bear on the culpability of the offender in such a way as to warrant mitigation under a theory of just deserts (von Hirsch and Ashworth 2005).

While the presence of mental or emotional conditions suffered by the offender may be evidence of lessened culpability, they probably will not be a valid source of mitigation because, in most situations, they will serve to increase the need for incapacitation. Likewise, while the drug or alcohol dependence of the offender arguably could serve to reduce culpability (see the chapter by Padfield in this volume for discussion), such dependence is typically not factored as a discount into the determination of desert.

Mitigation and deterrence

Section 3553 defines deterrence as the need for the sentence imposed to afford adequate deterrence to criminal conduct. The theory of general deterrence justifies a particular punishment based on its ability to deter others from committing the same crime (Bentham 1843). General deterrence depends on a number of factors, including the severity of the penalty, the swiftness with which it is imposed, the probability of being caught and punished, the target group's perceptions of the severity, swiftness and certainty of punishment; the extent to which members of the target group suffer from addiction, mental illness or other conditions which significantly diminish their capacity to obey the law; and the extent to which these would-be offenders face competing pressures or incentives to commit crime (Frase 2005).

Most of the disfavoured categories of mitigation have little effect on the determination whether a sentence deters others from committing the same crime. The exception would be where an individual offender's characteristics make the case such an outlier that it would be unlikely to achieve the same deterrent value as the typical case. For instance, consideration of an offender's prior good works as a community hero or leader might provide evidence that the same deterrent value might not be achieved by a long sentence in that case. Generally speaking, though, the prohibited or disfavoured evidence of mitigation would have little bearing on deterrence and thus not be relevant to that part of the section 3553 determination.

Mitigation and incapacitation

The third purpose of sentencing that section 3553 requires a sentencing court to consider is incapacitation, defined as the need for the sentence imposed to protect the public from further crimes of the offender. The concept of incapacitation is a justification for punishment based on the potential threat an offender will be likely to pose *in the future* (Ashworth 2010). The rationale, then, for punishing someone based on their dangerousness is that the state needs to protect its citizens from the threat that the offender poses to society. In other words, the state chooses to incapacitate an offender in order to ensure that the offender does not commit the same or another criminal act.

In terms of mitigation, several of the disfavoured and prohibited categories could provide evidence of the 'dangerousness' of the offender. First, the offender's education and vocational skills and employment history could provide for mitigation based on the degree to which such evidence could prove a reduced likelihood that the offender might reoffend, as such categories may be indicia of an absence of dangerousness. Similarly, prior good works of an offender could provide evidence of a reduced need to incapacitate the offender. In addition, the age of the offender could provide mitigating evidence on the issue of dangerousness, particularly where the offender is elderly.

Mitigation and rehabilitation

Finally, section 3553 articulates a fourth purpose that must be considered during sentencing – rehabilitation – which it defines as the need for the sentence imposed to provide the offender with needed educational or vocational training, medical care or other correctional treatment in the most effective manner. Asking the question of the kind of sentence necessary to ensure that the offender has been 'corrected' enough to rejoin society, the goal of rehabilitation provides a final justification for introducing previously disfavoured or barred mitigation evidence.

A number of such categories can provide persuasive evidence mitigating the length of time an offender needs to serve before being rehabilitated, including the offender's education and vocational skills, the employment record of an offender, and the family ties and responsibilities of the offender. All of these can be indicia of the ability of the offender to rejoin society and can be a basis for mitigating a sentence.

Several other categories of mitigating evidence might also be relevant to the degree that they are 'treatable' conditions that could be rehabilitated in a lesser time frame than the advisory guideline sentence. For instance, where an offender has mental or emotional conditions that can be remedied with medication and other forms of treatment, the ability to remedy these conditions may be grounds for mitigating a sentence. Likewise, the ability to remedy the drug or alcohol dependence of an offender may serve as grounds to mitigate a sentence on the basis of rehabilitation.

The theoretical puzzle of the advisory guidelines

The expanded availability of categories of mitigation explicitly disfavoured or prohibited still does not address the problem of how federal trial judges should determine sentences. Much has been made of the sentencing commission's (and Congress's) failure to choose a guiding rationale for sentencing offenders, and arguably this failure has come back to haunt it (von Hirsch, Knapp and Tonry 1989). The four purposes of punishment (just deserts, deterrence, incapacitation and rehabilitation) often dictate different and contradictory outcomes in sentencing (Ashworth 2010; Berry 2007). Given these four competing mandates, the parsimony clause and the presence of the advisory guidelines, how then should a judge calculate the appropriate sentence? One cannot assume that the guidelines reflect the appropriate balance of the purposes of punishment in every case, because, as discussed, some categories of mitigation previously disapproved by the guidelines must now be taken into account.

One possible approach would be to read the parsimony language of 3553 ('[t]he court shall impose a sentence sufficient, but not greater than necessary, to comply with the purposes' of just deserts, deterrence, incapacitation and rehabilitation) to mean that the court should apply the shortest sentence that would comply with *all* the purposes. In other words, the court would determine the purpose that dictated the longest sentence and apply that purpose. A contrary approach would to be to read the same language to mean that the court should apply the sentence that would comply with *any* of the purposes. This approach would result in the court choosing the purpose that dictated the shortest sentence and applying that purpose.

A third approach would be to assume that the guidelines encompassed most of the purposes and to depart from the guidelines only in situations where the additional mitigating evidence was such that the guideline sentence would seriously offend one of the purposes. This might occur, for instance, where an offender's personal characteristics reduced his or her culpability in such a way as to make the guideline sentence excessive. Of course, in certain situations, such as the crack cocaine guidelines, the guidelines themselves can be found to be excessive by a court (see *United States* v. *Kimbrough*).

A final approach would be to prioritize among the purposes for a particular crime, and then adjust the sentence within a range defined by that purpose. One example of such an approach is the limiting retributivism approach practised in Minnesota (Morris 1977). The result of all of these possible interpretations could be confusion and inconsistency. The courts, however, as explained below, have largely chosen to ignore this advisory guideline puzzle and instead simply apply the advisory guideline sentence.

The practical outcome of advisory guidelines

The practical outcome of the advisory guidelines, however, has been largely a preservation of the prior pre-*Booker* status quo. Despite the broader discretion offered and even required of judges under Booker and section 3553, judges have adopted the guideline sentence in an overwhelming majority of cases. As one federal appellate judge lamented in the case of *U.S.* v. *Sexton*,

> the old system is just continuing on as though nothing had happened – continuing under the pretext that the guidelines are only 'advisory' instead of being considered only as a starting point against the backdrop of the more sensible and humane penological goals set out in § 3553(a), Title 18. This case is one more example of the continuing problem, the problem of guidelineism, or 'guidelinitis,' the inability of most federal courts to break their habit of mechanically relying just on the guidelines alone. (Merritt J dissenting)

Statistics in the five years since *Booker* support this conclusion. In 2009, for instance, judges used their additional discretion to depart downward using *Booker* in only 12 per cent of cases (see US Sentencing Commission 2010). Further, the average sentence length post-*Booker* has actually increased, with judges choosing to depart upward in more cases than before. In most cases, then, federal trial judges sentence within the six-month advisory guideline range, and then provide boilerplate language explaining how they considered all four of the section 3553 purposes of punishment in determining the sentence.

What explains the collective decision by federal judges to adhere largely to guidelines that are no longer mandatory? At first glance, it is surprising to see that judges have chosen not to use additional discretion accorded to them. Several factors may explain the pervasiveness of what may be termed 'guidelinitis'.

First, the threat of reversal on appeal under a 'reasonableness' standard, even when the review is for an abuse of discretion, may contribute to the trend simply to apply the guideline sentence in the typical case. With all of the judges having life tenure, though, this certainly cannot be the only explanation. Second, the phenomenon of status quo persistence and the relative ease of simply calculating the sentence under the guidelines may provide a sense of predictability and legitimacy for trial judges. The judges, after having used them for many years, may simply just have become comfortable with the guidelines. Finally – and perhaps most significantly – is the potential confusion created by actually trying to apply the four competing purposes of section 3553 to determine a sentence. As described above, there are at least four broad approaches a judge could take in trying to determine what the appropriate sentence may be. Given the potential for confusion, it may prove easier to apply the guidelines in most cases and then use boilerplate language to justify that decision.

CONCLUSION

The *Booker* decision has, in theory, had a dramatic impact on mitigation in federal sentencing by allowing offenders to introduce evidence of a number of categories of mitigation previously disfavoured or prohibited by the guidelines. In other words, categories of mitigation such as the offender's age, educational and vocational skills, employment record, family ties and responsibilities, and any prior good works – all are now part of the sentencing calculus of the judge, to the extent that they inform the judge's application of the purposes of punishment (desert, deterrence, rehabilitation and dangerousness).

Unfortunately, the internal inconsistency of the statute and its parsimony principle has made this new advisory guideline system difficult to apply. The result of the confusion in how to analyse the application of the guidelines in the light of competing purposes of punishment has been a decision, in most cases, simply to apply the guidelines. In other words, the absence of clarity in determining how to apply the guidelines has resulted in a decision not to exercise broader judicial discretion in many cases. So far, then, while the availability of mitigation evidence in federal sentencing has dramatically increased, the overall effect on sentencing outcomes has been quite limited. Until the reluctance of judges to move beyond the guidelines in a large majority of cases diminishes, the real impact of *Booker* will remain largely theoretical.

REFERENCES

Anello, R. J. and Peikin, J. M. (2006). 'Evolving Roles in Federal Sentencing: The Post-*Booker/Fanfan* World', *Federal Courts Law Review*, 1: 301–17.

Ashworth, A. (2010). *Sentencing and Criminal Justice*, 5th edn. Cambridge University Press.
Bentham, J. (1843). *The Works of Jeremy Bentham, Published under the Superintendence of his Executor, John Bowring*. Edinburgh: William Tait.
Berry III, W. W. (2007). 'Discretion Without Guidance, the Need to Give Meaning to 3553 after *Booker* and its Progeny', *Connecticut Law Review*, 40: 631–73.
Frase, R. S. (2005). 'Punishment Purposes', *Stanford Law Review*, 58: 67–84.
Luna, E. (2005). 'The Overcriminalization Phenomena', *American University Law Review*, 54: 703–46.
Morris, N. (1977). 'Towards Principled Sentencing', *Maryland Law Review*, 37: 267–85.
Nagel, I. H. (1990). 'Structuring Sentencing Discretion: The New Federal Sentencing Guidelines', *Journal of Criminal Law and Criminology*, 80: 883–943.
Roberts, J. V. (1994). 'The Role of Criminal Record in the Federal Sentencing Guidelines', *Criminal Justice Ethics*, 13: 21–30.
Robinson, P. H. (2009). *Distributive Principles of Criminal Law*. Oxford University Press.
Stuntz, W. J. (2001). 'The Pathological Politics of Criminal Law', *Michigan Law Review*, 100: 505–600.
Tonry, M. (1996). *Sentencing Matters*. Oxford University Press.
US Sentencing Commission (2010). *Federal Sentencing Statistics*, available at www.ussc.gov/linktojp.htm.
von Hirsch, A. and Ashworth, A. (2005). *Proportionate Sentencing: Exploring the Principles*. Oxford University Press.
von Hirsch, A., Knapp, K. A. and Tonry, M. (1989). *The Sentencing Commission and its Guidelines*. Boston, MA: Northeastern University Press.
Zimring, F. E. (1982). *The Changing Legal World of Adolescence*. New York: Free Press.

TABLE OF CASES

Rita *v.* United States, 551 US 338 (2007).
United States *v.* Apprendi, 530 US 466 (2000).
United States *v.* Booker, 543 US 220 (2005).
United States *v.* Kimbrough, 552 US 85 (2007).
United States *v.* Sexton, 512 F3d 326 (2008).

CHAPTER FOURTEEN

THE DISCRETIONARY EFFECT OF MITIGATING AND AGGRAVATING FACTORS: A SOUTH AFRICAN CASE STUDY

Stephan Terblanche

The sentence imposed in a South African court depends primarily on the discretion of the presiding judicial officer, the sentencer. The sentencer is expected to come to a reasonable decision regarding an appropriate sentence, based on all the facts relevant to the case. These facts might be aggravating, mitigating or even neutral in their effect on the sentence. The sentencer should explain in the judgment why the eventual sentence is appropriate. This judgment usually states that all the relevant facts and factors have been taken 'into account' or have been considered, but the extent to which such factors actually affect the sentence usually remains a mystery.

However, the purely discretionary sentencing model is not the only model in place, as South African law currently employs two different but parallel sentencing models, where the roles of mitigating and aggravating circumstances are not quite the same. The first model could be described as the traditional position; the second manifests itself within a wide-ranging scheme of minimum custodial sentences that affect most of the more serious crimes. Within the traditional model the sentencer's discretion determines the complete creation of the sentence,[1] but with the minimum-sentences scheme the starting points are provided by the legislature. Whereas the details of the minimum sentences are uniquely South African (Terblanche and Mackenzie 2008), the same is not true

[1] The discretion is not equally wide for all sentences, but it is widest in the case of fines and imprisonment (the most frequently imposed sanctions).

of discretionary sentencing – here South African law has much in common with other parts of the world.

A large number of factors have at times been described as either mitigating or aggravating, or even both, depending on the circumstances. One sentencing text in South Africa has identified fifteen 'considerations of prime importance' and an additional twenty-nine 'miscellaneous considerations' (Rabie et al. 1992: 301–46).[2] Beyond the most obvious such factors, the prime considerations also include circumstances such as the social status of the offender, remorse, the prevalence of the offence and the cumulative effect of multiple sentences. Included in the miscellaneous considerations are examples such as when the accused person is an alcoholic or a foreigner or even a university student, and the overcrowded state of prisons. However, few of these factors consistently affect the sentence imposed and it is not possible to predict their effect on the sentence with any certainty, or within any acceptable range of accuracy. As I concluded elsewhere, '[i]t is almost impossible to assess what weight the different mitigating factors have on a particular sentence, since it is never known what the sentence would have been in the absence of those factors' (Terblanche 2007: 194–5). To put it differently, an independent observer is unable to determine what starting point, if any, was used by the sentencer in the sentencing process. One cannot claim that no starting points are used, as it is quite possible for individual sentencers to develop their own starting points. This is particularly true of district magistrates' courts in larger cities, where an individual sentencer may repeatedly hear similar cases. However, even if they were developed, such starting points are rarely mentioned.

CHAPTER OVERVIEW

This chapter considers the role of mitigating and aggravating factors or circumstances within such a dual sentencing system. To that end it is first necessary to explain the basic principles guiding sentencing in South Africa. This explanation is followed by examples of how these principles are used in practice to determine sentence. In the course of this exercise it will be shown that it is usually impossible to isolate the effect of individual factors, whether mitigating or aggravating. Finally,

[2] In another work seventeen mitigating and seventeen aggravating factors were addressed (Hiemstra 1987, pp. 590–604).

the opportunity is taken to make certain recommendations, based on the proposals of the South African Law Commission, towards improving the application of sentencing factors.

BASIC PRINCIPLES OF SENTENCING

The traditional approach

The traditional approach to sentencing requires the sentencer to exercise his or her discretion in order to determine an appropriate sentence. The sentence should be neither too lenient nor too severe. The guiding principles are judge-made and are contained in what has become known as the 'triad of *Zinn*', from the judgment in *S v. Zinn* (1969). The court held that '[w]hat has to be considered is the triad consisting of the crime, the offender and the interests of society'. This statement has become trite[3] and does not require further discussion here. Suffice to say that the three basic elements in the construction of any sentence are (i) the seriousness of the crime; (ii) the offender's personal circumstances; and (iii) the wider interests of society.

As so often happens in the case of principles that are stated in broad terms, the difficulty lies in their application. Therefore, although the court will take into account the crime and its seriousness, no further principles have been developed in terms of which the conversion of the crime into a sentence can take place. It is accepted that the severity of punishment should reflect the seriousness of the crime. In theory this reflects a proportionality requirement (which has also been elevated into a constitutional requirement[4]). Clearly, some mitigating and aggravating factors affect the seriousness of the crime. Examples include the extent of violence used in perpetrating a robbery, whether murder was premeditated, or whether a theft involved an item of much value or a breach of trust.

As far as the second element of *Zinn's* triad is concerned, the basic premise is that the sentence should also fit the offender. As a result, a youthful offender is not punished as severely as an adult offender (Rabie et al. 1992: 290, 304–7; Van der Merwe 1991: 5–20–5–21; South

[3] See, e.g., *S v. M (Centre of Child Law as amicus curiae)* 2007 ('However, all the parties to this matter agreed that the classic *Zinn* triad is the paradigm from which to proceed when embarking on "the lonely and onerous task" of passing sentence'); *DPP, KwaZulu-Natal v. P* 2006 ('The so-called traditional approach to sentencing required (and still does) the sentencing court to consider the "triad"'); Van der Merwe (1991), 5–1–5–4.

[4] The issue of proportionality in sentencing as a constitutional requirement is most directly addressed in *S* v. *Dodo* 2001. The court found that proportionality between the seriousness of the offence and the measure of punishment goes 'to the heart of the inquiry as to whether punishment is cruel, inhuman or degrading'.

African Law Commission 1999: para 2.57) and a first offender not as severely as a repeat offender (Rabie et al. 1992: 301–4; Kriegler and Kruger 2002: 683). It is standard practice for sentencers to include a range of factors related to the offender in their sentencing judgments. Apart from the offender's age and whether he is a first or repeat offender, the list would typically include references to the offender's marital status and whether there are any dependants, his employment history, financial situation and facts related to personal character. Most of these facts and factors would tend to be mitigating, and listing them in the sentence judgment would indicate that they have been taken into account in the sentencing process. However, their effects are unpredictable and, once sentence has been imposed, usually very hard (if at all possible) to isolate. Often, when the crime is really serious, one can only conclude that they made no difference to the sentence.

The third element of the basic sentencing principles is the interests of society. Usually, 'interests of society' is considered by the courts as a synonym for giving expression to society's view of the seriousness of the crime (e.g. *S* v. *Sinden* (1995); *S* v. *Dhlamini* (1988); *S* v. *Maseko* (1998)). The preferred view should be that the sentence should promote the interests of society in some way (*S* v. *Mafu* (1992)). To this end the interests of society are often linked to the traditional purposes of punishment (Terblanche 2007: 137, 155), but even when they are not, the sentencer is still expected to consider the general purposes of punishment, namely retribution,[5] deterrence, rehabilitation and incapacitation or prevention (e.g., *R* v. *Swanepoel* (1945); *S* v. *Rabie* (1975); *S* v. *M (Centre for Child Law as amicus curiae)* (2007). Typically, a sentence judgment will include a reference to all four purposes, despite the fact that a single sentence rarely has the potential to achieve more than one or two of them (Law Commission 2000a: 48–52; American Law Institute 2007: 4–10). When the crime is serious, the sentencer would typically state that deterrence and retribution are emphasized (see, e.g., *S* v. *Makwanyane* (1995); *S* v. *Kgafela* (2001); *S* v. *Swart* (2004)). Serious crime also frequently results in a conclusion that society needs to be protected against the offender, emphasizing incapacitation (see, e.g., *S* v. *Bull* (2001); *S* v. *Makwanyane* (1995)). In the end, few factors related purely to the interests of society could be considered either mitigating or aggravating. The prevalence of the crime could arguably be one of the

[5] Although retribution is usually included in the list of 'purposes of punishment', it should probably not be seen as a 'purpose', but rather as a more foundational notion (Ashworth 2007, pp. 992–3).

few exceptions, as it is directly connected to the deterrent effect that the sentence is aimed to achieve.[6]

The minimum sentences regime

In 1998 legislation was introduced prescribing minimum sentences for a wide range of the more serious crimes in South Africa (Du Toit et al. 2010, 28–10V ff.). The mechanics of this scheme is not of current importance, but the role of aggravating and mitigating factors is relevant. For example, life imprisonment is prescribed for aggravated forms of murder such as premeditated murder, murder following a rape or robbery 'with aggravating circumstances', or murder as part of organized crime. The extent of violence involved, the kind of weapon that was used, or the suffering of the deceased are not included within this legislation. In the absence of the specifically mentioned aggravating factors, the minimum sentence prescribed for murder is fifteen years' imprisonment (Criminal Law Amendment Act 105 of 1997, s. 51). Life imprisonment is also prescribed for rape accompanied by certain aggravating factors, for example when the rape is repeated or takes the form of a gang rape, where there is a rape by a person knowing he is HIV-positive or where the victim is under the age of 16 years. Again, the extent of the violence employed by the rapist is not included as an aggravating factor.[7]

Various financial and drug offences are also included in the legislation, but generally only once a certain monetary limit is exceeded. Throughout, these monetary limits are reduced if the perpetrators are involved with organized crime or law enforcement. For example, the minimum sentence for theft is fifteen years' imprisonment if more than 500,000 rand (currently about £46,000) are involved. If the theft is part of an organized crime, this limit is reduced to R 100,000 and if a law enforcement officer committed the offence, the threshold lies at R 10,000 (s. 51 read with Part II of Schedule 2 of the Criminal Law Amendment Act 105 of 1997). The legislation also caters for previous convictions, which increase the minimum sentences in increments of years. With the above-mentioned theft example, the minimum sentence

[6] Whether increased punishment provides any deterrent effect is doubtful (Walker and Padfield 1996: 101), but this fact has not prevented the courts from relying on deterrence as a valid purpose of punishment.

[7] It is instructive to contrast these provisions with the guidelines of the English Sentencing Council. In addition to the circumstances mentioned above, the Council's guidelines include abduction or detention and a sustained attack accompanying the rape, and indicate a starting point of eight years' imprisonment for all these offences (it is increased to ten years' imprisonment if the victim is under thirteen years of age) (Sentencing Guidelines Council 2007: 25).

for an offender with one previous conviction increases from fifteen to twenty years' imprisonment and, in the case of an offender with two or more previous convictions, to twenty-five years' imprisonment. In this way the legislation makes specific provision for aggravating circumstances, but in relation to a limited number of factors only.

The minimum sentences legislation does not apply to children under 18 years of age,[8] nor to cases heard in the lowest trial courts (district magistrates' courts – see Terblanche 2007: 55). It also provides for the courts to depart from the prescribed sentences if there are 'substantial and compelling circumstances' that would justify the imposition of a lesser sentence (s. 51(3)(b)). The seminal judgment regarding this departure test is *S* v. *Malgas* (2001). According to this judgment the sentencers should generally use the prescribed sentences as the point of departure. However, in determining whether a departure from the prescribed sentence is required, the court should have regard to *all* the factors that would traditionally affect sentencing. None of the normal mitigating and aggravating factors is excluded from this consideration. These factors that would traditionally affect sentences have generally been understood to refer to the triad of factors referred to in *S* v. *Zinn*. However, the sentencing court must have regard to the legislature's decree that these crimes should generally be punished more severely (e.g., *S* v. *Abrahams* (2002); *S* v. *Malgas* (2001)).

APPLYING THE BASIC PRINCIPLES OF SENTENCING

In what follows a number of reported judgments are employed to show how the above-mentioned principles are used in practice to shape sentences.

A renowned case, justifiably famous for its pure application of the principles established in *Zinn*, is *S* v. *Rabie* (1975). The local supreme court convicted the accused of fraud involving a scheme described as 'ingenious and simple'. The ill-gotten gains amounted to about R 3,000 (then the equivalent of about £1,000). The trial court sentenced the accused to a fine of R 5,000, plus one year's effective imprisonment and two years' suspended imprisonment. On appeal, the Court attempted to quantify the seriousness of the crime, the first component of the *Zinn* triad. Relevant factors included that the relevant legislation permitted a

[8] In terms of s. 51(6), the minimum sentences legislation does not apply to children under 16, but the Constitutional Court found this provision to be unconstitutional and increased the limit to 18 years of age in *Centre for Child Law* v. *Minister of Justice* (2009).

suspect to be arrested without a warrant, indicating that the legislature considered the crime to be serious. Certain aspects aggravated this particular fraud: pre-planning, the extended period over which the offence was perpetrated (nineteen times over a period of seventeen months), the substantial amount involved and the fact that the victims were poor and vulnerable. The offender (the second component of the *Zinn* triad) was characterized as a deceitful person, but he was also 60 years of age, a first offender and regretful about what had happened, and he had made restitution. His conviction had also resulted in certain professional disadvantages. Regarding the third component of the *Zinn* triad – the interests of society – the court held that the sentence should serve as a deterrent. Balancing all these considerations, the Court found no reason to interfere with the trial court's sentence.

Although *Rabie* is highly regarded as a sentencing judgment, it is not possible to isolate any of the aggravating and mitigating factors and to predict how a difference in these factors would have affected the sentence. For example, it is not possible to state what the sentence would have been had the fraud involved only ten counts and not nineteen, or if the amount of the illegal gain was half or three times the actual R 3,000, or if the appellant had been 40 instead of 60 years old.

In a case decided under the minimum sentences legislation, the appellant was convicted of robbery and sentenced to the statutory minimum of fifteen years' imprisonment. *S* v. *Nel* (2007) relates how he armed himself with a firearm and held up the staff of a local entertainment centre and robbed them of R 32,595 (the current equivalent of about £5,300). He explained during the plea process that he committed his crime because of financial difficulties, partly as a result of a gambling addiction. He urgently needed money to pay some of his employees on the day of the robbery. He obtained a small loan, which he attempted to increase through gambling. Not surprisingly, he lost everything and then decided that the robbery represented his only chance of acquiring the necessary funds. Many mitigating factors were present: the firearm was not loaded, the money was recovered, he was a first offender, had led an exemplary life and had shown remorse by pleading guilty. With all these mitigating factors present the trial court's finding that there were not substantial and compelling factors to justify a lesser sentence is surprising. Unsurprisingly, the Supreme Court of Appeal reversed this finding and imposed ten years' imprisonment.

Again, it is the totality of aggravating and mitigating factors that brought the Court to its sentence. None of the factors were highlighted as being particularly influential in reducing, for example, the offender's level of blameworthiness. One cannot say whether the sentence would have been any different if he had robbed R 100, 000, or if he had not suffered from a gambling problem, to mention only two possible examples. It is also not possible to say on what basis the Court decided to impose imprisonment for as long as ten years, since this robbery was a far cry from the typical armed robbery perpetrated in South Africa.

I want to refer to one further case to explain how the basic sentencing principles are employed in the sentencing process. In *S* v. *Kunene* (2001), the court utilized an approach that is used from time to time to increase consistency in sentencing, namely to compare explicitly the sentences imposed in similar cases previously sentenced. The value of this comparative approach to the current enquiry is that it isolates the mitigating and aggravating factors that are really influential with respect to a certain kind of crime.

COMPARING CASES MORE DIRECTLY

The *Kunene* case relates to an offender who was found in possession of some of his employer's property, such as items of clothing, cigarettes and batteries, to the value of R 1,200 (then the equivalent of about £115). The trial magistrate convicted him of theft and in the sentencing judgment emphasized his breach of trust as well as the extent of the total losses that the employer suffered through theft. As to his personal situation, the only factor mentioned was that he was a first offender. He was sentenced to twelve months' imprisonment. On appeal, the Court accepted that theft from an employer is a serious crime as it involves a breach of trust, but held that this fact by itself did not make imprisonment imperative. The Court then compared other judgments dealing with theft from an employer and concluded that imprisonment was mainly imposed when the dishonest acts were committed over a period of time, when they involved substantial amounts of money or when the offender was in a particular position of trust, such as a bookkeeper. However, it is clear from the comparison that sentences were mainly influenced by the breach of trust (as an aggravating factor) and whether the thief was a first offender (as a mitigating factor). The other factors, despite being mentioned, were not nearly as important. In the present matter the appellant was a first offender, married, and had two dependent children and a stable employment record. The Court then replaced the trial court's sentence with a fine of R 3,000, plus six months' imprisonment, suspended.

The 'comparative' approach followed in *Kunene* was by no means new. However, in practice there is a widely followed approach that each case should be considered according to its own facts.[9] The comparative approach did receive considerable impetus a few years after *Kunene* in a number of judgments from the Supreme Court of Appeal.[10] As the Court held in *S* v. *Xaba* (2005), '[i]t has often been pointed out that no two cases are alike and this is self-evidently true, but the fact remains that courts must strive for some consistency in punishment'. It is to this quest for greater consistency, and what this teaches about the role of aggravating and mitigating factors, that we turn next.

In *S* v. *Xaba* the Court held that, in order to 'translate' the blameworthiness of the offender into a sentence, sentencing courts must be aware of the sentences considered 'socially appropriate or desirable' in other cases. A 'general and necessarily rough comparison' of such cases could provide the presiding officer with some starting point, which then has to be adjusted for 'the special circumstances of the case, most prominent of which are the special circumstances of the accused: his record, his contrition and that kind of thing'. The two appellants were caught trading in cannabis (marijuana) during a sting operation. Almost 600 kg of the drug were involved. A major aggravating factor was that the appellants intentionally involved the local police in their operation. The trial court had imposed twenty years' imprisonment and eighteen years' imprisonment on the two appellants respectively.[11] The Court noted that these sentences were very close to the maximum sentence permitted by the penalty clause for the offence, namely twenty-five years' imprisonment (Drugs and Drug Trafficking Act 140 of 1992, s. 17). As the same maximum also applied to dealing in much more dangerous drugs (such as heroin), the imposed sentences were problematic.

The Court found assistance in establishing an appropriate starting point for its own sentence in *S* v. *Morebudi* (1999), which involved a

[9] See Terblanche (2007, pp. 127–30) for a discussion of this principle and its history: 'It was generally considered an "idle exercise" to try matching the facts of one case to another in order to find an appropriate sentence.'

[10] Such as *S* v. *Jimenez* (2003); *S* v. *McMillan* (2003); *S* v. *Gerber* (2006) (the desirability of broad guidelines is self-evident); *S* v. *Smith* (2003) (the sentences imposed for other severe crimes had a role to play in the present case: '[t]he level of sentencing generally resorted to in even more serious cases has to be borne in mind when considering what sentences should be imposed in a case such as this. Unless that be done, all sense of proportion may be lost and a sentence imposed which, by comparison, is too harsh').

[11] The first appellant received a higher sentence as she was considered to be the leader of the organization.

drug dealer who transported nearly one-and-a-half tons of cannabis in a secret compartment in a trailer specifically modified for this purpose. The sentence of fourteen years' imprisonment was confirmed on appeal and is described in *Xaba* as 'the high-water mark for a [cannabis] sentence confirmed by this Court in recent years'. It then concluded as follows,

> The aggravating features of the appellants' offences, in particular the evidently widespread corruption of the local police, warrant a sentence up to that level [of fourteen years' imprisonment] but not beyond.

It then imposed the same sentence of fourteen years' imprisonment on the first appellant. However, the other 'aggravating features' of the appellants' offences, apart from the corruption of the local police, are not identified. The frequent references in the judgment to the amount of drugs involved strongly indicate that this was aggravating, but no others can be deduced from the judgment itself.

The comparative approach was also emphasized in S v. *Nyathi* (2005), a case that dealt with culpable homicide arising from negligent or reckless driving. The appellant was the driver of a motor car that crashed into a minibus taxi, in a failed attempt to overtake another vehicle on a blind rise. As a result the taxi overturned, killing six of its occupants. The Supreme Court of Appeal described the appellant's conduct as just about the most dangerous form of driving imaginable. The Court reiterated that in this kind of case the degree of blameworthiness of the accused should be the basic criterion of an appropriate sentence. However, the death of another person is a particularly serious consequence of the negligent act, which would aggravate the crime. In determining how much more severe a sentence would be justified by such aggravation, the Court held, 'it is useful to have regard in a general sort of way to sentences imposed by this and other courts'.

The Court then considered a range of similar cases and their sentences. In all instances but one of these cases the numbers of people killed and seriously injured are mentioned; all instances briefly relate the manner in which the offender drove negligently. Clearly, these two factors are the most important determinants of an appropriate sentence. It would invariably be aggravating when more people died, and when the driving becomes more reckless. In the end the Court found that none of the comparable cases involved negligence as gross nor consequences as grave as the present case. It therefore confirmed the trial court's sentence of five years' imprisonment of which two years were conditionally suspended.

It should be evident from this discussion that when comparing similar cases courts typically refer to a small number of shared factors only. For example, in the case of theft from an employer the court mainly compared whether the thefts occurred over a period of time, whether substantial amounts of money were involved, or whether the offender was in a particular position of trust (*S* v. *Kunene*). In the case of culpable homicide resulting from negligent driving, the court really only compared the number of people killed and seriously injured, and the extent to which the offender's driving deviated from the reasonable person norm (*S* v. *Nyathi*).

Despite its advantages in terms of providing the sentencing court with a starting point for its own sentence, the comparative approach has lost much of its momentum since 2006, and when it is used nowadays, the court is unlikely to highlight the importance of such a comparison.

ASSESSMENT AND PROPOSED IMPROVEMENTS

To summarize, sentencing in South Africa suffers from inconsistency and unpredictability, mainly because the general principles are too vague and unsophisticated (Van Rooyen 1980; Van der Merwe 1991: 5–12). Although all factors are taken into account in the sentencing process, it is rarely possible to know which of them really made the difference. Instead, the vagueness of the general principles permits a sentencer to decide on a sentence instinctively or intuitively and then to use the explanations in the sentence judgment to justify the sentence (Van der Merwe 1991: 1–15; Terblanche 2007: 118). Clearly, a useful set of general principles must provide the sentencer with some point of departure or starting point, which can then be adjusted according to the special circumstances of the case (*S* v. *Xaba* above). From this starting point, to state the obvious, the mitigating factors should reduce the sentence and the aggravating factors increase the sentence.

One of the first steps that is required to improve a largely discretionary sentencing system is to develop clarity regarding what is meant by 'the seriousness of the crime' and how this seriousness can be 'translated' into a sentence. Such clarity, it is submitted, will contribute to making a discretionary system substantially more rational and predictable. It is not necessary to reinvent the proverbial wheel in this process, as the South African Law Commission thoroughly investigated and reported on the issue in 2000 (South African Law Commission 2000b). Although this investigation resulted in a wide-ranging set of recommendations (for an assessment, see Terblanche 2008), few are as topical as simply the proposals regarding the seriousness of the crime. In this regard the Law Commission proposed that the seriousness of the crime should be established with reference to the harm caused or risked by the offence, as well as the extent to which the accused could be blamed for that harm (South African Law Commission 2000b, paras. 3.1.4, 3.1.12).[12]

As is well known, this approach is widely accepted internationally (e.g. *Solem* v. *Helm* (1983, at pp. 293–4); Frase 2005: 580; Canadian Sentencing Commission 1987: 154; Criminal Justice Act 2003, s. 143(1) (England and Wales); Ashworth 2010: 104–5) and is no doubt more specific than the open approach currently employed by our courts. It consistently provides a starting point from which to develop a sentence more rationally. Whereas aggravating and mitigating factors are currently simply added to the larger mix of sentencing 'ingredients', under the proposals many of these factors will have to be allocated specifically to determine either the harm involved or the blameworthiness of the offender.

Applying the analysis

The practical application of the above-mentioned standard for the seriousness of the crime, and how the aggravating and mitigating factors should find their role in the process, is best explained with reference to a couple of practical examples. *S* v. *Thebus* (2002) involved a group of vigilantes who decided to take the law into their own hands against drug dealers operating in their township. At one point a suspected drug dealer fired a shot at the motorcade of these vigilantes and when they returned fire an innocent girl was killed. The Cape High Court convicted two accused of murder[13] and sentenced them to eight years' imprisonment, totally suspended on condition that community service be performed.

The state appealed against these sentences. In the Supreme Court of Appeal the majority found that the prescribed sentence of life imprisonment would be manifestly unfit under the circumstances and had to be

[12] It is notable that the recent Child Justice Act 75 of 2008 relates the seriousness of the crime, specifically with reference to the imposition of imprisonment on children, directly to '(i) the amount of harm done or risked through the offence; and (ii) the culpability of the child in causing or risking the harm' – s. 69(4)(*a*). These principles have not yet received any notable judicial attention, but it is unfortunate that it has been limited to the imposition of imprisonment.

[13] The accused were convicted of murder based on the so-called common purpose doctrine, and as they were 'part of a group acting in furtherance of a common purpose', it meant that life imprisonment was prescribed (s. 51(1) read with Part II of schedule 2 of the minimum sentences legislation).

overturned.[14] Although the offenders had participated in the violent action, they did not fire the shot that killed the deceased and were not seen using a firearm. Thus their participation in the crime was significantly limited. In addition, their personal circumstances (first offenders, in stable employment, with families to support) had to be taken into account. On the other hand, the Court held, the trial court's sentence was grossly inadequate, and had to be replaced with fifteen years' imprisonment. In complete contrast, the minority judge would have imposed the prescribed sentence of life imprisonment. In his view the minimum sentences legislation was directly aimed at 'mob . . . rule and general lawlessness'. The offenders acted in a violent and dramatic manner and it was fortuitous that more people had not been killed. In this context the offenders' personal circumstances could not be seen as being substantial and compelling.

If the seriousness of the crime were judged according to the Law Commission's proposals instead of the traditional approach, such an outcome would have been unlikely. In accordance with these proposals the sentence could be structured in the following manner. Major harm was clearly caused by the conduct of the offenders. Causing the death of another human being itself indicates a starting point at or close to the maximum sentence that may be imposed. In South Africa this means a starting point of life imprisonment. The mitigating factors involved do not affect the harm, but are all related to the blameworthiness of the offenders. One such factor would be the offenders' motive, which was to reduce the level of criminality in their community. The fact that they used the wrong means to achieve their goal does not change their motive. In addition, they did not have a direct intent to kill the deceased.

These mitigating factors can now be used to make a rough estimate of the offender's blameworthiness. If, for argument's sake, the blameworthiness is set at 50 per cent, then a sentence in the range of ten to fifteen years' imprisonment would be indicated.[15] If further mitigating and aggravating factors have not been accounted for at this stage, the sentencer should have the discretion to use such factors to further fine-tune the sentence. However, the proposed basic principles no longer

[14] In accordance with the considerations discussed above under the minimum sentences scheme.

[15] One is mindful of the extensive debates that have taken place about the connection between the seriousness of the crime and the severity of punishment, on issues such as ordinal and cardinal proportionality, whether it is possible to determine proportionality mathematically, and so forth (see essays by Davis (2002) and von Hirsch (2002). The examples used here are inevitably somewhat simplified.

include the person of the offender within its framework, with the result that personal factors that do not affect the offender's blameworthiness are no longer given prominence. Nevertheless, two important mitigating factors with regard to murder have been taken into account and, as shown above, reduced the offenders' blameworthiness, justifying a very substantial reduction in sentence.

The facts of *Nel*'s case, discussed above, can be used as a second practical example. It will be remembered that this case involved a robbery with aggravating factors (as the offender 'armed' himself with an unloaded firearm and robbed the staff of an entertainment centre of almost R 33,000). The harm risked is that of a substantial amount of money (it is a moot point whether its recovery should serve as a mitigating factor). Armed robbery also contains a risk of bodily harm to the victims, but, when the firearm is not loaded, such risk cannot be said to be any greater than the risk of bodily harm when no firearm or other weapon is involved (see also Sentencing Guidelines Council 2006: 6). Thus the resultant harm is much closer to an ordinary robbery than to a typical armed robbery. However, merely having a firearm aggravates the offender's conduct, as the victims' perception that they are in great physical danger is certainly a harm that should be accounted for in the sentence.

It is difficult to attach a specific starting point to this crime based purely on harm without the context of comparable crimes. Although the minimum sentences legislation contains a minimum of fifteen years' imprisonment for robbery with aggravating circumstances, it only affects theft once an amount in excess of R 500,000 is stolen. Here that amount is much lower. Based on harm and risked harm, it is suggested that a sentence of no more than five years' imprisonment would be an appropriate starting point, although comparison with other harm-to-punishment translations might well indicate a lower starting point. To reach this point involves the consideration of several mitigating factors that are directly connected to the harm that is caused or risked by the offence, such as the lack of violence associated with the robbery, its amateur nature and the fact that the firearm was not loaded. Depending on the nature of the crimes that are used for comparative purposes, the amount of money involved could indicate that either an increase or a decrease from the starting point is required.

Having established a tentative starting point of five years' imprisonment, the offender's blameworthiness remains to be determined. As noted earlier, he was a first offender who pleaded guilty. He also had a gambling addiction, but otherwise led an exemplary life. If any of these factors would reduce the extent to which he can be blamed for the harm caused or risked, they would be truly mitigating. Whether this should be the case requires fundamental answers to some crucial questions, such as the following:

- Could blameworthiness be increased above 100 per cent?
- Is being a first offender a factor that reduces the offender's blameworthiness, or do previous convictions increase blameworthiness?
- Does it affect the blameworthiness of the offender when he pleads guilty?

It is not the purpose of this chapter to provide answers to these difficult questions, which have already received considerable attention elsewhere. The arguments advanced in such writings should inform the answers to these questions, but the answers need to be given locally and, in South Africa's case, preferably by the Supreme Court of Appeal. Whatever the answers, there are no factors in the case of *Nel* that could conceivably be said to increase his blameworthiness so as to justify a sentence in excess of the starting point, with the result that a sentence of nothing more than half that imposed by the Court is indicated.

CONCLUSION

The sentencing systems in most common law jurisdictions still operate without any meaningful guidelines, and South Africa is one such example. Without such guidelines it is barely possible to account for mitigating and aggravating factors rationally and predictably. The proposals by the South African Law Commission regarding the seriousness of crimes represents a small but significant step forwards. It is a step that would enable courts better than the current system to distinguish between aggravating and mitigating factors that affect sentences substantially, and should do so. It is surely a step worth taking.

REFERENCES

American Law Institute (2007). *Model Penal Code: Sentencing (Tentative Draft No 1)*. Philadelphia: American Law Institute.

Ashworth, A. (2007). 'Sentencing', in M. Maguire, R. Morgan and R. Reiner (eds.), *The Oxford Handbook of Criminology*, 5th edn. Oxford University Press.

(2010). *Sentencing and Criminal Justice*, 5th edn. Cambridge University Press.

Canadian Sentencing Commission (1987). *Sentencing Reform: A Canadian Approach*. Ottawa: Minister of Supply and Services.

Davis, J. (2002). 'The Science of Sentencing: Measurement Theory and von Hirsch's New Scales of Justice', in C. Tata and N. Hutton (eds.), *Sentencing and Society: International Perspectives*. Aldershot: Ashgate.

Du Toit, E. et al. (original service 1987, updated to revision service 44, 2010). *Commentary on the Criminal Procedure Act*. Cape Town: Juta.

Frase, R. (2005). 'Excessive Prison Sentences, Punishment Goals, and the Eighth Amendment: "Proportionality" Relative To What?', *Minnesota Law Review*, 89: 571–651.

Hiemstra, V. (1987). *Suid-Afrikaanse strafproses*, 4th edn. Durban: Butterworths.

Kriegler, J. and Kruger, A. (2002). *Hiemstra: Suid-Afrikaanse strafproses*, 6th edn. Durban: LexisNexis Butterworths.

Rabie, A. et al. (1992). *Sentencing: An Introduction to Principles*, 5th edn. Pretoria: Lex Patria.

Sentencing Guidelines Council (2006). *Robbery: Definitive Guideline*, available at www.sentencingcouncil.org.uk/.

(2007). *Sexual Offences Act 2003: Definitive Guideline*, available at www.sentencingcouncil.org.uk/.

South African Law Commission (1999). *Discussion Paper 79 (Project 106): Juvenile Justice*. Pretoria: South African Law Commission.

(2000a). *Discussion Paper 91 (Project 82): Sentencing (A New Sentencing Framework)*. Pretoria: South African Law Commission.

(2000b). *Report (Project 82): Sentencing (A New Sentencing Framework)*. Pretoria: South African Law Commission.

Terblanche, S. (2007). *A Guide to Sentencing in South Africa*, 2nd edn. Durban: LexisNexis.

(2008). *Report on the Sentencing Framework Bill*. Cape Town: Open Society Foundation.

Terblanche, S. and Mackenzie, G. (2008). 'Mandatory Sentences in South Africa: Lessons for Australia?', *Australian and New Zealand Journal of Criminology*, 41: 402–20.

Van der Merwe, D. (original service 1991, updated to 1997). *Sentencing*. Cape Town: Juta.

Van Rooyen, J. (1980). 'The Decision to Imprison: The Courts' Need for Guidance', *South African Journal of Crime and Criminology*, 4: 228–35.

von Hirsch, A. (2002). 'Scaling Punishments: A Reply to Julia Davis', in C. Tata and N. Hutton (eds.), *Sentencing and Society: International Perspectives*. Aldershot: Ashgate.

Walker, N. and Padfield, N. (1996) *Sentencing: Theory, Law and Practice*, 2nd edn. London: Butterworths.

TABLE OF CASES

Centre for Child Law *v.* Minister of Justice 2009 (2) South African Criminal Law Reports 477 (CC).
DPP, KwaZulu-Natal *v.* P 2006 (1) South African Criminal Law Reports 243 (SCA).
R *v.* Swanepoel 1945 AD 444.
S *v.* Abrahams 2002 (1) South African Criminal Law Reports 116 (SCA).
S *v.* Bull 2001 (2) South African Criminal Law Reports 681 (SCA).
S *v.* Dhlamini 1988 (2) South African Law Reports 302 (A).
S *v.* Dodo 2001 (1) South African Criminal Law Reports 594 (CC).
S *v.* Gerber 2006 (1) South African Criminal Law Reports 618 (SCA).
S *v.* Jimenez 2003 (1) South African Criminal Law Reports 507 (SCA).
S *v.* Kgafela 2001 (2) South African Criminal Law Reports 207 (B).
S *v.* Kunene 2001 (1) South African Criminal Law Reports 199 (W).
S *v.* M (Centre of Child Law as amicus curiae) 2007 (2) South African Criminal Law Reports 539 (CC).
S *v.* McMillan 2003 (1) South African Criminal Law Reports 27 (SCA).
S *v.* Mafu 1992 (2) South African Criminal Law Reports 494 (A).
S *v.* Malgas 2001 (1) South African Criminal Law Reports 469 (SCA).
S *v.* Makwanyane 1995 (2) South African Criminal Law Reports (1) (CC).
S *v.* Maseko 1998 (1) South African Law Reports 1 (A).
S *v.* Morebudi 1999 (2) South African Criminal Law Reports 664 (SCA).
S *v.* Nel 2007 (2) South African Criminal Law Reports 481 (SCA).
S *v.* Nyathi 2005 (2) South African Criminal Law Reports 273 (SCA).
S *v.* Rabie 1975 (4) South African Law Reports 855 (A).
S *v.* Sinden 1995 (2) South African Criminal Law Reports 704 (A).
S *v.* Smith 2003 (2) South African Criminal Law Reports 135 (SCA).
S *v.* Swart 2004 (2) South African Criminal Law Reports 370 (SCA).
S *v.* Thebus 2002 (2) South African Criminal Law Reports 566 (SCA).
S *v.* Xaba 2005 (1) South African Criminal Law Reports 435 (SCA).
S *v.* Zinn 1969 (2) South African Law Reports 537 (A).
Solem *v.* Helm 463 US 277 (1983).

INDEX